Advance Praise

"Again, Louis Cozolino is helping clinicians understand themselves, their clients, and their brains better. In *Executive Functioning and Psychotherapy,* he reenvisions the neuroscience of executive function beyond the frontal lobe to include the amygdala and the attachment network, creating a more integrative view where both stress management and improved relationships are crucial to improved cognitive *and* interpersonal functioning. A must-read for anyone doing clinical work with children and adults."

—**Amy Banks, MD,** founding scholar of the International Center for Growth in Connection and coauthor of *Wired to Connect: The Surprising Link Between Brain Science and Strong, Healthy Relationships* and *Fighting Time*

"Written with the practicing therapist in mind, this compelling volume reframes executive functioning as an embodied, relational process central to every therapeutic encounter. Cozolino, Drulis, and Trissler offer a three-system neurobiological model that helps clinicians see beyond deficits, access deeper client strengths, and tailor interventions with greater precision. A vital resource for therapists seeking to integrate brain-based insight with compassionate, effective care."

—**Mary L. Meador, MD,** board-certified family physician and founder, Good Doctor, Healthy Soul, LLC

"Cozolino, Drulis, and Trissler have written an extremely important book which revamps the concept of executive functioning, aligning EF strongly with neuroscience 2.0: the science of big brain networks. With thoroughness and clarity, the authors review the three core brain networks and then propose a new three-system model of EF. Finally, they apply this model to the work of therapists and coaches, moving seamlessly from the theory to practical applications. I highly recommend this book to all mental health professionals."

—**Jonathan Baylin, PhD,** psychologist and coauthor of *The Neurobiology of Attachment-Focused Therapy* and *Brain-Based Parenting*

"Each of Lou Cozolino's books offers a masterful synthesis of current neuroscientific knowledge combined with development psychology and psychotherapy research. This book prophetically steps toward the future with a superb blend of cutting-edge science by explaining how a mental health practitioner may apply this knowledge. He and his coauthors, Chloe Drulis and Carly Trissler, provide vignettes and helpful summaries that illustrate and teach. They take an illuminating dive into the historical background and new insights of our executive networks. This excellent book ushers in a renaissance in mental health care."

—**John Arden, PhD, ABPP,** author of *Mind–Brain–Gene*

Executive Functioning
and Psychotherapy

The Norton Series on Interpersonal Neurobiology
Louis Cozolino, PhD, Series Editor
Allan N. Schore, PhD, Series Editor (2007–2014)
Daniel J. Siegel, MD, Founding Editor

The field of mental health is in a tremendously exciting period of growth and conceptual reorganization. Independent findings from a variety of scientific endeavors are converging in an interdisciplinary view of the mind and mental well-being. An interpersonal neurobiology of human development enables us to understand that the structure and function of the mind and brain are shaped by experiences, especially those involving emotional relationships, as well as the relational mechanisms by which interacting and communicating brains synchronize with and align their activities with other individuals.

The Norton Series on Interpersonal Neurobiology provides cutting-edge, multidisciplinary views that further our understanding of the complex neurobiology of the human mind. By drawing on a wide range of traditionally independent fields of research—such as neuroscience, attachment, the unconscious mind, genetics, memory, complex systems, anthropology, and evolutionary science—these texts offer mental health professionals a review and synthesis of scientific findings often inaccessible to clinicians. The books advance our understanding of human experience, identity, and relational connections by finding the unity of knowledge, or consilience, that emerges with the translation of findings from numerous domains of study into a common language and conceptual framework. The series integrates the best of modern science with the healing art of psychotherapy.

Executive Functioning
and Psychotherapy

The New Neuroscience of
Adaptive Intelligence

LOUIS COZOLINO

CHLOE DRULIS

CARLY TRISSLER

Norton Professional Books

An Imprint of W. W. Norton & Company
Independent Publishers Since 1923

Note to Readers: This book is intended as a general information resource for professionals practicing in the field of psychotherapy and mental health. It is not a substitute for appropriate training or clinical supervision. Standards of clinical practice and protocol vary in different practice settings and change over time. No technique or recommendation is guaranteed to be safe or effective in all circumstances, and neither the publisher nor the authors can guarantee the complete accuracy, efficacy, or appropriateness of any particular recommendation in every respect or in all settings or circumstances.

All patients and case studies discussed in this books are composites. Any URLs displayed in this book link or refer to websites that existed as of press time. The publisher is not responsible for, and should not be deemed to endorse or recommend, any website other than its own or any content that it did not create. The authors, also, are not responsible for any third-party material.

This book is dedicated to our children:
Caden, Coco, Georgia, Julian, and Sam

Contents

Often Used Abbreviations: **EF**, executive functioning; **ES1**, first executive system; **ES2**, second executive system; **ES3**, third executive system; **SN**, salience network; **DMN**, default mode network

Introduction

A story must be exceptional enough to justify its telling.
—Thomas Hardy

Executive functioning (EF) is a term used to describe the inner navigation system we use to guide us through life. It allows us to evaluate and select goals, focus our attention, create action plans, and carry them to completion. We employ EF at school and work, in personal relationships, at the grocery store, and during moments of self-reflection. Although cognitive and intellectual processes are central contributors to EF, so are emotional regulation, self-awareness, and social connectedness. EF is not simply a cognitive ability housed in our frontal lobes, but a complex set of skills that arise from our brains, bodies, and relationships.

Consider all the things you had to do to get to the point in life where you are curious about EF. In addition to persevering through decades of schooling, you had to decide on and train for a career, navigate relationships with family, friends, and partners, take countless tests, and pay for it all. As the CEO of your life, you have made thousands of strategic decisions, performed millions of tasks, and kept the complex enterprise called "you" up and running. Your successes require that you understand and regulate your emotions, and use your skills to connect with others, while sustaining a safe inner world: all important ingredients of EF.

Given that EF is essential to our ability to love and work, it is always at the core of psychotherapy. Most people come to therapy when their life isn't working well. Perhaps they suffer from depression or anxiety, lack the necessary skills to play well with others, or have difficulties choosing a direction or following through on their commitments. Although we may not use the term "EF" in day-to-day practice, we are constantly referring to it with concepts like ego strength, empathy, resilience, and boundaries. These and many other therapeutic concepts involve our ability to set goals, navigate challenges, enlist the cooperation of others, and persevere toward our goals.

Until recently, theories of EF have focused almost exclusively on verbal expressions of conscious rational thought. While certainly important, it turns out to be just one aspect of EF. The majority of people that come to treatment with complaints about EF are not suffering from brain lesions or medical illnesses, but from an array of physiological, emotional, and relational challenges that undermine their ability to navigate life. Many of these challenges are unconscious, manifesting symbolically through behaviors and psychological symptoms, and getting played out in self-destructive ways. Focusing exclusively on rational thought and thinking of people as purely conscious beings has failed us time and again.

The best way to assess EF is in the real world of the people, places, and things our clients navigate each day. Instead of fitting them with diagnostic labels, we have to approach each client as a unique experiment of nature. This requires spending the time to get to know them, the context of their lives, and the positive and negative adaptations they have made during development. This whole-person-in-context approach naturally involves an appreciation of human diversity in general and of neurodiversity in particular—and the diversity not just of individuals but of situations, environments, and cultures within which we are all embedded. The neglect of these broader factors is why standardized testing and a cognitive approach to EF fails with a majority of our clients.

The Evolution of Executive Functioning

> Life comes from physical survival; but the good
> life comes from what we care about.
> —Rollo May

As social animals, our survival depends upon our ability to cooperate and compete with others. It simultaneously depends upon the ability of our tribe to cooperate and compete with other tribes. If we are to survive as individuals, we have to become a viable member of our tribe, fortunate enough to be a member of a successful tribe, and balance our personal needs with the needs of others. The complex and often contradictory demands of being a social animal have guided the evolution of our brains, minds, bodies, and relationships. Juggling these competing needs is why our brains are so complex, relationships so challenging, and why EF and intelligence are social and emotional as well as cognitive.

Countless genetic and biological factors need to fall into place during conception and gestation to lay down the necessary neural templates for the nascent brain. Attachment relationships continue the developmental journey by nurturing the body and generating the proper state of mind and brain to optimize the chemical, biological, neural, social, and emotional building blocks of EF. Years of experience with play, exploration, interacting with others, and adapting to particular physical and social environments shape our EF. Making contributions, first to the family, then to the peer group, and later to society, engenders an expanding sense of purpose and solidifies our social identity. The ultimate test of EF is at the heart of Freud's goals for a good life—to love and work. This is how EF was assessed throughout history, before school systems and standardized tests.

To say that someone has problems with EF is to highlight one or more challenges in a particular context but tells us little about how to address it, and nothing about its cause. At a neurobiological level, EF is a set of functions distributed throughout the nervous system. As such, disruptions in physiological, sensory, motor, emotional, and relational abilities can all undermine EF. At an interpersonal and community level, failures of EF can be caused or enhanced by neglect, prejudice, conflict, scapegoating, bullying, and ostracism. They can also occur in situations of bad person-environment fit, when an individual's abilities have no avenue of expression, or when people are not seen or appreciated. For example, someone may be perfectly articulate in a one-on-one conversation but freeze up when they address a small group. A child may be able to focus on a task when sitting in a quiet place at home but find it impossible to pay attention in the classroom.

We know that Steve Jobs was a college dropout, van Gogh only sold one painting a few months before his death, and Satchel Paige didn't pitch in the major leagues until his 40s. While none of us doubt their particular talents, their "failures" in college, the art world, or sports say more about the biases and limitations of others than it does about their intelligence, abilities, or

EF. How their minds worked, their particular quirks and idiosyncrasies, and the values of the worlds they lived in are all relevant to understanding their challenges and genius. This is why we need to understand EF within a specific context and across a spectrum of variables from the biological to the cultural.

Imperialistic powers have always known that the best way to subjugate or destroy a people is to remove them from their land, take away their sources of meaning, and erase their history. When indigenous communities are removed from their native lands, they tend to lose a sense of purpose and identity. When put on reservations or separated from traditional forms of accomplishment, they often suffer from anxiety, depression, and addiction. As the adaptive skills and abilities of their EF lose relevance, they can easily lose their ability to thrive or survive. A parallel phenomenon on a much smaller scale occurs when children with active and curious temperaments are forced to sit at a desk all day, given drugs to help them focus, and have their abilities evaluated using tests of information retention. These are the children and adolescents who, in the past, would likely have grown up to be hunters, warriors, and healers—or, more recently, Jobs, van Gogh, or Paige.

Executive Functioning as Cliché

> *Last, but not least, avoid clichés like the plague.*
> —William Safire

In recent years, the concept of EF has gone public. It is generally seen as a brain-based problem requiring proper testing, diagnosis, medication, and intervention. As a result, psychotherapists, educational counselors, and executive coaches are seeing a growing number of clients referred with what are believed to be deficits in EF. Because we lack an agreed-upon definition of EF, and because it consists of so many diverse abilities, these referrals open a wide range of possibilities. Given that most of our theories and assessment tools focus on the cognitive aspects of EF, it is left to clinicians to explore the relevant, yet unaddressed, psychological, social, emotional, and cultural factors. It is also up to the clinician to educate clients and their families about the complexity of EF and help to connect the dots between the presenting problem, the assessment data, and the client's development, strengths, vulnerabilities, and current challenges.

Imagine that a fifth-grader comes to you who is having trouble sitting still and completing her assignments. Her parents and teachers are concerned about her grades and the possibility that she has a learning disability. She admits to having difficulty focusing in the classroom, but what is the cause and how do we help her? Do her challenges arise from her brain, mind, body, relationships, community, or some combination of all five? Is it because she has ADHD or sustained a concussion on the playground? Her symptoms could be the result of abuse or neglect, being bullied, or the stress caused by a parent's recent illness. Perhaps she feels that her teacher doesn't like her or is disturbed by some violent content she came across on the internet or her father's unexplained absence from the home. All of these (and many more) factors can trigger deficits with attention, focus, and task perseverance. But who will take the time to find out?

When it comes to EF, mental health and educational professionals tend to overindex on cognitive assessment and pharmacological interventions. Stimulant medications often help a child focus better during class, regardless of whether or not they have ADHD or are experiencing neglect or abuse at home. However, this "solution" runs the risk of masking or ignoring other, more fundamental life challenges. There certainly are children with brain-based difficulties that are helped by medication. However, this has become the go-to solution instead of utilizing an in-depth exploration of the whole child and the world they must navigate. Parents are extremely vulnerable to following this advice out of anxiety and desperation to help their child. It also helps some parents avoid blame for their child's difficulties or having to confront their own childhood trauma. ADHD may run in families, but so do anxiety, depression, forms of spectrum disorder, insecure attachment, and trauma.

Another example is a business executive who comes to therapy complaining of struggles at work. Despite her obvious intelligence and extensive industry knowledge, her promotion to a management position six months ago has led to overwhelming distress, anxiety, and social withdrawal. Although she has taken management courses and read a mountain of books, nothing seems to make a difference. She now wonders whether she is executive material, or, as her jealous husband suggests, is only smart enough to be a stay-at-home mom. The prior coaching she received, focusing on her business platform and management skills, have not proven helpful because her social anxieties, marital stressors, and past trauma were the real issues that needed to be addressed.

As we all know, relating to and managing others requires much more than cognitive intelligence. It also calls for empathy, perspective taking, and self-esteem. Emotional regulation, staying calm under pressure, and self-awareness are also necessary for success at work as well, especially when you reach the managerial level. Without these social and emotional resources, industry knowledge can only take you so far. What if the distress in their marriage or a child's illness has created stress that compromises their work performance? Is your client dealing with unconscious struggles with shame that prevent them from establishing boundaries, being assertive, or utilizing their skills?

Most would agree that a strictly cognitive model of EF is based on outdated notions of functional neuroanatomy and rooted in the adage "I think, therefore I am." This is why clinicians find it so difficult to translate and utilize the results of neuropsychological testing. In reality, executive functioning is the result of cooperation among many cognitive, social, and emotional neural systems that are influenced by our past, our present context, the broader culture, and even our vision of the future. If EF is the ability to target important goals, focus attention, create action plans, and carry them to completion, it is obvious that this always occurs within the context of a complex life. If there were no contexts, there would also be no environment to navigate, no goals to attain, and no need for EF.

In addition, there is the internal environment to consider, with its temperaments, emotions, moods, memories, and bodily states. There is also the social environment expressed via peer pressures, conscious family expectation, and unconscious loyalties passed down through the generations. These and other internal dynamics might keep us from doing the very things our executive systems direct us to do. The familiar conflict between our heads and hearts can result in the anxiety, ambivalence, and procrastination that can sabotage EF. Fluctuations of moods and states of mind may make what was easy to accomplish yesterday impossible to do today. These psychological dynamics make EF an embodied process that goes beyond anyone's objective analysis of a situation.

Executive functioning is like a Swiss Army knife—an interrelated set of tools with many purposes, rather than a single specialized cognitive skill confined to one part of the brain. While our abilities, knowledge, and goals change through time, our need to navigate daily life remains the same. Because each of us is an experiment of nature, there will always be a kaleidoscope of factors to consider with each of our clients across different situations. A deeper understanding of EF requires expanding our point of view to include an acceptance of diversity, both neurobiological and cultural, as well as an examination of how well a person is matched to their social and physical environments. And finally, when it comes to our experience, everything is ultimately connected to everything else, and the arbitrary lines we draw between mind, brain, and relationships may keep us from discovering the true nature of EF. Simplistic solutions seldom solve complex problems.

The Three-System Model

Human behavior flows from three main sources:
desire, emotion, and knowledge.
                                                —Plato

The three-system model of executive functioning described in the chapters ahead reflects a significant shift from the concept of a single executive located in the frontal lobes. We will be describing a dynamic relationship among three interconnected neural systems distributed throughout the brain. The first executive system (ES1), also referred to as the salience network, contains the amygdala and portions of the insular and cingulate cortices. It is responsible for the control of basic survival processes and approach-avoidance choices, and serves coordination and cooperation among the three systems.

The second executive system (ES2) is centered in networks of the parietal and frontal lobes. It is responsible for our sensory-motor navigation of the environment and is the seat of higher-order problem-solving and abstract thinking. The third executive system (ES3) is made up of what is also called the default mode network (DMN) and runs front to back through the middle regions of the brain. It appears to organize many inner experiences, including self-awareness, theory of mind, and imagination. Optimal EF requires the participation and cooperation of all three systems, in a complex and dynamic relationship.

The primary purpose of this book is to provide you with an expanded framework for understanding, working with, and optimizing EF in all of your clients. Although EF emerges within a complex dynamic system, we will first take a step-by-step journey through its various structures and functions. In later chapters, we will use the three-system model as a guide to a naturalistic assessment of a client's strengths and weaknesses combined with strategies for interventions and positive growth. The three-system model also serves as a neurobiological foundation for understanding a client's developmental, environmental, psychological, and social experiences that impact their current functioning. A guiding focus will be to explore the individual in context and an examination of skills and abilities they require to navigate their lives. EF always requires an ecosystem, and the sources of deficits are just as likely to exist outside as they do inside an individual.

If working with EF challenges seems overwhelming or outside your area of expertise, consider this: The majority of EF challenges are caused by difficulties with emotional dysregulation and/or chronic anxiety. If you have been trained to treat these symptoms, you already have many of the tools necessary to help clients with EF challenges. What remains is to learn to assess for hyperarousal and determine if it is the primary cause of EF dysfunction. Addressing emotional and family conflicts, examining the client's situation, and forming a strong alliance are all necessary skills in that work, many of which you already possess. The three-system model will guide us as we gather information, generate hypotheses, and develop treatment plans to address and treat deficits in executive functioning.

Executive Functioning and Psychotherapy

Part I
Theory and Historical Context

Chapter 1

The Exploration of Executive Functioning

*It's not what happens to you, but how
you react to it that matters.*

—Epictetus

What is executive functioning (EF), and how do we think, make decisions, and navigate our lives?

The current predominantly cognitive view has limited our ability to grasp the complex evolutionary, developmental, and psychosocial contributions to our understanding of EF. This perspective is perpetuated by cultural biases and reinforced by the separate scientific silos that study EF. While neuroscientists hone in on the latest brain research, neuropsychologists focus on measuring specific cognitive abilities, and social scientists are exploring the interpersonal effects on perception. There is little collaboration or communication among these research communities, and their diverse perspectives, languages, and academic departments keep them separated.

In fact, an understanding of EF requires the inclusion of many fields of study. In light of this, we're taking a deep dive into the notion of EF through the holistic lens of interpersonal neurobiology (IPNB). Interpersonal neurobiology was developed as a response to the segregation of scientific fields that are relevant to understanding human experience. It's an interdisciplinary approach that draws from the work of biologists, cognitive scientists, neuroscientists, evolutionists, developmental psychologists, and many others.

IPNB is not a therapeutic approach but an attempt to create a consilient framework that can be applied across treatment modalities. IPNB offers "a practical view of the underlying basis of mental suffering and the scientific mechanisms of change to improve mental well-being. These core principles are building blocks of clinical evaluation and treatment that can be applied across multiple theoretical orientations and client populations" (Siegel & Drulis, 2023).

For the purposes of this book, our working definition of EF is as follows:

Executive functioning is a broad set of skills and abilities that allow us to navigate our lives, environments, and relationships using conscious and unconscious input from our thoughts, bodily sensations, and emotions, as well as the beliefs and behaviors of those around us. This highly complex and integrative process includes both the internal and external forces that guide our moment-to-moment decision-making. The development of EF involves a complex interaction between genetics and experience, and encompasses all forms of emotional, social, and adaptive forms of intelligence.

While we certainly have evolved a degree of top-down organization and control offered by the frontal lobes, many levels of automatic and non-conscious forms of intelligence have been conserved from our mammalian ancestors. Consider the fact that when three or more males are present, female chimps respond loudly and aggressively to potentially threatening sounds. By contrast, they choose to quietly retreat in similar situations when two or fewer males are present (Hauser et al., 2000; Rossano, 2012). Thus, their executive decisions are influenced by social and contextual variables.

How we respond to threats is a key element driving the evolutionary adaptation of EF. These female chimps are assessing the situation, doing the math, and responding in a way that has likely been shaped through millions of years of natural selection. History has probably played out in such a way that three or more males are needed for a successful encounter with a predator or another group of chimps. In this situation, their primary value is to be a danger alert. With two or fewer, survival is served by sneaking away to live another day.

These more primitive levels of evaluating situations and making choices still exist within us and remain interwoven with later-evolving conscious mechanisms of problem-solving. While neurology offers little credence to the value of implicit knowledge in guiding our decision-making, what we call intuition represents an upward flow of information from our bodies, emotions, and signals we received in the past and are currently receiving from the external world. At the same time, why do we often fail to do what we know we should? Could our procrastination, deficits of attention, and failures of judgment have their sources in these same upward flows of information? Any comprehensive explanation of EF must include an openness to the contributions of all levels of our nervous system, including the kind of social and mathematical mechanisms we share with our primate ancestors.

The Executive Functioning of Phineas Gage

Knowledge is of no value unless you can put it into practice.
—Anton Chekhov

Although the term "executive functioning" gained popular usage in the early 1970s, interest in its neural foundation dates back to the 19th-century case of Phineas Gage. Gage became well-known in the field of neurology after suffering a gruesome injury while working as a railroad foreman. An explosion drove an iron rod upward into his left cheek, exiting through the top of his skull. Incredibly, Gage's capacities for attention, perception, language, motor function, and intelligence remained intact. Just as surprising was that after his physical recovery, "Gage was no longer Gage!" Changes in his personality, judgment, and EF left neurologists baffled.

The belief at the time was that personality was an innate and unchanging aspect of the soul, unrelated to the brain and body. However, Gage transformed from a sober, sensible, and moral person to a volatile, unpredictable, and unethical man who lacked a sense of purpose and forethought (Harlow, 1848). His case was clear evidence that damage to the brain could alter a person's behavior, judgment, planning ability, and character. His symptoms were so out of line with the beliefs of his time that Harlow's letter about the case to the *Boston Medical and Surgical Journal* in November 1848 was largely ignored. Since the 1990s, advances in theory and methodology within neuroscience have helped us to understand how and why Gage was so profoundly affected by his injury despite his intact cognition (Damasio, 1994). The case now serves as a foundation for a view of EF that goes far beyond cognition and the prefrontal cortex to include the entire body, relationships, and our multiple forms of intelligence.

The Current Dogma

Step with care and great tact, and remember
that life's a great balancing act.
                              —Dr. Seuss

Although there is no single accepted definition of EF, there is considerable overlap among the ideas proposed by leading theorists (Barkley, 2012a; Lezak, 1995; Luria, 1973; Stuss & Benson, 1986). First, there is a focus on the prefrontal cortex and its role in attention, rational thought, and logical reasoning (Pribram, 1973). Second, there is an assumption that EF is a solely conscious process in the service of goal-directed behavior (Shallice et al., 1994). In other words, we choose a goal, create a plan to achieve it, and execute our plan until the goal is reached. Third, there is a belief that EF is a solely top-down cognitive control of the other functions of the brain and body (Roth et al., 2005).

While most theorists recognize the importance of inhibition and impulse control for successful EF, physiological, emotional, and social input are rarely thought to be influencing our judgment and decision-making. This belief is held in neuropsychology despite the thousands of studies from other fields that demonstrate the significant impact of interpersonal experience on everything from selective attention, to emotional reasoning, to how long it takes to recover from surgery. The top-down model assumes both the primacy of conscious cognition in human behavior and its dissociation from the body and relationships. This model, sometimes referred to as "cold cognition," is a holdover from the dogma of a century ago maintained within the silo of cognitive psychology.

There is no doubt that the frontal lobe plays a central role in EF. However, research has consistently demonstrated that it must coordinate with many other neural networks to plan, problem-solve, and make advantageous decisions. The mental formulation of a plan will not get us far if we aren't able to navigate time and space, manage emotions, coordinate with others, and adapt to the demands of an ever-changing environment. This is why many of us are mentally aware of what we should do to be healthier, happier, and more successful, yet never bring our plans into action. So many of us have had the experience of saying, "I know it up here" (pointing to the head), "but not down here" (usually the heart). Using the cover story of being lazy or a chronic procrastinator only labels the behavior while telling us nothing of its origin.

The notion that executive functioning is a fully conscious process is driven by the common assumption that we are totally aware of and in control of all of our actions and behavior. In other words, there is total free will and no unconscious mind. While a comforting thought, this belief is far from accurate. There are countless implicit processes that impact our thoughts and actions outside of conscious awareness, such as in instances of racial bias, transference, and love at first sight. The same is true when we pursue unavailable partners because of a fear of rejection or postpone taking on challenges to avoid the possibility of failure. All of these instances point to the fact that our EF is being influenced by unconscious physiological, social, and emotional processes.

Human beings evolved as social creatures with brains shaped within a matrix of relationships. Like tuning forks, our nervous systems resonate with and attune to the nervous systems of those around us. Social interactions build the architecture of our brains and regulate our physiological and psychological states. These social signals also impact our experience, emotions, and behaviors and thus, our EF. The way that we think, feel, act, and behave will be directly impacted by the context of where we are and who we are with. Just think about how emotions and behaviors can be modified, in opposition to our usual way of being, when we are in a crowd, gang, or mob. Optimal EF has always necessitated striking an appropriate balance between our needs and the circumstances and demands of our tribe.

Past Theories of Executive Functioning

A man does not consist of memory alone. He has
feeling, will, sensibility, and moral being.

—Alexander Luria

The present three-system model is inclusive of a century of experimental and clinical research in EF. Most of this past work focuses on the cognitive aspects of EF and applies primarily to what we will be referring to as the second executive system (ES2). Over time, there has been a gradual inclusion of social and emotional influences on EF, but these aspects were generally seen as tangential. The three-system model includes and expands upon this past work, balancing its cognitive focus with the emotional, social, and experiential aspects of functioning. We'll begin with an overview of the history of the study of EF around the middle of the 20th century.

The modern conception of EF can be traced to the work of the Russian psychologist Alexander Luria, who gained extensive experience in brain-behavior relationships while treating brain-injured soldiers during and after World War II. Luria's work established the central role of the frontal lobes in regulating arousal, directing attention, and navigating time and space. Alongside his mentor and colleague Leo Vygotsky, Luria mapped out a dynamic and multifactorial landscape of the mind and its multiple interdependent neural networks. Vygotsky encouraged Luria to include the social nature of the brain in his studies of development as well as the role of language and communication in self-regulation. They both believed that the development of this system of networks reflected an interplay of both genetic and environmental factors including social relationships and culture. They also agreed that the internalization of language becomes an inner dialogue used to guide thinking and complex problem-solving.

Luria's biopsychosocial developmental model and its integration of the subjective elements of experience stood in stark contrast to the dominant behavioral view. Although Luria acknowledged the importance of behavior in learning, he considered it as only one of many elements of EF. Just as important, Luria argued, were the mediating variables of speech, objects, signs, and symbols between stimulus and response. The nature of these mediating tools would arise from the adaptations of each individual and be unique to the individual within their sociocultural context. Self-regulation was understood as a developmental process where a child would learn to apply strategies for impulse control, planning, and deliberation while discovering socially acceptable strategies to meet their needs. Luria's contributions to our understanding of brain development as a dynamic, interactive system that is impacted by social and cultural factors remain essential to our three-system model of EF.

Cognition Hot and Cold

Man is a rational animal who always loses his temper when
called upon to act in accordance with the dictates of reason.
                                                    —Orson Welles

Despite Luria's articulation of the complex and dynamic elements of intelligence, neuropsychologists remained fixated on assessing conscious thought and the prefrontal cortex. The dominant behavioral and cognitive models in psychology largely ignored his broad, inclusive perspective in favor of cold cognition, which assumes that our thinking is separate from our bodies, emotions, and relationships. In opposition to this central dogma, there was a gradual shift toward a warmer model of cognition. In regard to assessing cognitive functioning, the pioneering neuropsychologist Muriel Lezak (1982) noted the importance of purposive action, self-regulation, and social intelligence. Although it was subjective and difficult to assess, she elected to include information about personal history, reports from collaterals, and her clinical observations along with the results of the objective testing she organized and developed.

At the same time, the work of Donald Stuss and neurologist Frank Benson (1986) focused on the regulation of arousal and attentional control. Their research led them to an expanded focus from the frontal lobes to the limbic system and other subcortical regions guiding these central aspects of EF. Another important contribution was made by the neuroscientist Joaquin Fuster (2000), who explored the integration of sensory, motor, and cognitive behavior across time. Fuster's work expanded the notion of EF from an abstract pursuit of the mind to the coordination of sensation, movement, memory, and action in space and time.

Meanwhile, Antonio Damasio became fascinated by individuals with damage to areas of the prefrontal cortex who performed well on standardized tests but experienced difficulties in situations that required judgment and decision-making. Although their abstract reasoning was intact based on neuropsychological testing, they struggled with real-life tasks requiring emotional and somatic input, similar to what had been witnessed in Phineas Gage. To explore this dimension of EF, Bechara and Damasio (2005) developed a gambling task measuring decisions related to risk and reward. While healthy participants were quickly able to discern risk-reward patterns, those with injuries that blocked input from the body's physiological stress response made riskier and less advantageous choices. This bodily input, which Damasio came to call somatic markers, guided healthy participants to gamble more successfully (Bechara & Damasio, 2005). These results clearly showed the important contribution of unconscious bodily input to decision-making, the safe navigation of the environment, and overall EF.

In his 1994 book *Descartes' Error*, Damasio described the interactive contributions of the mind and the body in intelligence and EF. Descartes's error was to believe, "I think, therefore I am," because we also act, react, experience, and feel. Minds are always embodied within brains and bodies, and contextualized within families, communities, and cultures. This suggests that there is no cold cognition, only a degree to which other factors contribute to EF. Thanks to Damasio's research, the notion of hot cognition (thinking influenced by the body and relationships) has become more widely accepted.

Using a different approach, research by the neuropsychologist Paul Eslinger and his team has focused on the social and emotional consequences of dementia. His work has led to the delineation of four specific functional domains they call "social executors": (1) *social self-regulation*, processes needed to manage social interactions; (2) *social self-awareness*, insight into the impact of one's behavior on others; (3) *social sensitivity*, the ability to understand another's perspective, point of view, or emotional state (similar to empathy and theory of mind); and (4) *social salience*, the regulation of somatic and emotional states that impart meaning to social situations (Eslinger et al., 2012). As you will see, these social-emotional executive abilities are included in the three-system model and organized by the first and third executive systems.

Finally, Russell Barkley, who has spent his career in the research and treatment of ADHD, conceptualizes EF as a kind of extended phenotype. This means that it is shaped by evolution, embedded in relationships and culture, and updated by our ongoing adaptation to our ever-changing physical and social environments (Barkley, 2010). While still favoring a top-down perspective, Barkley considers nuances of EF that are beyond the traditional cognitive view. He points out, for example, that the problems faced by those with EF deficits have more to do with not using what they know at critical points rather than not knowing what to do. Essentially, abstract knowledge does not equal self-regulation or the ability to make good choices. Our model will build on Barkley's line of thinking and attempt to address these questions: Why is it not enough to know what to do? What gets in our way? How are these conflicting directives organized within our brains, and how do we address these issues in psychotherapy?

All of the theorists discussed in this chapter have made valuable contributions to our understanding of the nature of intelligence and executive functioning. The throughline of their work to our own is an expanding development from the belief in a disembodied rational intelligence to embodied capacities that allow us to navigate the real world of people, places, and things. Our hope for this book is to take a next step in developing an inclusive and useful way of understanding and utilizing EF in clinical practice, one that can also be integrated with existing forms of cognitive assessment, psychotherapy, and ancillary forms of treatment.

Chapter 2

An Expanded View of Executive Functioning

Wholeness is not achieved by cutting off a portion of one's being, but by the integration of the contraries.

—Carl Jung

For a broader perspective of executive functioning, we will be utilizing the consilient framework of interpersonal neurobiology (IPNB). As mentioned in Chapter 1, IPNB incorporates a broad range of perspectives from neuroscience to evolution, anthropology, and attachment theory. From neuroscience, we learn about brain-behavior relationships and the underlying neurodynamic processes of EF. Cultural anthropology, attachment theory, and epigenetics provide a framework to consider how our brains and minds are shaped by relationships and culture. Biology sheds light on the biochemical processes that drive and guide human behavior and decision-making. Developmental psychology gives us essential information about how the brain and mind develop across the lifespan. Just as the instruments of an orchestra come together to create an infinite complexity of sound, together, the different fields of science reveal a deeper, more inclusive understanding of human experience.

In IPNB, the synthesis of theory and research across these and other fields of study is guided by a number of fundamental assumptions about the human condition. Here are seven such principles to keep in mind as we move ahead:

1. Our Brains Are Social Organs of Adaptation

The human brain is a social organ of adaptation, shaped by natural selection to support the survival of both the individual and the group. As we evolved to be increasingly social, our ancestors became more reliant on their tribe to survive. At the level of group selection, tribes of individuals that connected and communicated in more sophisticated ways gained a survival advantage over rival groups. These developments also gave rise to our increasing ability to build the brains of our children (epigenetics) and regulate the brains of those around us (sociostasis). Linked together as a group, we became a "super-organism," better able to cope with changing environments, protect ourselves from predators, and fight our enemies.

2. Evolution Is a Problem-Solving and a Problem-Creating Process

Over millions of years, evolution has armed us with effective survival strategies; initially in the physical environment and later in our emerging social world. These navigational strategies are what we now call executive functioning: the thoughts, feelings, and behaviors that guide us through our day-to-day lives. The result is that we have complex and heterogeneous brains that retain primitive and nonconscious processes, interwoven with later-evolving conscious and rational abilities. The same primitive fight/flight response that helped our ancestors escape from predators now helps us rapidly avoid an auto accident. A second later, we become conscious of what just happened because conscious cortical processing takes longer than primitive reflexes.

These two executive systems, and a third that guides our social and emotional functioning, can work independently, process different information, and run on separate clocks. Each of our executive systems has evolved in different eras, develops at different rates during life, and is expert in different tasks. While the brain's complexity and specialized functions allow us to cope with many challenges, these same factors have led to the creation of new problems. These problems are often the reason for mental distress and seeking therapy.

3. The Brain Functions at Conscious and Nonconscious Levels

The majority of neural processing is automatic and nonconscious. It does, however, influence and often guide our conscious experience without our awareness. This is not only true in psychotherapy; it is also at play in EF when reflexes, habit patterns, stress, anxiety, and unresolved trauma mix with cognitive and abstract thinking. For example, an executive may continue to bring conflict into the boardroom because of the activation of implicit memories of childhood family conflict. After work, he may be drawn to the same unhealthy romantic partners or addictive coping strategies as he struggles with unconscious fears of abandonment and shame. We all have parallel narratives that guide our experience: the conscious narrative we tell ourselves and others, and the unconscious narratives expressed in our nonadaptive thoughts, feelings, and behaviors. Our multitrack processing is one of evolution's most troublesome legacies.

The fact that unconscious fear is usually more powerful than our conscious thoughts is an example of the primacy of our earlier-evolving survival systems. We can't simply think ourselves into better decision-making until we learn to manage the fear-based reflexes that contaminate our reasoning. For example, if I know that eating healthier will improve my health and make me feel better, I will struggle to put this into practice until I uncover the fact that I am using food as a coping mechanism for anxiety. In this case, the primitive executive system will drive me toward what will reduce anxiety (food), and my conscious desire to be healthier will be unable to inhibit it. I first need to find a way to identify the problem and find an alternative way to manage anxiety (e.g., meditation, exercise, medication) before I am able to act in my own best interest.

4. Our Minds Are Embodied and Relational

Our minds arise from the interaction among our brains, bodies, and relationships. Our brains are simultaneously a part of our bodies and also live within a matrix of other brains. This is why our EF is impacted by both our physiology and our relationships. We know that we do not perform our best when we are under high levels of stress or when we are tired or ill. An inconsiderate coworker or a bad mood of a partner can undermine our attention, motivation, and abilities. Similarly, if we are struggling, a kind word or the encouragement of an employer can turn us around. This is why any model of EF must include executive systems involved in both bodily regulation and social connectedness.

5. The Brain Consists of a Government of Neural Systems

Although we think of the brain as a monolithic structure, it is actually a complex government of neural systems, each with its own realm of functioning, evolutionary history, and developmental trajectories. This complexity has contributed to our species' greatest accomplishments and most grievous mistakes. The various activities and roles we engage in require a range of contributions and activation patterns across multiple neural systems. The neural systems engaged when we negotiate a pay raise will not be identical to those which become activated when trying to soothe a loved one. Successful EF requires an ever-changing and dynamic relationship among our three executive systems, the rest of our body, and those around us.

6. The Brain Retains Plasticity Throughout Life

Research in neuroplasticity supports the idea that neuroplasticity, learning, and development continue to occur throughout life. For example, having grandchildren activates attachment circuitry to change and grow later in adulthood, serving the purpose of supporting our children's children. On the other hand, learning new information unrelated to what you already know seems to become more difficult in midlife. However, we retain the ability to add to structures of knowledge we already have. Thus, we can become more expert in a particular field as we age, while it is more difficult to change fields and start from scratch at 40 than it was at 20.

Because our brains are organs of adaptation, they require new and challenging situations to adapt to. In the absence of ongoing challenges, the biological resources required to build new neurons and neural connections are directed elsewhere in the body. As therapists, we rely on this ongoing plasticity to allow for changes in dysfunctional thoughts, feelings, and behaviors with our clients. Positive outcomes rely on our ability to reorganize neural networks in new and more adaptive ways.

7. The Importance of Social-Emotional Intelligence

The cognitive elements of EF are necessary but not sufficient to success-fully navigate contemporary life. A good manager, teacher, or therapist must know the techniques of their trade and possess the self-awareness, awareness of others, and the social-emotional intelligence to apply them. From boardrooms to classrooms, people seldom care what you know until they know that you care. We need to be effective at perceiving, interpret-ing, and expressing emotions to exhibit true social-emotional intelligence. The importance of emotional intelligence in everyday life underscores the integral role of qualities such as self-awareness, empathy, motivation, self-regulation, and social skills. Additionally, good decision-making usually involves ethical consideration and gut feelings in business and leadership. Social-emotional intelligence involves an integration of emotion and cog-nition that is key to optimal EF.

Neurodynamic Integration

> *We are always in a perpetual state of being*
> *created and creating ourselves.*
>
> —Dan Siegel

As we discussed earlier, the brain is a government of systems with shifting patterns of neural activation triggered by the demands of each situation we encounter. Flexibility and adaptation across various tasks is at the core of EF. At a dinner party, our brains will connect to others and activate the thoughts, behaviors, memories, and emotions that help us connect, relax, and enjoy the evening. In a job interview, alternative activation patterns will allow us to present what we know and conduct ourselves in a profes-sional manner. Each of our experiences contributes to mental models and neurodynamic patterns that will become activated in future situations. This is how both positive and negative past experiences, habit patterns, and defenses come to contribute to maladaptive behaviors.

The more pervasive negative attitudes we have internalized, like poor self-esteem, feelings of abandonment, or being fearful of abuse, the more likely we are to be overwhelmed by these negative emotions when they are triggered in the present. When these echoes of the past stored within our nervous system become activated, we are much more likely to engage in maladaptive, negative, and self-destructive behaviors. We see this occur in just about all of our clients and ourselves from time to time, and it can be quite confusing if we are unaware of the historical origins and emotional underpinnings of our actions. One day we might be patient, compassionate, and emotionally attuned with our tantrumming toddler, and the next, react in a way that is far from our best self.

Although we expect ourselves to be consistent across time and situations, this is a far cry from how we actually function. States of mind can be chaotic; our reactions are influenced by fleeting emotions, and we can never predict when an implicit association from the past will be triggered and direct our attention in surprising ways. The disparity between our expectations and the realities of experience can lead to feelings of confusion, shame, and the fear that we are disappointing others. This is one of the reasons why every therapeutic relationship presents new challenges. It is also why therapists need their own therapy and supervision to learn as much as possible about their unconscious triggers and biases.

Rather than striving to be a singular, consistent self, it is best to accept the multiplicity of experience and the ever-emerging emotions, bodily states, and states of mind that arise. If we can step back from the illusion of consistency, we gain the opportunity to work toward an inclusive and coherent equilibrium among them. The goal is not consistency but openness, flexibility, and balance. Keep in mind, however, that stress, anxiety, and fear can inhibit cortical functioning and undermine these abilities. Because life is often challenging, maintaining a state of integration requires consistent attention to self-awareness, learning, and remembering ourselves.

The Three-System Model

The mind is like an iceberg, it floats with one-seventh of its bulk above water.

—Sigmund Freud

Most clients come to therapy with an extremely limited understanding of their own brains and minds. Many imagine a homunculus—or "Mini-Me"—who lives behind their eyes, directing their thoughts, words, and actions. This is a handy illusion shaped by evolution to create the experience of self-direction and free will. We identify with our homunculus and assume we are one with it. The concept of autonomous, top-down, and cognitive EF is based on this illusion and expectation of a single experience of self. The majority of current educational systems are based on this belief. As such, intelligence is measured by IQ scores, and standardized tests are thought to be predictors of academic and career success. We tend to gloss over the fact that there are many contradictions to this view.

Many of the limitations of the current views of both EF and intelligence rest on the denial of our descendance from our primitive ancestors and the obvious reality that we are embodied, social, and emotional creatures. In other words, the homunculus doesn't live in our heads; we are the human living in the real world. Our EF has evolved over many millions of years across all levels of our nervous system and adapted to the physical and social environments to which our ancestors needed to adapt. Although below conscious awareness, the influence and input of our entire nervous system, our bodies, and those around us continue to contribute to our EF. Our EF is both impacted by and embedded within the relationships, emotions, and impulses inherited by our ancestors and learned during our lives. Our technical skills (oh, what a beautiful spreadsheet!) are only one expression of a vast and complex matrix of intelligences and represent but a fraction of EF.

What we are now proposing is that successful executive functioning requires the participation of (at least) three interacting neural systems, each of which receives and processes a wide range of input to control different aspects of EF. These systems must communicate and cooperate in order for us to achieve optimal EF. As we widen the lens through which to examine EF, we have to include bottom-up contributions of the body and extended nervous system. Our primitive decision-making systems that support physical survival and bodily well-being also play a role. Consider this: How do we return a 100-mph tennis serve? How do we know when to respond to someone with our hearts rather than our minds? These decisions require a model that includes the role of reflexes, somatic states, feelings, and input from our physical and social worlds. More importantly, why can someone have a great deal of cognitive intelligence and still be socially inept or completely dysfunctional? Any comprehensive model of EF has to account for why intact cognitive functioning doesn't always translate into effective life skills.

This new model of EF requires a shift in thinking from a unidirectional, top-down hierarchy to a distributed model spread across multiple processing hubs. Information can flow up and down, left and right, and from the middle out and back in again. Our vision of the self as a homunculus is replaced by a holistic view of a person who thinks, feels, and senses their way through life. From this perspective, we can also expand our focus from linear cause-and-effect relationships to the complexity of thinking of the individual in the context of their social and physical environments. Optimal EF requires the development of each system and their ability to work together or selectively stand down, depending on the requirements of the task. Nothing about the way we function is simple and straightforward, and this is why a three-system model may bring us a step closer to understanding how EF works.

Clinical Applications

We do as we have been done by.
—John Bowlby

Thinking about our clients within this three-system model might sound complicated or intimidating at first. In reality, you likely already have experience working with key aspects of this model. For example, a workaholic father may come to therapy despairing over the lack of an emotional connection with his wife and children. Rather than suggesting some social skills techniques, we consider the larger picture of his adaptational history.

Perhaps he grew up in a family where emotions were not expressed or discussed, and this environment led him to seek purpose and reinforcement from his career rather than his loved ones. He is smart, successful, and active, but also lonely and insecure. He realizes that he needs to find a way to connect with his family but lacks the connection with his own inner emotional world to build a bridge to them. Within the three-system model, he possesses the EF skills to be successful at work, but not the ones required to be a husband and father. Cases like this show us that EF is not a monolithic function but a diverse set of skills and abilities that differ across situations.

Another client with a difficult history is experiencing chronic anxiety and frequent panic attacks. Her unresolved trauma is impacting her emotional regulation, empathy, and cognitive processing. She comes to therapy believing she may have ADHD, which is making her unable to function at home and at work. In reality, her first executive system—hypervigilant for danger—is inhibiting her emotional and cognitive functioning. She does, in fact, have a deficit in attention, concentration, and EF, but it isn't due to a lack of intelligence or prefrontal development. It is due to a lack of neurodynamic balance among her executive systems and the inhibition of her cortical executive processing. The best way to improve her EF would be to process past trauma and provide her with more helpful tools for affect regulation.

Consider a young girl who comes to therapy due to emotional outbursts, inattentiveness, and trouble taking direction at school. The referral calls for a diagnostic workup to rule out ADHD, anxiety, and depression. Her neuropsychological evaluation reveals deficits in attention, concentration, and challenges with impulse control (which she has also demonstrated in therapy). Rather than honing in on her cognitive functioning, let's zoom out and consider the larger picture. A conversation with her father reveals that her problems at school developed around the same time he and his wife were going through a contentious divorce. The client was having to adapt to shifting between two houses, getting used to a new nanny, and dealing with the emotional volatility of her parents. Because she had no history of developmental difficulties or symptoms of attentional problems, the focus of treatment should be her attachment relationships, sense of security, and creating a healthy narrative for her new life.

Just as the brain is an organ of adaptation, EF is a process of adaptation to our physical and social worlds. As our brains and minds take shape during the early years of life, the structures and strategies of our survival become the behavioral templates and internal logic we use going forward. As most of our early learning is nonconscious, the influence of our early experiences is often obscure and difficult to bring into conscious awareness. If these templates are flexible enough to adapt to adult challenges, they usually go unseen and unexplored. If they are too rigid or a bad fit for life beyond our families of origin, we struggle, become distressed, and seek solutions. This dilemma is what psychotherapy was originally created to address.

Consider the development of a child's executive functioning as their brains and minds adapt to an insecure parent—one who attempts to soothe their own anxieties by trying to control everything around them. These parents are usually intolerant of alternative opinions and ways of doing things. They are also prone to experiencing differences of opinions from others, including their children, as critical and/or rejecting. Through countless interactions, their children learn that their ideas, interests, and autonomy trigger negativity and rejection from their parent. Because they are completely dependent and have no other frame of reference, they soon learn that their well-being hinges on compliance with the demands of their caregivers. Internally, they learn that their connection with the parent is best served by avoiding having their own thoughts, opinions, and desires.

Normal attempts at autonomy or individuation by this child will be met with the parent's emotional dysregulation and threats of physical and financial abandonment. The compliant child is terrified by these manipulations and does their best to stay in their parent's good graces. If they are clever enough, they fine-tune their dependency by conforming to the parent's psychological needs. They will learn to avoid making choices, neglect life's demands, and sabotage personal successes out of their invisible loyalty to their parent's needs. This family dynamic makes it more likely that the child will have been excluded from learning most of the psychological and professional skills that would allow for their independence.

This adaptation shapes the networks, strategies, and structures of their executive functioning. On the surface, it looks as if the child lacks the intelligence, motivation, and EF to be competent and autonomous. What is not seen is that they have been quite successful in adapting to the invisible emotional requirements of the family system. When their parents search for answers to their children's failures at school and work, they seldom consider the family as a source of problems. When they are told by professionals that their child has problems with attention, concentration, and EF, they naturally accept it as the probable cause. This directs the solutions to focus on medication, executive coaching, and forced discipline for their child's "neurological" problems. They generally come to believe that their child's problem is a result of an unfortunate genetic inheritance, from the other parent's side of the family.

When these children enter psychotherapy as adults, they are often characterized by feelings of insecurity, emptiness, and a lack of motivation. Once the scaffolding of the controlling parent is removed, they lack the skills and experience to take over this function. Not only have they been punished for attempts at autonomy, but they have never had to face the confusion, uncertainty, and failures of everyday trial-and-error learning. If they never rebelled against control earlier in life, they will usually be afraid of the anger, energy, boundaries, and power required for autonomy. For autonomy to grow during adulthood, assertiveness, boundaries, and anger need to be accessed and utilized. If not, it is possible to stay in a frightened and dependent state throughout life.

The diagnostic labels, medication, and failure at school and work usually trigger shame, erode self-confidence, and reinforce the need to rely on the parent. Because these children lack boundaries, assertiveness, and a sense of their own power, they learn to get what they want through passive manipulation, a lesson learned at the knee of their parent. Ironically, the parent will see their child's attempts at manipulation as a sign of bad character, antisocial personality, and more evidence for their lack of proper EF. The child's stellar emotional awareness of the parent and their successful adaptation to their parent's unconscious world is never recognized for the high level of EF it actually represents.

Chapter 3

A Three-System Model of Executive Functioning

Teamwork makes the dream work, but a vision becomes a nightmare when the leader has a big dream and a bad team.
—John C. Maxwell

Picture a mother scanning a recipe while stirring vegetables on the stove. At the same time, she talks with her third-grader about his geography homework and responds to a text from her teenage daughter about soccer practice. This is an everyday example of the broad attention required for adaptive multitasking. The benefit of her simultaneously juggling multiple tasks in this situation is clear. However, attention is a limited resource, and each task will receive some fraction of her focus and concentration. There is a chance she will tell her son that the capital of Peru is asparagus, or not remember when her daughter said she would be home. A moment later, when her four-year-old comes into the room wailing, she turns her attention exclusively to him, getting down at eye level to soothe his distress. After her son is reregulated, she turns back to dinner and geography, while trying to remember what time her daughter told her to pick her up.

This complex pattern of EF and the adaptive intelligence it generates reflects

1. second executive (ES2) abilities in cooking, geography, and temporal planning,

2. third executive (ES3) skills in emotional attunement and soothing, and
3. first executive (ES1) capacity to maintain emotional regulation while orchestrating the activation and participation of the other two.

This everyday example of multitasking highlights the fact that although we can discuss the executive systems separately, adaptive intelligence in the real world requires that they work together within a complex and dynamic system.

Localization of Functions Versus Dynamic System Interaction

Simplicity does not precede complexity, but follows it.
—Alan Perlis

Until recently, neurology and neuroscience were preoccupied with finding a specific brain region responsible for each of our skills and abilities. The search for specific brain-behavior relationships, also known as localization theory, began with phrenology in the 1800s, was adapted by Broca and Wernicke at the dawn of neurology, and continued to guide theory and research through the 20th century. Scientists raced to lay claim to some area of this unexplored territory for a specific task. The slew of exceptions and contradictions arising from this simplistic perspective were glossed over by the need to establish a knowledge base.

For basic functions, like reflexes and startle responses, simple nervous system-behavior relationships are somewhat accurate. By contrast, increasingly complex abilities, like sustained attention, language, or theory of mind, make clear the inadequacy of localization theory. The gap only grows larger when you explore higher-level abilities like creativity, social intelligence, or consciousness. Most human abilities once sought in specific regions of the brain are actually dependent on widespread neural networks. Similarly, structures previously thought to perform only one function have been shown to participate in many others. In addition, an understanding of systems neurodynamics—their ability to communicate, cooperate, and modulate one another—is essential.

The human brain is a grayish lump of tissue weighing just a few pounds. Not very impressive at first glance, until you realize that you are looking at 100 billion neurons, another 100 billion glial cells, and connections numbering in the trillions. Then there is the additional dimension of time—an evolutionary process that has been experimenting with how to navigate the world for a billion of years. If you multiply the brain's computational power by the time it has had to test and develop adaptational strategies, the complexity is beyond comprehension. It is easy to see how many come to believe that it must have been designed by an intelligence far greater than our own.

As a rule of thumb, the more complex an ability:

1. the longer it took to evolve,
2. the more widely distributed it is throughout the brain,
3. the more likely it is to involve cortical structures, and
4. the more its development and current functioning are influenced by social and emotional experience.

Executive functioning checks all of these boxes, which is a primary reason why defining it as a cognitive function of the prefrontal cortex has such limited clinical utility. We believe that expanding EF to a three-system model is a step in the right direction; more complex, yes, but the value of this new model is that it accounts for more of the data and provides greater clinical application. In this chapter, we will explore an overview of the three-system model, followed by a deeper dive into each system.

The Three-System Model: An Overview

> Finding good players is easy. Getting them
> to play as a team is another story.
> —Casey Stengel

In exploring how our brains evolved to navigate, adapt, and survive, it appears that instead of one executive area controlling our behavior, we possess at least three interwoven executive systems. Each system participates in a broad set of abilities, has a particular evolutionary history, and follows a unique developmental trajectory. Depending on the task, these three systems interact with one another in ways that can be *inhibitory*, *excitatory*, *cooperative*, or *synergistic*. In addition to rational thought, EF includes our ability to regulate our bodies and emotions, be self-reflective, and connect with others. Optimal EF requires the development, integration, and participation of all three systems. We have chosen to call these systems the first, second, and third executives for simplicity but will associate them with many of the labels used in neuroscience research.

The First Executive System (ES1)

The first executive is a primitive system with the amygdala at its evolutionary core. The role of the first system is to make positive and negative associations to all of our experiences to guide future behavior. This is the system that may motivate us to move away from a dog if we have had a bad prior experience and toward ice cream if we have enjoyed it in the past. It receives information up from the body and down from the cortex to trigger associations and appropriate behaviors in response to stimuli in the outer world and from within our own minds. Areas of the frontal, insular, and cingulate cortices evolved to cooperate in these approach-avoidance decisions and trigger appropriate physical actions. ES1 controls our arousal, the focus of our attention, and fight/flight/freeze responses.

As the cortex grew and became more complex, these structures also came to guide the activation and inhibition of the other two systems in line with our moment-to-moment needs. This is why ES1 is often referred to as the *salience network* (SN). This simply means that it directs our attention and brain activity in line with the importance (salience) of each situation and the adaptational intelligence it requires. As the earliest conductor of EF, ES1 maintains veto power over the other two systems and is capable of inhibiting them. This is why, if we are walking down the street texting a friend and a growling dog appears out of nowhere, we forget about texting, and our complete focus shifts to the dog. This is the amygdala and salience system at work.

In a dangerous situation, the amygdala takes over and largely inhibits the other executive systems until the immediate danger has passed. This veto power has been referred to as "amygdala hijack" in the trauma literature. Because the first executive receives input from systems of implicit memory, it can be triggered by associations from a traumatic history. This phenomenon helps explain why stress, anxiety, and fear have such a detrimental impact on our ability to sit still, attend, and learn, as well as our ability to connect with others. When this primitive executive system is overactive and/or chronically aroused, we experience anxiety disorders, panic attacks, and posttraumatic stress disorder (PTSD) flashbacks. The inclusion of this system in EF helps to explain why so many of our clients with normal cognitive functioning experience EF deficits.

The Second Executive System (ES2)

A second system, alternatingly referred to in the research literature as the central executive, task-positive network, or parietal-frontal circuit, is centered primarily within the frontal and parietal lobes and the white matter tracts that connect them. This expanded circuit has recently come to be seen as performing the roles previously thought to reside solely in the prefrontal cortex. The second executive integrates the brain's processing of space (parietal) and time (frontal), allowing us to navigate our physical, conceptual, and imaginal environments. This second executive receives information from the entire cortex and motor networks, allowing us to navigate space and time. ES2 has been the primary focus of intelligence and neuropsychological testing designed to assess the cognitive aspects of EF.

Over the course of evolution, the second executive system leveraged its growing neural complexity in the service of increasingly sophisticated problem-solving. While the first executive motivates us to approach a goal, the second makes it possible for us to reach it. The first executive system remembers that a coconut is something positive, while the second remembers it is edible and learns how to find, gather, store, and open it. Far down the evolutionary path, this system figured out a way to make machines do all this as well as bottle its milk. The second executive system contains mirror neurons in both the frontal and parietal lobes that allow us to imitate others and learn through observation and imitation.

Damage to the second executive can result in an array of deficits in problem-solving, navigating the environment, and a loss of abstract reasoning. The damage may be physical, such as a penetrating head wound or a closed head injury. Functional deficits can be a result of biochemical imbalances, as in schizophrenia, depression, or drug addiction. They can also occur in states of chronic arousal where the first executive inhibits this system through sustained high levels of cortisol and adrenaline. This is why many children and adolescents fail in school despite a healthy brain and others fail to attain their career potential due to life stressors and unresolved trauma. It is the ability of the first executive to inhibit the second that leads to so many misdiagnosed instances of anxiety and depression as ADHD.

The Third Executive System (ES3)

Our third executive system got its name, the default mode network (DMN), because it was first discovered while research subjects were lying in scanners "doing nothing" between experimental tasks. Although its name reflects our cultural bias that favors doing over being, the discovery of the DMN has led researchers to explore internally focused brain activity. We have learned that our DMN is at work when we daydream, reflect on ourselves, replay old memories, or think about others. It appears to specialize in the experience of self-awareness, social awareness, and mental travel through space and time. It seems to be centrally involved in aspects of social intelligence related to understanding, empathy, and compassion for others and ourselves. Like the second executive, the third can also become inhibited by high levels of ES1 arousal.

While originally thought to be active only when the second executive was at rest, it now appears that the two also cooperate in ways that serve cognition and integrate our personal experience and problem-solving abilities. Think of the DMN as the system we attempt to activate and communicate with during insight-oriented therapy. We do this first by working to deactivate the first executive system through the development of a safe and trusting relationship. Next, we encourage clients to orient away from a focus on the outside world and consider their experience in the present moment. Third, we help them shift their focus to the realities of the here and now—their thoughts, feelings, and the therapeutic relationship. From these insights, we also use the participation of the second executive to problem-solve and take new learning into their day-to-day life.

For reference and review, Table 3.1 contains lists of the core neurological structures and executive functions of each of the three systems. In the chapters to come, we will be exploring each in more detail as well as their interactive and dynamic relationships with one another.

TABLE 3.1
The Three Executive Systems

	Core Structure	Functions
First (ES1)	Amygdala	Rapid evaluation of negative and positive stimuli
	Anterior cingulate cortex	Attention to novel and dangerous stimuli
	Anterior insular cortex	Interruption of ongoing activity
	Medial prefrontal cortex	Redirection of attention to novel and dangerous stimuli
	Autonomic nervous system	Fight/flight/flee responses
	Vagal system	Regulation of bodily arousal
Second (ES2)	Frontal lobe	Space-time navigation, problem-solving
	Parietal lobe	Sustained attention, task perseverance
	Hippocampus	Concentration, abstract thinking
	Temporal lobe	Working: narrative and autobiographical memory
Third (ES3)	Medial prefrontal cortex	Self-awareness, social awareness, perception, and cognition
	Posterior cingulate cortex	Empathy, compassion, attunement
	Parietal lobe	Autobiographical memory, self-reflection
	Medial temporal lobe	Mental time travel, imagination, daydreaming

The Three Systems in Action

You are only as good as your team.

—Dominique Wilkins

When my (LC's) son started preschool, my task was to drop him off each morning on my way to work. This meant that in addition to getting myself ready, I would be helping my wife get him washed up and dressed, fed, packed up, and on his way. This would take place alongside my showering, drinking coffee, brushing my teeth, getting dressed, making sure I had everything I needed for work, and finding my shoes, keys, and glasses before leaving the house. All of these things needed to be accomplished to allow time to drive to his school, park, take him into the school, sign him in, store his supplies for the day, and settle him in so he wouldn't be upset by my leaving him behind.

Most parents recognize some version of this routine where they sequence multiple tasks, keep an eye on the clock, and alternate between putting on their shoes and changing diapers, while remembering to brush their own teeth. Successfully managing all of these tasks and accomplishing the goals of getting us both where we need to be on time is an expression of the array of tasks organized by the second executive—attention, concentration, problem-solving, and persevering until we attain our goals. (Occasionally my second executive would fail me, and I'd show up at work with only half of my face shaved, wearing two different socks, or without my phone.)

You may also recognize that it is not always easy to stay calm and remain flexible to lapses of cooperation from your child, or some tension with the spouse. A smooth morning requires not only being able to perform the mechanical aspects of getting ready but also regulating your emotional reactions (first executive) and having an empathic understanding of your child's and spouse's reaction to the morning and the stressors they are experiencing (third executive). While some parents may have a completely intact second executive organizing their morning, a failure of optimal participation of the other two systems can turn mornings into a disaster for the entire family. This is why failures in successful functioning often occur because of difficulties in the first and third. Here is just one example.

With my second executive system in control, my son and I would exit the front door, backpack in one hand, Sam's tiny hand in the other, and walk slowly down the pathway to the car. When we would arrive at the back door of the car, I would put down my backpack and open the door so he could jump up into his booster seat. The next steps were to buckle him in, walk around to the back of the car, put our stuff in the trunk, walk around to the driver's door, get in, and drive to his school. On some mornings, however, Sam had other plans.

The opened door and the sight of his booster seat seemed to trigger a desire for conversation. So instead of getting in, he would plop down in the driveway and begin to ask me questions about my work, the color of the sky, or how the wind managed to be invisible. As an older father, I had plenty of time to think about having a child and looked forward to conversations like these. The problem was that we were on a tight schedule and these were better discussions for bedtime talks or weekend strolls. I wasn't in a relaxed state of mind but in my "get to work on time by sticking with the planned sequence" mode—completely second executive of me. The fact that he was blocking my progress triggered a stress response and a picture in my mind of the looks I would get from the saintly sisters of Montessori for being late.

Being thwarted in my plan, a fear of being late for work, and an image of the disapproving preschool teachers in mind, my first executive sounded the alarm. The voice in my head that usually said, "What cute questions," was drowned out by the irritation and impatience driven by my anxiety— "Get in the car!" In this state of mind, which contained no self-awareness of my internal state nor any empathy for my son, getting him into his car seat became a power struggle. A flurry of protests, flailing legs, and an arched back only increased the distress for both of us. Similar interactions occurred over the next couple of days, turning what could have been a fun time into a dreaded morning ritual. By the third day, I realized something had to change, but what?

It was time to call a meeting of my three executive systems and do some problem-solving. What was going on here? What was I missing? Was there a better way? I questioned my dedication to the schedule and lists of tasks and wondered why it triggered so much agitation in me. My first executive reminded me of my early experiences with my father. I remembered how irritable and impatient he always seemed to be and how scared, sad, and invisible it would make me feel. There was never time to relax and always pressure to move on to the next thing. There was always a fear of doing something wrong and not living up to his expectations.

My third executive reminded me that these early interactions of mine made me feel unseen and unimportant to the point where I had promised myself never to do the same to my kids. Yet, here I was. I somehow became *that* guy. The faces of the preschool teachers evoked the same shame in me as had my teachers, my father, and all the critics that still filled the jury box in my head. Sitting with this awareness, and the empathy for myself as a child, my father, and my son, I finally became better able to consider the morning ritual from my son's point of view and have empathy for his feelings.

Armed with these memories, thoughts, and insights, it became clear that taking time to talk with Sam was both more important and better for both of us than getting to school or work on time. In reflecting back on his gestures and facial expressions in the mornings, I realized that he did look anxious. I wondered if going to school was as stressful for him as taking him was for me. I realized that my anxiety (first executive) was inhibiting my ability to be empathic and compassionate (third executive). Maybe he needed a few more minutes of transition time. In light of these insights from my three executives, I decided to leave the house five minutes earlier the next morning and sit and talk if he hesitated at the car door instead of pressuring him to be on time.

The next morning, after I opened the car door, I sat down on the curb and started talking to him about his day and what I was going to do at work. He stood next to me, listening, with a quizzical look on his face. He eventually smiled and went on happily talking and asking questions for a minute or so. Out of nowhere, he said, "Let's go Dad, we're gonna be late" and hopped into his car seat. We exchanged smiles, he felt seen and understood, and I felt both happy and relieved. With a good second executive, we can be a very successful human doing, but living as a human being requires a collaboration between all three executive systems.

This very small and personal example may seem to have little to do with adult relationships, work success, or international relations. But if you look closely, the good parent, the successful CEO, and any good leader needs to do the same thing; get all three executive systems involved, regulate emotions, be self-aware, have empathy for others, and apply your problem-solving skills in the context of human interactions. This brings us up from the level of intelligence to wisdom—the practical application of knowledge in the service of human experience—and requires the participation of all three executive systems.

From Intelligence to Wisdom

Most people say that it is intellect which makes a
great scientist. They are wrong: It is character.
                                    —Albert Einstein

We in the Western world tend to value intelligence over most other abilities. Many masters of the universe in finance, engineering, and technology scoff at the value of social skills, relationships, and self-reflective capacity. "After all," they might say, "I don't have any of those abilities and I'm a billionaire." There are, in fact, countless examples of the fact that living exclusively within the realm of the second executive can be professionally and financially rewarding. In contrast, the integration and synthesis of the three executives allow us to attain other kinds of knowledge, one of which is wisdom.

Although we know it when we see it, defining wisdom can be a challenge. Wisdom can mean many things to many people. In fact, a book edited by Yale psychologist Robert Sternberg (1990) on the topic presented a slightly different definition in each chapter. In the East, wisdom has traditionally focused on understanding and controlling one's thoughts and passions to promote inner and social harmony. In Western cultures, wisdom has been represented in the form of good advice, codes of social behavior, and an understanding of the natural sciences. More recently, Eastern and Western notions seem to be combining to create a view of wisdom as a blending of knowledge and compassion expressed in the context of relationships. While knowledge gives us the capacity to understand what we are doing, wisdom helps us to attain a correct, prudent, and just application of that knowledge.

Who comes to mind when you think of a wise person? When a group of undergraduates were asked to name well-known wise individuals, their top 10 choices included Gandhi, Jesus, Solomon, Martin Luther King Jr., Socrates, and Oprah Winfrey (Paulhus et al., 2002). You may notice that we don't see Napoleon, Einstein, or Elon Musk on this list, which suggests that power, intellect, or wealth isn't synonymous with wisdom. With these thoughts in mind, I asked a group of graduate students to list the qualities they felt made someone wise. They were quick to point out that wisdom brings together both intellectual and emotional intelligence in ways that maximize affiliation, compassion, and a recognition of our common humanity. They perceived wisdom as emerging in the context of interacting hearts and minds coming together to comprehend and solve complex human problems. Some of the descriptors they used fell into these three categories:

1. A broad perspective (self-awareness, seeing the big picture, and maintaining doubt)
2. Personal attributes (moral courage, resilience, and appropriate detachment)
3. Attitudes toward others (empathic, compassionate, and forgiving)

According to this small and informal survey, attaining wisdom involves being able to see past the surface of things to deeper levels of meaning. Wise individuals are also able to discard notions of a singular correct perspective and remain open to new learning while recognizing the limitations and distortions in their own thinking. To the extent that this perspective is accurate, it highlights the important integration and synergy of the three executive systems, which together foster a type of metacognition that includes an awareness of both self and other in a broad existential context. In other words, it results in the maintenance of a broad perspective that includes both life, death, and the passage of time.

Social science research suggests that wisdom coalesces from a complex pattern of personality variables, life experience, and inner growth (Staudinger, 1999). Those judged to be wise in any age group excel in higher-order thinking and grasp the relativism of values (Baltes et al., 1995). They tend to have good social abilities, with a rich internal life, and are open to new experiences (Staudinger et al., 1998). Someone with wisdom is capable of sustaining focus on a problem as they consider its multiple dimensions and meanings, and their personal responsibility in the matter at hand (Holliday & Chandler, 1986). Given that navigating complex and difficult relationships is one of life's most enduring challenges, much wisdom is expressed in how people interact with and treat one another. This requires the participation, development, and integration of all three executive systems over time. As a friend once told me, wisdom is thought to show up with age, but sometimes age shows up all by itself.

If wisdom is the integration of intelligence and compassion in the service of others, it deserves a central place in the issues we address in executive functioning. While intelligence serves solving particular problems, wisdom addresses the broader challenges of our existence. Wisdom is the coming together of those things we hold most dear in the exploration of the brain, mind, and relationship. Wisdom is social glue, a sacred communication, a gift from one generation to the next. Becoming wise requires emotional regulation, minimizing ego, mindfulness, secure attachment, and being the safe base that allows others to explore, play, love, and work.

Part II

Neuroscientific Foundations of the Three-System Model

Chapter 4

The First Executive System

Emotional intelligence is the ability to recognize
and understand emotions in yourself and
others, and your ability to use this awareness to
manage your behavior and relationships.

—Travis Bradberry

Although generally ignored by cognitively oriented researchers, the foundation of optimal executive functioning rests on our ability to regulate bodily and emotional arousal, especially under stress. The best-trained therapists, the smartest CEOs, and the most loving parents devolve to primitive and unproductive behaviors when dysregulated, anxious, or afraid. The reason for this comes down to the fact that when our amygdala senses danger, it triggers our salience network (SN) to inhibit our other executive systems (ES2 and ES3), which downgrades our intellectual and interpersonal functioning. It also activates our fight/flight/freeze alarms, which further diminishes our adaptive functioning in the absence of a real threat. This is usually why, when facing a challenge without adequate emotional regulation, smart people do dumb things.

Prior research on this three-system model has focused on the SN as an integrated executive system. In the pages ahead, you will see that we will sometimes refer to the amygdala alone as a shorthand for the entire SN. The reasons for this include the fact that the amygdala is a well-known structure in the clinical community and that its relationship to stress, anxiety, panic, and PTSD are well understood. Another factor is that the complexities of the internal neurodynamics of the SN and their role in psychiatric disorders are not yet clear. Keep in mind that when we refer to either the amygdala or ES1, we are assuming the involvement of the entire salience network. For now, let's first look at the SN and what we know about its structures and functions.

The Salience Network (ES1)

Every man builds his world in his own image. He has the power to choose, but no power to escape the necessity of choice.

—Ayn Rand

The role of the SN (sometimes referred to as the ventral attention network) is to detect and evaluate survival-relevant stimuli (both external and internal) and trigger rapid adaptive responses. The SN integrates information from our body and senses to guide our actions and emotions based on what it deems to be the most relevant (salient) stimuli (Menon & Uddin, 2010). The SN consists of the amygdala, the anterior insula, the dorsal anterior cingulate cortex (ACC), and areas of the prefrontal cortex (PFC). The SN is an evolutionary extension of the amygdala, which is our most primitive organ of appraisal. It is likely that the SN expanded from the amygdala as cortical structures created the need for higher level processing and organization.

The amygdala contains primitive stimulus-response associations (implicit memories) and modulates our physiological arousal via its control of the autonomic nervous and vagal systems (LeDoux, 1996). The other components of the SN work together to detect both novelty and discrepancies between past and present experiences (Etkin et al., 2010). This makes us orient to the unfamiliar and unexpected, both of which are important to read the environment for potential threats and the possibility of new resources. The areas of the SN in the inferior PFC are thought to be involved in amygdala regulation and the updating of existing memories based on new learning (Tops et al., 2014).

The reason why early caretaking experiences play such a large role in EF is because they shape the hierarchical networks connecting the PFC and amygdala. The quality of these connections determines our ability to regulate our bodily and emotional arousal in response to stress. They also contain our implicit memories of early relationships (attachment schema), which influences the accuracy, quality, and positive/negative valence of our experiences with others. For these and other reasons, early childhood experiences are capable of influencing the nature of our emotional stability and interpersonal abilities throughout life. Regardless of how advanced our intelligence and cognitive functioning may be, they remain reliant on these more primitive mechanisms.

A role of the SN that is central to our discussion of executive functioning is its orchestration of the appropriate neurodynamic activation of ES2 and ES3 for optimal adaptive responses. In other words, it acts as a conductor to mobilize the correct neural system(s) to adapt to and navigate each situation. In the face of imminent danger, the amygdala alerts the SN to inhibit ES2 and ES3, as it signals the hypothalamus to mobilize the autonomic nervous system for a fight, flight, or freeze response. Depending on the task, it can activate or deactivate ES2 and ES3, or allow them to work together (Sridharan et al., 2008).

If sustained focus on an external task is needed, the anterior insula of the SN engages (ES2) and suppresses activity in the default mode network (ES3). This allows for an ongoing focus and the manipulation of information in working memory required for a cognitive task (D'Esposito, 2007; Fuster, 2000; Sridharan et al., 2008). On the other hand, being thoughtfully and emotionally engaged in psychotherapy requires the SN to activate a unique balance of a calm amygdala and a synergistic engagement of both ES2 and ES3. This allows us to feel safe and calm, reflect on our inner experience, and bring our memories and problem-solving abilities to benefit from our therapeutic insights and apply them in real life.

When the SN and the many systems providing it with information are working properly, we are able to direct our attention to inner and outer experience, cognitive and/or emotional tasks, self-reflection, or attention to others. Adaptive functioning of the SN depends on the proper modulation of the amygdala, so that it doesn't sound the alarm and signal the SN to inhibit ES2 and ES3. When it is provided with misinformation or misjudges internal or external events, it will trigger inappropriate responses that disrupt adaptive functioning and put us at risk for anxiety, depressive rumination, and other psychiatric symptoms and disorders (Menon, 2011). The next section goes a bit deeper into the structures and functions of the ES1, aka the salience network.

The Components of the Salience Network

Tell me what you fear, and I will tell you what happened to you.
                                        —Donald Winnicott

This first executive system is centered around and expanded from the amygdala, an ancient structure that can be traced in evolution back to early amphibians. Its dense connectivity with the autonomic nervous system allows it to rapidly trigger fight/flight/freeze reactions in the face of danger. In early mammals, its influence extended to the regulation of maternal caretaking, attachment, and other aspects of sociality. As we discuss the individual components of the first executive system, you will see how they cooperate and complement one another. See Table 4.1 for an overview of the structures and functions served by the first executive system.

The Amygdala

The amygdala is an organ of appraisal, with the role of associating the things we experience in our environment, in our relationships, and within ourselves with positive or negative value. The amygdala is fully developed before birth and retains a central role in fear processing throughout life. This is why we are born fully capable of experiencing intense emotions yet lack the cortical development to regulate or contextualize them. The amygdala associates emotional value with the object of the senses based on

TABLE 4.1
ES1: The Salience Network

	Core Structure	Functions
First executive	Amygdala	Rapid evaluation of negative and positive stimuli
	Anterior cingulate cortex	Novelty detection
	Anterior insular cortex	Interruption of ongoing activity
	Inferior prefrontal cortex	Redirection of attention
	Autonomic nervous system	Fight/flight/freeze responses
	Vagal system	Regulation of bodily arousal

instincts and learning history, and translates these appraisals into bodily states and survival-based reactions (Adolphs, 2003; Barrett et al., 2007; Davis, 1992; LeDoux, 1986; Winstanley et al., 2004).

The amygdala becomes active in response to pleasant or positive stimuli as well as perceived danger (Davis & Whalen, 2001; Garavan et al., 2001; Zald, 2003). It stores past negative experiences in a manner that is highly resistant to updating, any of which can be reactivated later in life and influence our conscious experience (Brodal, 1992; Davis, 1997). This is likely why negative memories are more powerful than positive ones. As primates' brains expanded and became increasingly social, the amygdala connected with the rest of the brain to facilitate complex social interactions (Brothers, 1997; Dolan & Vuilleumier, 2003). Damage can result in a loss of social judgment, inappropriate social behavior, and an absence of evaluating the trustworthiness or dangerousness of others (Adolphs et al., 1998; Bauman et al., 2004; Gur et al., 2002; Whalen et al., 2004).

One of the aspects of the amygdala most relevant to executive functioning is its connectivity with networks of implicit memory. Implicit memories are stored within networks separate from conscious awareness, such as those from early childhood and traumatic experiences later in life. Remember, the amygdala's role is to protect us in the present from those things which have proven dangerous in the past. This could be a visceral memory related to meeting an angry dog on a dark street, or experiences related to abandonment, loss, or shame from early relationships. When the amygdala becomes activated by a memory of danger, our cortex becomes inhibited, and we regress to the state of a frightened child or a helpless victim. This can completely undermine our reality testing, judgment, and our ability to successfully navigate our lives.

The Anterior Cingulate Cortex

The anterior cingulate is an early-evolving cortical association area that receives visceral, motor, tactile, autonomic, and emotional information from throughout the brain (Kennard, 1955). It first appeared during evolution in animals exhibiting maternal behavior, nursing, play, and social sounds (MacLean, 1985). Together, the anterior cingulate cortex, the medial prefrontal cortex, and the amygdala synthesize emotion, learning, and memory, linking motivation with goal-directed behaviors (Bush et al., 2000; Paus et al., 1993; Sutherland et al., 1988). This is how our brains connect the desire to achieve something, like taking a drink from a cup, with the cognitive and motor behaviors required to bring it to our lips. The caretaking and resonance behaviors made possible by the cingulate cortex support the neural infrastructure for social cooperation, empathy, and the experience of self (Rilling et al., 2002). Destruction of the anterior cingulate in mammals results in mutism (loss of speech), a loss of maternal responses, and emotional instability (Bush et al., 2002; Joseph, 1996; Jürgens & von Cramon, 1982).

The Anterior Insular Cortex

The insula is an early-evolving region of the cortex that receives input from the body and the senses and has extensive reciprocal interconnections with the anterior cingulate and the amygdala. It is involved in a wide array of functions, from our awareness of bodily states to self-awareness, emotional expression, empathy, and consciousness (Bechara & Naqvi, 2004; Carr et al., 2003; Critchley et al., 2004; Gündel et al., 2004; Phan et al., 2002). The insula is involved with mediating the entire range of emotions from disgust to love, as well as reading facial expressions, the meaning of eye gaze, and the evaluation of the untrustworthiness of others (Bartels & Zeki, 2000; Calder et al., 2003; Kawashima et al., 1999).

The Inferior Prefrontal Cortex

The inferior prefrontal cortex is vital to interpreting complex social events, linking them with emotional value and the appropriate activation of the autonomic nervous system (Hariri et al., 2000; Mah et al., 2004). The inferior prefrontal cortex also stores representations and expectations of rewards and maintains goal-directed behavior (Gallagher et al., 1999; O'Doherty et al., 2001, 2002; Rolls, 2000; Schultz et al., 2000). The medial portion of the inferior prefrontal cortex calculates the magnitude of reward or punishment value, such as winning or losing money or whether others are sources of safety, as in the development of attachment schema (Damasio, 1994; Rolls, 2000; Tremblay & Schultz, 1999; Watanabe,

1996). The inferior prefrontal cortex expands the primitive functions of the amygdala into conscious appraisal and decision-making.

Central Regulatory Systems

Happiness is not a matter of intensity but of
balance, order, rhythm, and harmony.
                                        —Thomas Merton

The salience network integrates bodily information with cognitive processing in the service of broadened awareness and directing attention. We rely on the salience system to provide us with an experience of our bodies and the associated conscious emotions. It becomes active when we experience resentment, guilt, embarrassment, and shame, as well as when we see others are scared, in pain, or treated unfairly. When we are trying to make a decision, this network (along with the somatosensory cortex) allows us to access our intuition or "gut feelings" about the consequences of whatever choice we are about to make.

The salience network is always vigilant, working with the amygdala for rapid reactions to novelty, things we desire, and threat. This means that we are constantly vigilant for external or internal cues of meaning or danger. At the same time, this system likely functions as an executive switchboard by modulating amygdala activation while coordinating the participation of the second and third executive systems dependent on the needs of each task. The SN may also direct the simultaneous involvement of different systems. For example, when we are working with someone who has a negative emotional reaction to a suggestion about their performance, we may have to shift from primarily ES2 focus to the activation of ES1 and ES3 to access our emotional attunement and interpersonal skills. It is in this way that the SN allows us to solve problems requiring combinations of abstract, personal, and interpersonal variables.

Via the amygdala's inputs to the autonomic and vagal nervous systems, the salience network monitors and regulates our arousal. The *autonomic nervous system* has two branches: the sympathetic and parasympathetic systems. The sympathetic system controls neural activation in response to negative or positive stimuli, driving avoidance and approach behaviors. The parasympathetic system supports the conservation of bodily energy, immunological functions, and the repair of damaged systems. The autonomic nervous system serves as an on-off switch for activation, driven by short-term (fight/flight/freeze) and long-term (rest and restoration) survival.

Relevant to executive functioning are the negative impacts of sustained autonomic arousal on the brain and the body. Sustained high levels of cortisol impede protein synthesis, necessary for building new brain structures and immunological functions, as well as damage to the hippocampus, which results in intellectual and memory deficits. Chronically elevated levels of adrenaline result in irritability, impulsivity, agitation, and panic, all of which diminish optimal EF. While an on-off switch for arousal may work well for asocial animals, social animals require a much more sophisticated "volume control" that serves the needs of pair bonding, child-rearing, and group cooperation.

The infinite subtleties of social interactions require a system of bodily and emotional regulation finely calibrated to the range of social complexities. In an attempt to explain the social evolution of affect regulation, Stephen Porges (2011) has proposed the central role of the *vagal system* in his polyvagal theory. At its core is the evolution of two regulatory systems: the "vegetative" vagus that controls bodily shutdown and immobilization, and the "smart vagus" that supports social engagement by modulating sympathetic arousal. According to Porges, it is this system that allows us to become excited and to stay engaged with others without triggering a fight/flight/freeze reaction. This makes sustained arousing engagement possible without activating states of defensiveness or attack (Blair, 1995).

In conjunction with oxytocin and vasopressin, vagal regulation mediates rapid and conscious control of heart rate and the fight/flight response based on experiences of safety and trust (Porges, 2011). The "tone" of the vagus refers to its ability to regulate the heart and other target organs. Children with poor vagal tone have difficulty suppressing emotions in situations demanding their attention, making it difficult for them to engage with their parents, sustain a shared focus with playmates, and maintain attention on important material in the classroom. Perhaps some children who receive a diagnosis related to disorders of attention, behavior, and sleep may suffer from insufficient vagal tone (Calkins, 1997; El-Sheikh & Buckhalt, 2005).

Good parenting and secure attachment not only teach appropriate responses in challenging interpersonal situations but lay the groundwork for autonomic and vagal regulation. This allows us to become upset, anxious, or angry without withdrawing or becoming physically aggressive. We all have the experience of disagreements and arguments when we become so angry that we need to go for a walk, count to 10, or put ourselves in time-out. In most instances we are able to experience our feelings and maintain adequate control over our emotions in order to continue communicating and working through a problem. The modulation and control of arousal and emotion are foundational to optimal EF and functional success in all of life's endeavors.

Getting Triggered and Amygdala Hijack

We may be done with the past, but the past may not be done with us.
—Bergen Evans

First executive system takeover, or amygdala hijack, is vital for survival in animals living among their natural predators. When a threat is detected, engagement in other activities is inhibited and all attention and energy are diverted toward immediate survival. This strategy has been conserved through evolution but now creates more problems for humans than other animals. The complexity of our brains, relationships, and the challenges of the modern world almost always requires the ongoing participation and integration of all three executive systems—especially when we are anxious and stressed. Many clients come to therapy and coaching because they regularly become triggered and "lose it," causing them to sabotage their relationships and careers. In this state, ES2 and ES3 are inhibited, leaving us to navigate the modern world with primitive reflexes and emotions.

When triggered, we express unmodulated emotions, lack perspective, and have little empathy for others. In essence, our brains regress to a more reptilian state, ill equipped for successful human interactions. Early in life, many of us learn to repress our emotions, especially anger, fear, and shame. This can leave us internally dissociated and result in (1) a lack of awareness of our feelings, (2) an inability to put words to them, and (3) a fear of having or expressing feelings. However, emotions create energy that require expression, and the emotions we resist, will persist. As much as we try to repress and deny strong emotions, they continue to generate energy until they are triggered or consciously released.

From the earliest days of psychoanalysis, it was recognized that the activation of unconscious memories can result in debilitating psychological and physical symptoms. This reaction is likely triggered by the amygdala's store of past negative memories becoming activated by present experience. The result is an undermining of the cognitive, emotional, and behavioral aspects of good EF. As clinicians, what can we do about this? The ability to become aware of, name, understand, and integrate our emotions with conscious awareness has been at the core of psychotherapy from its earliest days. This process allows us to create a narrative about what is going on in our bodies, emotions, and minds so that we can share with others, and with ourselves, what is happening inside us from moment to moment. The fact that this has been excluded from the study of EF reflects the cultural dissociation between cognitive intelligence, emotional intelligence, and self-awareness.

The collaboration of our three executive systems provides us with the capability to become aware of, name, and consciously process our emotions. We are not born with the ability to integrate our executive systems; we develop emotional intelligence through countless interactions with wise others. Optimally, this occurs during childhood or later in life in psychotherapy. Without this mentorship, we may enter adulthood lacking awareness as well as the ability to regulate and control our emotions. This makes us vulnerable to becoming triggered by unconscious emotional memories, which the first executive reacts to as if we are in danger in the present. This can result in us having extreme reactions to neutral and mildly challenging situations, damaging our personal and professional relationships.

Being triggered represents an immediate activation of our bodies by the amygdala without any intervening cortical (ES2 and ES3) involvement. When this happens, we often end up as a passive witness of the negative and destructive things we have just done. After becoming aware of our emotions, regulation requires that we insert thought and consideration between the stimulus and our response. We need to go from a pattern of *stimulus-response-reflection* to *stimulus-reflection-response*, in other words, thinking before we act. This is only possible when (1) the first executive has enough regulatory capacity to slow down or inhibit the initial impulse to act, and (2) when the other two slower cortical executive systems have the time, experience, and ability to consider our reaction. We may not possess the free will not to be activated, but we can learn to develop the free *won't* to inhibit our impulses and choose more adaptive responses.

A real-world example of this comes from the wisdom of Alcoholics Anonymous (AA) in a strategy called HALT. It is assumed that when an alcoholic reaches for a drink, it involves a conditioned response to some underlying physiological or emotional state. This results in drinking first and regretting it later, along with the resulting shame and an array of negative consequences (stimulus-response-reflection). The HALT strategy is to learn to notice yourself reaching for a drink, and instead of drinking, ask yourself the question, "Am I hungry, angry, lonely, or tired?" If you realize you are feeling one of these or some other negative emotion, deal with these feelings with an alternative behavior. If you are hungry, make dinner; lonely, call a friend; tired, take a nap; angry, express those feelings. In other words, insert reflection between the stimulus and response (stimulus-reflection-response).

Over time, the shift to a stimulus-reflection-response style of processing information becomes more habitual and requires less effort. At a neurobiological level, this change represents a move away from first executive control to the mutual participation, integration, and synergy of all three executive systems. This process applies to all of us, regardless of our challenges. Being guided by unconscious negative emotions is not usually a formula for a successful life. We immediately see the results of a stimulus-response-reflection strategy not only in substance abuse but also in panic disorders, depression, borderline personality disorder (BPD), and PTSD. Many of the treatment modalities for these challenges employ a range of interventions to alter executive functioning in just this manner.

Grounded in neuroscience, the three-system model can add to our diagnostic hypotheses, case conceptualizations and clinical work. As you learn more about each executive system, be thinking about both their contributions to EF and how they may be involved in the everyday clinical issues we encounter in the consulting room.

Chapter 5
The Second Executive System

*Space and time were bound together and formed an
inseparable whole which determined human life.*
—Octavio Paz

When we consider the standard elements of intelligence, such as having
a good memory, problem-solving abilities, and abstract thinking, we are
referring to the second executive system. Here we expand the traditional
frontal lobe focus to include the parietal lobes as well as the sensory,
motor, memory, and somatic networks that support our cognitive abilities. In this chapter, we will first explore the contributions of the frontal
and parietal lobes separately, how they work together, and what happens
when either area, or the fiber bundles connecting them, become damaged
or compromised.

As we proceed, you may notice that the three executive systems have
a number of overlapping neural territories. Keep in mind that each region
of the brain has numerous components and diverse connectivity across
multiple neural systems. This overlap supports connectivity, communication, and integration among our executive systems. This overlap helps us
to appreciate the limitation of localizing complex functions to a specific
area. This perspective brings us a step closer to understanding the complex neurodynamic relationships that characterize our brains.

The Frontal Lobes

In order to carry a positive action, we must develop a positive vision.
—The Dalai Lama

The frontal lobes are a diverse set of structures that play a central role in the cognitive, behavioral, and emotional aspects of EF. The prefrontal cortex is divided into two functionally related areas, the orbital-medial (ompfc) and dorsal-lateral regions (dlpfc). Although physically contiguous, they differ in their connectivity, biochemistry, and functional responsibilities (Wilson et al., 1993). While both play a role in action and inhibition, the dlpfc and ompfc specialize in attentional and social-emotional tasks, respectively. The participation of the prefrontal cortex appears necessary for theory of mind and metacognition (thinking about thinking), which includes observing our thoughts, revisiting memories, and changing our minds (Jenkins & Mitchell, 2011).

Although the dorsal and lateral areas of the human frontal lobes initially evolved to organize complex motor behavior, the expansion of the prefrontal cortex added capacities for working memory and strategic planning. Neural networks throughout the brain provide the prefrontal cortex with preprocessed somatic, sensory, and emotional information to guide goal-directed behavior (Alexander et al., 1986; Nauta, 1971). Neurons and neural networks within the prefrontal cortex organize our conscious sense of time through a combination of processes, including specialized timing neurons and working memory (Dolan, 1999; Fuster , 2000; Grinband et al., 2011; Watanabe, 1996).

The frontal lobes play a central role in the inhibition of motor movements, extraneous thoughts, and inappropriate emotions, allowing us to stay focused on a task until we reach a goal. It inhibits primitive reflexes, like the grasping reflex of infancy, so we can learn hand dexterity via our motor cortex. The reemergence of early reflexes after damage to the frontal lobes, referred to as cortical release signs, demonstrates the ongoing role of the cortex in inhibiting primitive reflexes throughout life (Chugani et al., 1987; Walterfang & Velakoulis, 2005). It also modulates amygdala activation in the organization of attachment schema and the regulation of arousal, anxiety, and fear (Ghashghaei et al., 2007). See Table 5.1 for an overview of the key functions of the frontal lobes.

TABLE 5.1
Functions of the Frontal Lobes

Orbital and Medial Regions

Attachment[1]	Estimating reward value and magnitude[8]
Social cognition[2]	Sensitivity to future consequences[9]
Thinking about a similar other[3]	Achieving goals[10]
Self-referential mental activity[4]	Stimulus-independent thought[11]
Appreciating humor[5]	Inhibitory control in
Encoding new information[6]	emotional processing[12]
Sensory-visceral-motor linkage[7]	Decisions based on affective information[13]

Dorsal and Lateral Regions

Cognitive control[14]	Learning motor sequences[20]
Directing attention[15]	Decisions based on
Organizing temporal experience[16]	complex information[21]
Organizing working memory[17]	Thinking about a dissimilar other[22]
Organizing episodic memory (right)[18]	The integration of emotion
Voluntary suppression of sadness[19]	and cognition[23]

[1] Minagawa-Kawai et al., 2008; Nitschke et al., 2004. [2] Berthoz et al., 2002; Mitchell et al., 2005. [3] Mitchell et al., 2006. [4] Gusnard et al., 2001. [5] Goel & Dolan, 2001. [6] Frey & Petrides, 2000; Nobre et al., 1999. [7] Öngür & Price, 2000. [8] Bechara et al., 1998; Gallagher et al., 1999; Gehring & Willoughby, 2002; Kringelbach, 2005; Krueger et al., 2006; O'Doherty, 2004. [9] Bechara et al., 1994; O'Doherty et al., 2002. [10] Matsumoto & Tanaka, 2004. [11] McGuire et al., 1996. [12] Dias et al., 1996; Simpson, Drevets, et al., 2001; Simpson, Snyder, et al., 2001; Quirk & Beer, 2006. [13] Malloy et al., 1993; Teasdale et al., 1999; Beer et al., 2006. [14] Koechlin et al., 2003. [15] Dias et al., 1996; Fuster, 1997; Nagahama et al., 2001. [16] Knight & Grabowecky, 1995; Rezai et al., 1993; Petrides et al., 2002. [18] Henson et al., 1999. [19] Lévesque et al., 2003. [20] Pascual-Leone et al., 1996. [21] Kroger et al., 2002; Malloy et al., 1993; Teasdale et al., 1999. [22] Mitchell et al., 2006. [23] Gray et al., 2002.

The orbital and medial (right behind our eyes) regions of the frontal lobes are at the apex of the basal forebrain and limbic system. They are densely connected with the amygdala and other subcortical structures involved in the regulation of arousal and attachment (first executive) and other social-emotional regulatory functions (third executive). The dorsal and lateral areas of the frontal lobes are densely connected with the rest of the cortex to integrate sensory and motor systems for successful environmental navigation. You can see by this pattern of connectivity how the prefrontal cortex is interwoven with the other two executive systems.

The cognitive and emotional functions in which each of these areas specialize have different sensitive periods during development. Orbital and medial prefrontal areas begin to organize in the context of interpersonal relationships during the first 18 months of life, sharing a sensitive period of development with the right hemisphere. Dorsal and lateral areas then have a growth spurt along with the left hemisphere that correlates with the development of language and the exploration of our physical and social worlds during the second year of life.

Problem-solving, which requires emotional regulation, sustained attention, and cognitive flexibility, is a second executive function that can become impaired with prefrontal damage. Some patients get stuck in a particular way of thinking (perseveration), while others have difficulty maintaining the direction of thinking (loss of set), or have difficulty utilizing abstract concepts (concrete thinking). They may have difficulty in remembering the outcome of past behaviors and repeatedly apply the same unsuccessful solutions to new challenges. Patients with frontal deficits often have a difficult time monitoring social interactions, such as keeping the listener's perspective in mind and abiding by social rules. See Table 5.2 for

TABLE 5.2
Manifestations of Prefrontal Compromise

Orbital and Medial Regions	Dorsal and Lateral Regions
Social and Emotional Disinhibition	*Loss of Focus and Planning*
Tactlessness or silly attitude	Forgetfulness
Decreased social concern	Distractibility
Sexual exhibitionism and lewd conversation	Decreased memory for the future
	Decreased anticipation
Grandiosity	Poor planning ability
Anger and irritability	Deterioration of work quality
Restlessness	
Apathy	*Loss of Abstract Abilities*
Decreased attention	Concreteness
Loss of initiative	Stimulus bound
Lack of spontaneity	Loss of aesthetic sense
Indifference	Perseveration
Depression	Set stuckness

a list of the behavioral consequences of damage to different areas of the prefrontal cortex.

The Parietal Lobes

There is more wisdom in your body than in the deepest philosophy.
—Friedrich Nietzsche

The human parietal lobes evolved from the hippocampus, which, in lower mammals, organizes a three-dimensional map of the external environment (O'Keefe & Nadel, 1978). They allow us to navigate a habitat and find, store, and retrieve food, as well as keep track of their children and identify and approach potential mates. The human hippocampus continues to serve this function while the parietal lobes have added conscious maps of internal imaginal space, internal somatic space, and of our bodies in external space (Husain & Nachev, 2007). Together, these maps allow us to create an increasingly sophisticated inner topography for self-reflection and expanded awareness. Many believe that our ability to navigate three-dimensional space created the infrastructure of higher-order cognition (Culham & Kanwisher, 2001; Jonides et al., 1998; Klingberg et al., 2002).

Johnson (1987) asserts that the experience of our bodies provides the basis for our sense of numbers, quantity, and space. Physical metaphors provide a context in which to "ground" our experience in time and space (Koziol et al., 2011). The balance provided by the vestibular system may be the internal working model for emotional stability (Frick, 1982). This is likely why many of the ways in which we describe our cognitive and emotional experiences are framed within space and time. For example, thinking requires *grasping* an idea, *framing* a concept, and *understanding* new ideas. When describing our emotions, we experience ourselves as *falling* in love, *flying* into a rage, becoming emotionally *unbalanced*, or having a hard time *handling* bad news.

Since our brains evolved to adapt within our four-dimensional environment (three dimensions of space and one of time), executive functioning originally emerged as a system of approaching and utilizing aspects of our environment in an adaptive manner (affordance). The parietal lobes, in connection with the rest of the cortex, allow for the integration of working visual memory, attentional capacities, and bodily awareness necessary for imagination. Athletes take advantage of these networks when they imagine making a difficult catch or working on their tennis serve. Mirror neurons in these inferior parietal regions respond to the hand position, eye movement, words, motivational relevance, and body position of others, supporting our learning from others through visualization and reflexive imitation.

The multimodal representation of four-dimensional space in posterior parietal areas also integrates our goal-directed behavior and attention with higher cognitive functions (Bonda et al., 1996; Corbetta & Shulman, 2002; Culham & Kanwisher, 2001). These regions weave together sensory input and motor action to help organize goal-oriented aspects of EF (Andersen et al., 1997; Brozzoli et al., 2012; Colby & Goldberg, 1999; Medendorp et al., 2005; Quintana & Fuster, 1999; Shomstein, 2012). They are also involved with the processes of the salience network when confronted by novelty, and calculating the probability of success of a choice or action (Platt & Glimcher, 1999; Snyder et al., 1997; Walsh et al., 1998).

Neural fibers connecting the middle portions of the frontal and parietal lobes also appear to serve a general integrative function of linking right and left hemispheres, limbic and cortical structures, and anterior and posterior regions of the cortex, possibly giving rise to a global workspace or "central representation" that allows for conscious working memory, self-reflection, and the conscious experience of self (Baars, 2002; Caspers et al., 2012; Cornette et al., 2001; Fedorenko et al., 2013; Lou et al., 2004, 2005; Taylor, 2001). See Table 5.3 for an extended list of parietal lobe involvements.

Albert Einstein, the archetypical absent-minded professor and a poor math student in his youth, went on to create some of physics' most influential theories. One of his major findings, $E = mc^2$, describes the previously hidden relationship between space, matter, and time, bringing us a step closer to understanding the invisible and nonintuitive workings of the universe. After his death, neuroscientists carefully studied his brain for anatomical clues to his abilities. Compared to other brains, Einstein's was different only in the larger size of his inferior parietal lobes and the ratios of glial cells that support neural functioning (Diamond et al., 1966, 1985; Witelson et al., 1999).

TABLE 5.3
Functions of the Parietal Lobes

Hemisphere	Function
Right	Analysis of sound movement[1]
	General comparison of amounts[2]
	Attention[3]
	Self-face recognition[4]
Left	Verbal manipulation of numbers[5]
	Mathematics[6]
	Multiplication[7]
	Motor attention[8]

Bilateral Findings

Visual-spatial work space[9]	Controlling attention to salient event and maintaining attention across time[17]
Visual-spatial problem-solving[10]	
Visual motion[11]	Preparation for pointing to an object[18]
Construction of a sensory-motor representation of the internal world in relation to the body[12]	Grasping[19]
	Movement of three-dimensional objects[20]
Internal representation of the state of the body[13]	A sense of numerosity, defined as nonsymbolic approximations of quantities (left)[21]
Verbal working memory[14]	Processing abstract knowledge[22]
Retrieval from episodic memory[15]	Perspective taking (right)[23]
Sequence and ordering of information in working memory[16]	Processing social information (right)[24]
	Taking a third-person perspective (right)[25]

[1] Griffiths et al., 1998. [2] Chochon et al., 1999. [3] Newman et al., 2003. [4] Uddin et al., 2005. [5] Dehaene et al., 2003. [6] Molko et al., 2003. [7] Chochon et al., 1999. [8] Molko et al., 2003; Rushworth et al., 2001. [9] Newman et al., 2003. [10] Newman et al., 2003. [11] Antal et al., 2008. [12] Grefkes & Fink, 2005; Wolpert et al., 1998. [13] Wolpert et al., 1998. [14] Jonides et al., 1998. [15] Wagner et al., 2005. [16] Marshuetz et al., 2000; Van Opstal et al., 2008. [17] Husain & Nachev, 2007. [18] Astafiev et al., 2003. [19] Mountcastle, 1995. [20] Orban et al., 1999. [21] Castelli et al., 2006; Fias et al., 2003; Lemer et al., 2003. [22] Fias et al., 2007. [23] Ruby & Decety, 2001. [24] Iaccoboni et al., 2004; Jackson & Decety, 2004. [25] Vogeley et al., 2004.

These findings are especially interesting in light of his reported use of mental imagery to solve complex mathematical problems. Einstein described translating numerical equations into visual images that he would manipulate in imagination in order to come up with solutions, and translate back into mathematical equations. It is highly likely that Einstein's larger and more complex parietal regions allowed for his superior visual-spatial workspace and abstract abilities (Nedergaard et al., 2003; Oberheim et al., 2006; Taber & Hurley, 2008).

Left parietal damage disrupts mathematical abilities, while damage to the right results in disturbances of body image and neglect of the left side of the body (hemineglect). Despite these debilitating symptoms, patients are either oblivious to or deny the significance of their deficits, suggesting that damage to the parietal lobes disrupts the experience of location, self-organization, and identity—in other words, where, what, and who we are. See Table 5.4 for an overview of some of the deficits experienced with parietal lobe damage.

TABLE 5.4
Manifestations of Parietal Lobe Damage

Left Parietal Compromise Results in:
Gerstmann syndrome, which includes the following symptoms:
Right-left confusion
Digital agnosia (inability to name the fingers on both hands)
Agraphia (inability to write)
Acalculia (inability to calculate)[1]
The symptoms of Gerstmann syndrome are linked through a unitary deficit in spatial orientation of body—sides, fingers, and numbers[2]

Right Parietal Compromise Results in Deficits of:

Mental imagery and movement representations[3]	Detecting apparent motion[9]
Visual-spatial awareness[4]	Analysis of sound movement[10]
Visual-spatial problem-solving[5]	Spatial-temporal abnormalities[11]
Temporal awareness and temporal order[6]	Contralateral neglect of the body and external space[12]
Spatial perception[7]	Denial of hemiparalysis and neglect[13]
Somatosensory experience[8]	

[1] Dehaene et al., 2004. [2] Victor & Roper, 2001. [3] Sirigu et al., 1996. [4] Colby, 1998; Driver & Mattingley, 1998. [5] Newman et al., 2003. [6] Rorden et al., 1997; Snyder & Chatterjee, 2004. [7] Karnath, 1997; Ungerleider & Haxby, 1994. [8] Schwartz et al., 2005. [9] Battelli et al., 2001; Claeys et al., 2003. [10] Griffiths et al., 1998. [11] Snyder & Chatterjee, 2004. [12] Andersen & Mountcastle, 1983. [13] Pia et al., 2004.

A Frontal-Parietal Executive System

It is only in the world of objects that we
have time and space and selves.
                              —T. S. Eliot

In the process of their research on the relationship between brain dam-age and intelligence, Jung and Haier (2007), found some significant brain region–performance correlations. Deficits of performance on three of the four broad factors of the Wechsler Adult Intelligence Scale (WAIS) revealed the following:

> verbal comprehension (left inferior prefrontal cortex), working memory (left frontal and parietal cortex), and perceptual organization (right parietal cortex). Only processing speed was found to be uncorrelated with specific parietal or frontal damage. This and other research points to a broader distribution of cognitive executive functioning beyond the frontal lobes. It is also a logical continuation of our increasing appre-ciation of the evolutionary foundation of cognition in the navigation of space and time. (Bartolomeo, 2006; Nachev et al., 2009; van den Heuvel et al., 2009)

The broadened neural contributions to the cognitive aspects of EF are cur-rently thought to include the dorsolateral prefrontal cortex, the inferior and superior parietal lobes, the anterior cingulate, and some regions within the temporal and occipital lobes, as well as the white matter tracts that connect them (Colom et al., 2009; Costa & Averbeck, 2013; Langer et al., 2012; Smith et al., 2011). The frontal and parietal lobes work together with the SN to interrupt ongoing behavior and redirect attention to new targets (Arif et al., 2021; Bush, 2011; Fraenz et al., 2021; Corbetta & Shulman, 2002; Peers et al., 2005). They also collaborate in deciding on and planning goal-directed actions (Andersen & Cui, 2009; Buneo & Andersen, 2006; Crowe et al., 2013; Goodwin et al., 2012; Whitney et al., 2012).

The volume of both frontal and parietal gray matter, as well as the white matter tracts that connect them, demonstrate the highest correlation with intelligence (Estrada et al., 2019; Glascher et al., 2009; Gray et al., 2003; Haier et al., 2004; Klingberg et al., 2002; Klingberg, 2006; Langeslag et al.,

2012; Lee et al., 2006; Olesen et al., 2003). The frontal-parietal network in the left hemisphere is responsible for verbal knowledge, verbal reasoning, working memory, cognitive flexibility, and executive control (Barbey et al., 2012). Parietal-frontal circuits are involved in the sustained focus and updating of information in working memory (Edin et al., 2007; Salazar et al., 2012; Sauseng et al., 2005) and work together to analyze the context and location of specific variables (Coull et al., 2014; Genovesio et al., 2014).

A properly functioning parietal-frontal network allows for the successful negotiation of our moment-to-moment survival and the ability to turn our attention to inner experience. From an evolutionary perspective, the complementary contributions of the frontal and parietal lobes reflect the brain's adaptation to simultaneously navigate space (parietal) and time (frontal) (Gregory et al., 2016). A compromised or poorly developed second executive system can ensnare us in "a noisy and temporally constrained state, locking the patient into the immediate space and time with little ability to escape" (Knight & Grabowecky, 1995, p. 1368). Without the ability to reflect on and sometimes cancel reflexive motor and emotional responses, there is little freedom from biological imperatives (Schall, 2001).

A similar phenomenon can occur in states of chronic anxiety where sufferers become "stimulus bound," unable to override reflexive fear reactions (Brown et al., 1994). The hyperactivation of the first executive system is capable of inhibiting the second, which can degrade the functioning of the frontal and parietal lobes. Test anxiety and stage fright are prototypical examples of this inhibition in our everyday experience. This is the reason why clients suffering with difficulties in attention, concentration, and problem-solving cannot be assumed to have an organic brain dysfunction. Anxiety disorders, depression, and an array of medical conditions that disrupt homeostatic and biochemical regulation can manifest the same deficits of EF. Thus, when the first and second executives are working properly, our third executive is also free to develop and expand its functioning.

Luis

Luis was in a serious auto accident a few days after his 20th birthday. He and his parents came in to see me (LC) after his neurologist suggested that they all might benefit from family therapy. At the time of their first appointment, I opened the door to find eight people packed tightly into my small waiting room. As Luis, his parents, and five younger siblings filed into my office, I noticed the scars and indentations across Luis's forehead and imagined the damage beneath them. I knew from talking with his neurologist that he had sustained severe injuries to his prefrontal cortex and that he had become impulsive, irritable, and occasionally violent. Luis now possessed limited inhibitory capacity, reasoning abilities, and recognition of social expectations.

After we all settled in my office, I turned to the father and asked how I could help him help his family. He immediately became tearful, shook his head slowly from side to side, and rubbed his hands together. "He drives too fast," he said quietly. "I don't!" exclaimed Luis. "Except for that one time!" Everyone in the family looked away and appeared embarrassed. It was immediately clear that talking back to his father was part of the problem. Although he had always been somewhat impulsive, his parents claimed that he was far worse than before the accident. I suspected that no matter how impulsive Luis might have been before the accident, the degree of his disrespectful behavior was new.

As the family discussed their situation, I found out that Luis's parents had moved to the United States from Mexico shortly before his birth and had adapted well to their new home. Despite their successful acculturation, they remained true to traditional Mexican values of loyalty to the family and respect for elders. In this context, Luis's reflexive and loud contradiction of his father was a source of shame for everyone except Luis. His injury had damaged the networks of his brain that allowed him to monitor and control his own behavior and take into account the expectations of his family. A year after the accident, he returned to his auto repair job but was unable to focus on his work or get along with coworkers and customers. For Luis, the descending neural networks of cortical inhibition had been compromised through the loss of so many prefrontal neurons.

Luis didn't remember anything about his accident and, in fact, had no memory of the weeks before or after the event. He read the police reports to discover that he had lost control of his car while street racing and crashed into a pole. His injuries were compounded by the fact that he was not wearing a seat belt and had installed a fancy steel steering wheel without an airbag. It's impossible to tell if this was the foolishness of adolescence or evidence reflecting his lack of judgment prior to the accident.

His mother reported that Luis spent most of his time at home with her and that his behavior was erratic and sometimes frightening. At times he would cry for no reason, yell at her and the others, or jump in her car and race off. A few times, he went into a rage and threw furniture around the house. He had also made sexual statements and cursed using Jesus's name during the holidays, upsetting everyone in the family. Family members were torn between their love for Luis and their disgust with his behavior.

Automobile, industrial, and recreational accidents, as well as community and domestic violence, all contribute to the increasing number of people who experience traumatic brain injuries. Because the frontal areas are located directly behind the forehead, they are also most likely to be damaged in fights and accidents. Although patients with head injuries come from all walks of life, young males are disproportionately represented. Their youthful impulsivity, risk taking, and lack of judgment make them more vulnerable to damaging the very regions required for understanding consequences and inhibiting impulses.

The massive reorganization of prefrontal brain areas along with biochemical and hormonal changes during adolescence likely contribute to these dangerous behaviors. Many of these young men may have already had frontal deficits or slowed frontal development prior to their accidents, amplifying typical adolescent risk-taking. In this way, frontal injuries often compound preexisting deficits of impulse control and judgment, complicating treatment and recovery.

Treatment with Luis and his family was multifaceted. I began by educating the entire family about the brain and Luis's particular injuries. The specific information was less important than labeling his behaviors as symptoms of his injury rather than moral failings. In particular, I targeted his cursing and sexual statements, which were, in their minds, connected to his character and spiritual health. By sharing case studies of others with them, I was able to show that Luis's symptoms were part of a pattern of pathological disinhibition related to his brain damage, not the result of moral lapses or bad parenting.

More specific interventions included enrolling Luis in an occupational therapy program to help him develop the instrumental and interpersonal skills needed to obtain and maintain employment. As the oldest son, it was important for him and the rest of the family that he be productive and regain a sense of self-worth. One of my goals was to reduce his resistance to taking medication that would help him with his anxiety and depression caused by his changed circumstances. I also worked with Luis and his family to develop skills related to stress reduction and anger management. We turned these exercises into family role-playing games that alleviated tension and allowed everyone to participate in helping Luis.

Over time, Luis was able to apply his knowledge of cars to a part-time job in an auto parts store. His occupational therapist helped him establish routines that allowed him to successfully use the computer. Antidepressants proved helpful with both his mood and irritability, and the role-playing games became woven into the family's everyday interactions. All of these improvements made the occasional outbursts more tolerable, and they could be seen more easily as a consequence of his illness. Luis was very fortunate to have the unquestioning love and support of a strong and involved family. The quality of a patient's support system plays a large role in the quality of his or her recovery.

Chapter 6

The Third Executive System

If I create from the heart, nearly everything
works, if from the head, almost nothing.

—Marc Chagall

The third executive system includes a group of neural structures located along the inner borders of the cerebral cortex. Commonly referred to as the default mode network (DMN), it contains a collection of "interacting hubs" that cooperate to serve a set of diverse yet interrelated functions (Andrews-Hanna, 2012; Gordon et al., 2020; Horn et al., 2013; Leech et al., 2011; Salomon et al., 2013). The DMN was first detected during functional brain scans of research subjects between tasks. Brain activity during these periods was initially thought to be background noise, or a default state, like having your car in neutral. It was later discovered that this activity was measuring the activity of a coherent neural system related a subject's subjective states (Beckmann et al., 2005; Beason-Held et al., 2009; Greicius et al., 2009; Smith et al., 2009).

The neural structures of the DMN include regions of the posterior cingulate cortex, the medial area of the prefrontal cortex and temporal lobes (including the hippocampus), and areas of the parietal lobes (Northoff & Bermpohl, 2004; Northoff et al., 2006). Subsequent research discovered that the DMN becomes active during reflection, daydreaming, imagination, and empathic understanding. It appears that both ES2 and ES3 participate in creating a foundation for our perception, cognition, and creativity. This reflective state of mind allows us to consider problems, rehearse solutions,

TABLE 6.1

Brain Regions and Their Contributions to DMN Functions

Medial prefrontal cortex	Self-relevant mentation, theory of mind[1]
Medial temporal lobe	Autobiographical memory
Hippocampus	Associations with past experiences[2]
Posterior cingulate cortex	Sensory integration
Parietal cortex	Self-awareness, self-other comparisons, memory source attribution, internal mentation, visual-spatial organization and coordination[3]

[1] Buckner et al., 2008; Wagner et al., 2012. [2] Greicius & Menon, 2004; Ward et al., 2013. [3] Buckner et al., 2008; Cavanna & Trimble, 2006; Laureys et al., 2006; Mason et al., 2007; Nielson et al., 2005; Zysset et al., 2002.

and process consequences. See Table 6.1 for a list of brain-behavior correlates of the DMN.

DMN activation has been detected as early as two weeks after birth, and establishes a pattern of coherent firing by around age seven (Chai et al., 2014; Fan et al., 2021; Gao et al., 2009). Its slow development suggests that its development is influenced by experience and is negatively impacted by chronic stress and adverse experiences (Pluta et al., 2014; Sambataro et al., 2010; Supekar et al., 2010). See Table 6.2 for a list of brain-behavior relationships thus far uncovered in DMN research.

Functional Neurodynamics

Nature is based on harmony.

—Bruce Lipton

Initially, the third executive system was thought to be completely inhibited by either high levels of amygdala activity (ES1) or intense attention to external tasks (ES2). This is why, when we are anxious, afraid, or preoccupied with external tasks, we are less likely to be aware of our emotions, bodily states, or even ourselves (Csikszentmihalyi, 2008). When we are in a resting state, ES3 activation will continue, while ES2 stands down until signaled to take over (Chen et al., 2013). ES3 shows decreased activation during goal-directed activities but becomes active during self-generated thought,

TABLE 6.2
Hypothesized Functions of the Default Mode Network

Self-Awareness

Conscious awareness[1]	Alterations in states of awareness[2]
Self-relatedness[3]	Self-awareness[4]
Self-reflection[5]	Autobiographical memory[6,7]
Self-referencing[19]	Sense of self[20]
Self-other distinctions[22]	Empathy[25]

Social Awareness

Processing social relationships[8]	Recognizing the faces of others[9]
Theory of mind processing[10]	Processing moral dilemmas[11]

Perception and Cognition

Visual fixation[12]	Resting with eyes closed[13]
Passive perception[14]	Spontaneous semantics[15]
Mnemonic processes[16]	Stimulus-independent thought[17]
Implicit processing[18]	Mental time travel[21]
Memory scene construction[23]	Navigation[25]
Semantic memory construction[24]	Prospection[24]

[1] Davey et al., 2016; Horovitz et al., 2009; Laureys et al., 2006. [2] Schneider et al., 2008; van Buuren et al., 2010. [3] Johnson, 2006; Qin et al., 2016; Whitfield-Gabrieli et al., 2011. [4] Van Buuren et al., 2010; Yoshimura et al., 2009. [5] Li et al., 2014. [6] Fiset et al., 1999; Chai et al., 2014. [7] Jardri et al., 2007. [8] D'Argembeau et al., 2011; Østby et al., 2012; Pardo & Fox, 1993; Spreng & Grady, 2010; Maguire & Mummery, 1999. [9] Quin & Northoff, 2011. [10] Iacoboni et al., 2004. [11] Li et al., 2014; Spreng & Grady, 2010. [12] Uddin et al., 2005. [13] Harrison et al., 2008; Moll et al., 2007. [14] Greicius et al., 2003. [15] Greicius & Menon, 2004. [16] Andreasen et al., 1995. [17] Baird et al., 2012; Corballis, 2013; Kucyi & Davis, 2014; Murphy et al., 2018; Smallwood et al., 2012; Yang et al., 2010. [18] Hassabis & Maguire, 2007. [19] Shapira-Lichter et al., 2013. [20] Laufs et al., 2003. [21] Bellana et al., 2017; McKiernan et al., 2003. [22] Courtney & Meyer, 2020; McGuire et al., 1996; Yeshurun et al., 2021. [23] Østby et al., 2012. [24] Spreng et al., 2009. [25] Esménio et al., 2019; Li et al., 2014. [26] Chen et al., 2020; Hamilton et al., 2015; Jacob et al., 2020; Zhou et al., 2020. [27] Kucyi & Davis, 2014. [28] Crittenden et al., 2015. [29] Smith et al., 2018.

self-reference, and attributing mental states to others. The signal for this change likely comes from the salience network if it detects threat or novelty (Fransson, 2005; Jilka et al., 2014; Sridharan et al., 2008).

Subsequent research supports the idea that the inhibition of each executive system is not total, except in extreme situations. It is more likely that patterns of shared activation are task dependent in ways that optimize their contributions of each system (Bellana et al., 2017; Singh & Fawcett, 2008). When we engage in external tasks, DMN activation varies with task demand and our degree of engagement (Greicius & Menon, 2004; McKiernan et al., 2003; Pfefferbaum et al., 2011; Uddin et al., 2009). Engaging in psychotherapy likely requires an integrated of focus on internal and external experience to expand awareness and apply therapeutic insights into our lives (Hampson et al., 2006).

The Experience of Self and Others

The most satisfying thing in life is to have been able
to give a large part of one's self to others.
—Pierre Teilhard de Chardin

The DMN (ES3) becomes active during self-reflection, autobiographical memory, and states of resting consciousness (Lou et al., 2004). Damage to particular parietal areas correlates with out-of-body experiences as well as disturbances of identity and the experience of self (Blanke & Arzy, 2005). For many clients with anxiety and spectrum disorders, the absence of a developed internal world can reflect inhibition of or damage to the DMN, robbing them of the ability to retreat from the world for self-reflection. Simultaneously, the DMN is also involved with the awareness of others, including face recognition, theory of mind, and interpersonal problem-solving.

There is evidence that the mirror neurons of the parietal lobes (ES2) participate in the creation of inner representations of the actions, intentions, and emotions of others (Cabeza, 2012; Shmuelof & Zohary, 2006). These inner images, which contain sensory, motor, and emotional components, likely reflect ES2 and ES3 cooperation, serving as a cornerstone of the construction and maintenance of our sense of self and others (Macrae et al., 2004; Tanji & Hoshi, 2001). While our awareness of others is reflexive and begins at birth, self-awareness develops gradually during early life. These findings strongly suggest that our experiences of self and others, as well as the concepts of internal objects, projections, transference, share a neurobiological infrastructure (Philippi, Tranel et al., 2015). A client's ability to simultaneously engage in a transference reaction and have insight into their projection likely reflects the cooperation of ES2 and ES3.

The addition of the DMN to our conception of executive functioning allows for a potential neural home for our relationship with ourselves and others. Social connectedness is a central aspect of EF which has been absent from most prior models. Many individuals with high levels of cognitive intelligence and worldly success fail to actualize their real potential in love and work because of social deficits. This may well reflect an underdevelopment, overinhibition or damage to ES3. The neglect of social and emotional functioning and intelligence have left many clients with EF difficulties unable to get the proper help from cognitively oriented physicians and mental health professionals.

The Third Executive System and Psychopathology

If isolation tempers the strong, it is the stumbling block of the uncertain.
—Paul Cézanne

Disruptions in the functioning and connectivity of the DMN (ES3) have so far been found in individuals suffering with ADHD, autism, dementia, depression, schizophrenia, stroke, and chronic pain (Balthazar et al., 2014; Lynch et al., 2013; Park et al., 2014; Whitfield-Gabrieli et al., 2011; Zhu et al., 2012). Its involvement across so many mental disorders reflects the central importance of the DMN and its sensitivity to neurodynamic disruptions. Whether DMN-related dysfunctions are a cause, effect, or collateral aspect of these disorders is currently unknown.

Attention-Deficit/Hyperactivity Disorder

Our ability to attend, focus, and persevere to the completion of a task is the result of the proper neurodynamic balance of activation and inhibition of all three executive systems and a range of other neural networks. These abilities depend upon the inhibition of distracting internal stimuli such as past memories and daydreaming. A number of studies with individuals suffering from ADHD have found insufficient anticorrelational regulation between the ES3 and ES2 (Brown et al., 2011; Duffy et al., 2021; Hoekzema et al., 2014; Mowinckel et al., 2017). In other words, what looks like a deficit of cognitive functioning may be an inadequate inhibition of the first and third executives, making it difficult to focus and inhibit impulses.

Schizophrenia

Given the disturbances of self in schizophrenia, it would be surprising if impairments of the DMN were not present (Bluhm et al., 2007; Garrity, 2007; Jang et al., 2011). Failure to activate and deactivate the DMN in a functional manner was found in schizophrenic subjects during memory tasks (Pomarol-Clotet et al., 2008). This could reflect their difficulties with differentiating between internal and external realities and the contamination of consciousness by preconscious and dreamlike states. These may be similar to the distortions of reality in the transition states between waking and sleeping and to the fluidity of a child's reality-testing before the DMN is fully developed and integrated. An interesting hypothesis is that the frontal/dopaminergic deficits in schizophrenia impair its proper neurodynamic relationship with the DMN, providing for the symptoms of hallucinations, thought withdrawal, and thought insertion (Manoliu et al., 2014).

Depressive Rumination

Functional abnormalities of the DMN have been found to be positively correlated with symptoms of sleep disturbances, hopelessness, depressive rumination, and negative self-focus (Chen et al., 2020; Grimm et al., 2011; Hamilton et al., 2015; Scalabrini et al., 2020; Zhou et al., 2020). Some have hypothesized that a failure of DMN inhibition during external tasks may result in depressed clients overpersonalizing their experiences (Jacob et al., 2020; Li et al., 2013; Sheline et al., 2009), which could enhance feelings of guilt and lower self-esteem. Some go as far as to postulate that DMN dysfunction may be a biomarker for depression and dysthymia (Nixon et al., 2014; Posner et al., 2016; Yan et al., 2019). This theory is supported by the fact that DMN functioning has been shown to normalize with successful selective serotonin reuptake inhibitor treatment (Posner et al., 2013; Silbersweig, 2013). Self-reflective capacity, while an important ability to possess, can become maladaptive when chronic and negative.

Anxiety Disorders / Posttraumatic Stress Disorder

The sustained hyperarousal of anxiety disorders likely inhibits both DMN functioning and executive system integration (Gentili et al., 2009). This can exile victims from their internal worlds, undermine a coherent sense of self, and limit the ability to connect with others. For example, clients with obsessive-compulsive disorder (OCD) demonstrate more DMN inhibition during tasks which could keep them from knowing what they want to do (Stern et al., 2012). Persistent anxiety about making a wrong choice can result in avoidance and procrastination. One example might be making endless lists of pros and cons concerning a specific choice, only to find that the two always end up being equal. This creates an inability to make a decision but saves the individual with OCD from the anxiety of making a wrong choice.

PTSD, usually characterized by amygdala hyperactivity, results in chronic inhibition of the DMN (Liao et al., 2013; Palaniyappan & Liddle, 2012; Patel et al., 2012; Rabinak et al., 2011). These clients also demonstrate deficits in the DMN functions of self-referential processing, autobiographical memory, and theory of mind. The DMN is usually inhibited during the encoding of episodic memory and active during retrieval and recall (Cabeza et al., 2002; Chai et al., 2014). If the DMN is active during memory encoding, it may trigger old memories while disrupting the processes involved in establishing new memories. This may be the neurodynamic interaction that is overridden during successful EMDR treatment.

It appears likely that early trauma interferes with the development, coherence, and functioning of the DMN (Daniels et al., 2011). For example, women with early-life trauma and adult victims of childhood maltreatment of both genders have been found to have decreased DMN development and connectivity (Bluhm et al., 2009). The severity of their PTSD symptoms correlates with less internal DMN connectivity (Akiki et al., 2018). Those with severe and chronic PTSD show deficits similar to schizophrenic patients when attempting to switch between second and third executive system functions (Daniels et al., 2010). In addition, resting-state connectivity between the DMN and the right amygdala correlates with symptoms of PTSD and predicts the occurrence and severity of future symptoms (Lanius et al., 2009).

Creating an Inner World

Feeling real is more than existing, it is finding a way
to . . . have a self into which to retreat for relaxation.
                                        —Donald Winnicott

Creating an inner world requires an internal space to which we can retreat for safety and reflection. Until recently, this ability, so prized in the Eastern world, has been mostly ignored in the West. Research has always focused on subjects engaged in tasks, while it rarely occurred to anyone to see what our brains are up to in the absence of doing. Together, the regions of the DMN appear to support a sensory experience of the body and internal world that allow us to enter an imaginal space within the flow of time. The medial prefrontal regions are capable of inhibiting the amygdala to allow the posterior cingulate cortex and parietal lobes to provide us with a platform for an internal three-dimensional workspace. Stimulus-independent thought is a prerequisite to imagination, where we can manipulate images, play out scenarios, and process emotions without interference. It also offers us the possibility to experience time travel through the juxtaposition in working memory of the present, past, and imagining the future.

What we call mind wandering and daydreaming may be the foundation of our sense of aesthetics, our creativity, and the background processing that helps us function in the world (Belfi et al., 2019). In the words of Michelangelo, "I saw an angel in the marble and carved until I set him free." This imaginative function, so vital to the experience of self and the development of culture, suggests that the adaptive functions of the DMN have exerted a strong influence on sociocultural evolution (Morcom & Fletcher, 2007a, 2007b).

The Mind of an Ultramarathon Runner

The affairs of the world go on forever. Do not
delay the practice of meditation.
                                        —Jetsun Milarepa

Optimizing executive functioning is essential to success in difficult tasks, as well as adapting to the unexpected aspects of life as they arise. Every challenge gives us the opportunity to enlist each of our executive systems and discover the best dynamic balance among them. This kind of self-reflective capacity can be called mindfulness, and requires remembering to be a human being and not falling into being a human doing. The human tendency to become a human doing is reflected in our obsession with stress reduction, the proliferation of meditation apps, and human resources posters touting work-life balance. If we chronically overwork or engage in long periods of intense activity, others may remind us that "life is a marathon, not a sprint." We need this advice because our brains have evolved with a bias toward action instead of thought and self-reflection. Good advice—obviously easier said than done.

The experts in pacing yourself are ultramarathon runners. One of us (LC) had the opportunity to work with Graham, a successful centurion marathoner (100-mile runner), and asked him what it takes to win in this extremely demanding sport. Of course, I was curious about what kind of executive functioning is required and what goes through your mind over the 20–25 hours of solitude it takes most competitors to complete a 100-mile course. Having a day job as a stock trader, Graham was extremely organized and a skilled communicator. Here is what he shared with me along with my reflections about EF:

> The two most important things are to have a training plan and a race strategy. The training plan is all about getting your body in proper shape, eating right, and getting the right amount of sleep. The race strategy is about studying the course terrain, being prepared for the weather, knowing ahead of time where the difficult sections are so you can be mentally prepared, as well as subtly adjusting your training schedule leading up to the race to the real-world conditions.

This first set of issues seem to primarily be the domain of the second executive system. There is a plan and a set of strategies that have been acquired through experience, mentorship, and study. They have to be held in mind, remembered day by day, and adhered to regardless of potential distractions and shifting moods. These are all skills and abilities that have traditionally been a part of the definition of executive functioning. In our attempts at being the CEOs of our own lives, we all need to develop short-, medium-, and long-term plans and have the discipline to stick to them, moment to moment, despite the fluctuations of moods and any of the 10,000 things that arise to divert our focus.

> The next challenge is to remember your plan during the actual race. You have to remember to pace yourself even though you might feel like running faster or keeping ahead of someone coming up from behind. You have to stay aware of your heart rate, what's happening in your GI system, keep properly hydrated, and stay mindful of how your feet and legs are doing. The endorphins can be a challenge in this regard because while they help you feel less pain, they also decrease feedback from your body. They can put you in a kind of trance and make it difficult to think clearly. You have to resist the urge to zone out and keep paying attention to your body mechanics.

Here Graham is sharing the importance of not only having a plan, but remembering and adhering to it during the race. I've heard other runners refer to this as an "ironclad mindset." He understands the impact of the endorphins released for the race and has to counteract them by being more focused on his body than he might be otherwise. He is also describing the importance of staying consciously aware of information from his body, for which he uses his first and third executive systems. How he understands and utilizes this information reflects the cooperation of his second executive to translate this interoceptive information into adjustments in his biomechanics and race plan.

Graham went on to describe an example of emotional regulation that likely involves the participation of all three executive systems:

> Even though I've been running for years, when someone passes me, I become anxious and have to fight the impulse to race them or stay in the lead. I still have to calm myself down and remind myself of my race plan. It's like holding on to stocks during a crash—the emotional impulse is to pull out, then you remember that you are playing a long game, especially with retirement funds, just like in a long race.

In these situations, the second and third systems cooperate to help the first executive downregulate anxiety and inhibit impulsive behavior not in line with his race plan.

I also have to pay attention if my thoughts stray into negative territory. You know, my father's health, the problems in my relationship, a challenging client I'm working with, things like that. There is no better way to forget your plan and become depleted of energy than to get caught in a negative thought loop about a problem that is out of my control, especially while I'm running the race. These runs are mostly on uneven terrain, poorly maintained trails, and go through an entire night. It can seem interminable, especially when pushing through fatigue and pain. You have to find a way to amuse yourself that doesn't distract you from paying proper attention to the race. If you can't figure this one out, ultramarathons are not for you.

While I had always focused on the physical challenges of ultramarathon running, Graham taught me that the mental hurdles are just as challenging. He clearly needed the participation and cooperation of all three executive systems. Successfully preparing for and running an ultramarathon requires constant shuffling among living in the past, present, and future, shifting focus between your internal and external environments, and synthesizing all of this information and implementing it appropriately. Having a plan and sticking to it, whether it is for a long run, career, or relationship, requires remembering the plan, maintaining oversight and regulatory control of your physical and emotional reactions, and having the necessary inner conversation among the three executive systems to be the CEO of a successful life.

Part III

Assessment of Adaptive Functioning

Chapter 7

Assessing the First and Second Executive Systems

The complexity of things—the things
within things—can seem endless.
　　　　　　　　　　　—Alice Munro

Clients are being increasingly referred to psychotherapy with vaguely defined deficits in executive functioning. Like ADHD and spectrum disorder, EF has become a cultural meme for a heterogeneous and poorly understood set of adaptational, learning, and behavioral challenges. How EF is understood and treated will largely depend on a therapist's training and orientation. A client might be given training in time management, medication, cognitive behavioral therapy (CBT), mindfulness training, brain scans, neuropsychological testing, psychoanalysis, or some combination of the above. Most everyone believes that whatever they do can help.

When a client appears to have difficulties in executive functioning, one or more of their neural executive systems may be underdeveloped, compromised, or improperly modulated. If clinicians diagnose and treat EF from a one-size-fits-all approach, therapeutic success becomes a matter of chance. Unfortunately, training programs have shifted from teaching how to think through complex clinical challenges to implementing assessment protocols. This trade school approach teaches students to navigate the algorithms of the *Diagnostic and Statistical Manual (DSM)*, write intake reports, and rely on treatment manuals. Very little time is spent on learning the art of case conceptualization, empathic attunement, or creative problem-solving. The reason for this is largely financial; it is far less expensive to teach and test content in a large classroom than it is to use traditional one-on-one apprenticeships required to guide the development of clinical acumen.

These kinds of educational experiences will lead you to search for a manualized method for the assessment and treatment of EF deficits. The problem is that executive functioning defies such standardization because it involves the whole person in their environment. This makes assessing EF a full-body process, requiring you to connect with your client, see the world through their eyes, and learn to think—or not think—as they do. You have to know their history, understand their adaptations, and get a personal sense of their emotional landscape. It is from this holistic perspective that you will be better able to identify problems and cocreate solutions.

Accept that in-depth assessments take time, knowledge, and a lot of trial-and-error learning. Instead of working to fit a client with the right label, approach each client as a unique experiment of nature who has adapted to their life experiences with a specific set of genetic and neuro-developmental strengths and weaknesses. Over their lifetime, these complex interactions have given rise to the person you see before you. Putting yourself in their shoes, seeing the world through their eyes, will give you the best perspective on their challenges and how you might be of help. This is obviously true for both assessment and psychotherapy, and the best assessments occur within therapeutic-like relationships.

While far from a panacea, the three executive system model does provide us with an open-ended strategy to guide brain-based diagnosis and treatment. The structures and functions of each system guide us to what to look for, think about, and explore with our clients. It can be used in educational, corporate, and psychotherapeutic contexts to pinpoint the source(s) of EF challenges, guide questioning, and develop a more comprehensive plan for structuring interventions. When faced with a complex human problem, there is no checklist, manualized treatment, or technical solution that can substitute for careful observation, exploration, and thought. We need to possess good executive functioning ourselves in order to recognize it, understand how to assess it, and use our own brains and minds to imagine and model possible treatments for our clients.

As you have already figured out from the previous chapters, functional deficits are logically related to the contribution of each neural system. Beyond this, we are also looking at the dynamic relationship among systems to identify possible origins of their problem. Sometimes there will be challenges in more than one system. This is why, in addition to the separate functions of each of the three systems, a understanding of how they interact is essential.

Assessing the Executive Systems

The good life is a process, not a state of being.
It is a direction, not a destination.

—Carl Rogers

We should begin with each client with the agenda of getting to know them. Initial interactions should involve open conversation, asking questions, finding out about their experiences, listening to their stories, and getting a sense of what it feels like to be with them. In the process, we work to establish a warm and trusting relationship, which maximizes the likelihood that our client will be both open and truthful about their experiences. When possible, it is also helpful to meet with a person or persons in their life (collaterals) who know them well and can speak as an observer of the client in their everyday life.

The *content* of their discussions involves all of the usual information we collect during the intake process—presenting problems (in this case, we are assuming that problems with EF are of major concern); psychological, medical, family, and social history; and treatment history, potential risks, and treatment goals. The *process* involves a client's appearance, behavior, cognition, mental status, and emotionality. At a somewhat deeper level, you're aiming to get a sense of ways they relate to you that may be indications of significant past relationships (transference) as well as the ways in which their language is coherent or incoherent for potential inferences about their attachment and parenting experiences.

Pay special attention to your personal reactions to your client, the internal reflections and inner dialogue that you typically wouldn't share and often ignore. Do you feel relaxed or nervous—settled or uneasy (ES1)? When they share their experiences with you, do they follow a linear course, or are you often surprised by how they understand, react to, or come to understand what happened to them (ES2)? Do they include self-reflection and evidence of an inner world, or do they describe situations via temporal sequences (ES3)? We can learn as much about our clients from what they don't say and the physiological states and emotions they evoke in us as we do through their expressed words and actions.

Whether due to a lack of time or experience, many of us get all of our information about a client from the client. The problem with this is that we are only seeing their world through their eyes. What we hear from our clients is always skewed by their memory, defenses, cognitive limitations, how they present themselves, and whatever cognitive problems they may be experiencing. This is why gathering information from others in the client's life is so vital. This is standard practice for those working with children but can be neglected when treating and assessing older adolescents and adults. Because EF is usually based in specific contexts, collaterals can describe both your client and the context (as they see it), providing aspects of situations that the client misses. These missing elements can be key to identifying deficits in EF.

Gathering collateral information is especially important if it appears that a client has problems with memory, affect regulation, and/or interpersonal skills. Examples of failures in these areas from collaterals can serve as valuable clues in assessment and diagnosis. It is always important, however, to consider the source of this information. Often, others in our clients' lives have their own challenges, limitations, and agenda—so always be mindful of the source of the information. These interactions will provide much of the basic information to form initial hypotheses about the origins of what has been labeled as their deficit in executive functioning.

As we begin to discuss the assessment of the three executive systems, remember that most of you have already been trained to assess multiple aspects of ES1 in your clinical training. What you are looking for is the degree of transient and chronic arousal your client experiences, which you already do by examining their symptoms of anxiety, stress, tension, and panic. It also relates to assessing for the presence of phobia, anxiety disorders, and CPTSD and PTSD. The second executive is usually assessed by neuropsychological and educational testing, which most of us refer out to others. The value of formal ES2 assessment is to rule out brain-based damage and dysfunction.

It is assessment of the third executive that may be where most of your learning needs to take place. The deeper questioning focuses on their experience of self and others, the nature of their internal world, and their ability to daydream and imagine alternative realities and different selves. These issues are largely ignored in most current forms of psychotherapy, and we have to rely on our familiarity with our personal experiences in these areas. Having experience with meditation, psychodynamic therapy, and other forms of self-reflective practices will be of assistance. The next challenge will be how to bring all of this information together to form a coherent picture of your client's executive systems and develop a treatment plan.

Assessing the First Executive System

What the mind doesn't understand, it worships or fears.
—Alice Walker

An understanding of the disruptions of the first executive relies heavily on an understanding of the neurobiology and psychology of arousal. For most clients, hyperarousal is experienced in both the mind and body, although the order of their appearance in conscious awareness can go either way. Some have physiological arousal that leads to anxious thoughts, while others have anxious thoughts that trigger their bodily arousal. Still other clients will be unaware of how highly aroused they are. This is usually because it has gone on so long that they can no longer consciously recognize it.

Clients with moderate to severe trauma histories may be completely dissociated from an awareness of both their body and their inner emotional experience. In these cases, you have to observe their bodily reactions through time, assess whether they live under persistent stress or keep themselves in constant motion, and explore stress-related physical problems that have accumulated over the years. See Table 7.1 for an outline of central aspects of the first executive system.

Successful executive functioning is established upon a foundation of physiological homeostasis and affect regulation. This is why it is important to begin with an assessment of ES1 functioning. Some clients are so agitated that they can't stay focused on one thought, understand the questions they are asked, or even stay seated. These same clients may find it incredibly difficult to sit through a class or a business meeting, or stay focused on a spouse

TABLE 7.1
First Executive System

Responsibilities	Affect regulation, attachment security, intrusive memories
Indications of deficits	Anxiety, panic, hypervigilance, social withdrawal, task avoidance
Situational variables	Past or present trauma, bullying, loss, life stress, family disruption, medical challenges
Diagnostic aids	Helpfulness of biofeedback, successfulness of breathing and mindfulness techniques
Possible interventions	Psychotherapy, medication, meditation, lifestyle changes
Common diagnoses	Anxiety disorders (OCD, GAD, PTSD, etc.), complications of medical disorders (cardiac illness, metabolic dysregulation, etc.)

who wants to have a conversation. Many have suffered with such high levels of arousal for so long that they have learned to hide it from others with an air of cool indifference. The only visible clues of this underlying arousal might be distractibility, physical agitation, or reports that they are unable to sleep or focus on their work. We can't necessarily rely on self-reported anxiety, because clients may not identify these experiences as anxiety.

Remember that the context of assessment or therapy itself is stressful for clients, especially early in the process before the establishment of a safe connection. This makes it a good opportunity to measure their regulatory capacities. As part of your assessment, you might try a breathing (or other) relaxation technique to assess your client's ability to regulate their physiological arousal. You can also use a simple biofeedback device that measures galvanic skin response (GSR). You can buy one online for around $75. It looks like an old computer mouse with two silver strips on top and measures subtle changes in the secretions of the sweat glands tied to autonomic arousal.

The basic idea of biofeedback is that clients will use the tone to learn to recognize their bodily arousal and achieve a more relaxed state of body and mind. Their inability to benefit from biofeedback could be an indication of the severity of their arousal, the possible need for medication, and even their readiness to engage in neuropsychological assessment. Use the biofeedback device yourself to get comfortable with how it works, your impression of the experience of the tone, and changes you are able to achieve in your own arousal.

If you decide to use it with a client, have them lie down and get as comfortable as they can. Next, have them rest their nondominant hand on the GSR device so that their index and middle fingers rest on the two silver strips. Once they find a comfortable position and can rest their hand on the device without movement, adjust the tone to a moderate level. Start by having them become alternatively tense and relaxed for five seconds at a time so that they can experience the tone change with their level of tension. Clients usually find the experience interesting and take on the challenge. Session by session, they learn how their breathing, muscle tension, and thoughts impact their bodily tension. I'll sometimes use it myself between clients to help me recenter and become more relaxed, especially after a difficult session or during some life challenge.

Most of us are able to learn to lower the tone over a 10- or 15-minute session. Clients often report that they are surprised by how much more relaxed they are able to become. Some even order one for themselves to use at home and work. By assessing your client's ability or inability to benefit from the GSR device, you are learning about the neurodynamics of their executive systems. Most specifically, you are learning whether they are able to leverage ES2 and ES3 to modulate ES1.

In contrast, clients suffering with various anxiety disorders are unable to change the tone of the biofeedback device no matter how long and how hard they try. There could be many possible explanations such as medical conditions, medication side effects, or how many energy drinks they had for breakfast. Regardless of the reason, it usually indicates that contemplative or self-focused techniques will likely fail until the underlying causes of arousal are addressed.

For highly anxious clients, directing them to clear their minds or focus on their breathing opens a Pandora's box of agitation, fear, and uncontrollable thoughts. Sitting quietly removes the distractions that they depend upon to distract themselves from the anxiety and fear that haunt them. The demons unleashed in any quiet moment are far worse than their usual state of anxiety and agitation. These clients will often report negative and even frightening experiences after taking recreational drugs or opioid-based pain killers. The fact is, clients with anxiety and affective disorders, manic defenses, or early histories of stress and trauma sometimes have brains that are so biased toward arousal that their minds lack the leverage to calm their brains. In these situations, medication may be an important first step in treatment, and you may want to assess their other executive systems until the first is stabilized so you can get a true measure of their abilities.

Second Executive System

Concentration is a fine antidote to anxiety.

—Jack Nicklaus

While the first executive is usually assessed through a clinical interview, the second has been traditionally evaluated via neuropsychological testing. On the other hand we can glean a great deal about someone's abilities to think, express themselves, and navigate their day-to-day life through inter-action and observation. But as clinicians, we realize that because we are biased by our own perspective and experience, it is also good to include more objective measures that can be compared to the performance of oth-ers. Of course, comparisons are tricky given how different people are, not to mention the impact of race, gender, culture, and even handedness. See Table 7.2 for an outline of central aspects of the second executive system.

We always have to keep in mind that an aroused first executive sys-tem will inhibit the activation and functioning of ES2. Anxiety, arousal, and fear often result in a decrease of multiple aspects of cognitive intel-ligence. This is why it is so difficult for us to perform cognitive tasks in states of anxiety (like test anxiety) or why we may freeze while doing public speaking or giving a performance (stage fright). Functioning of the second and third executives is always modulated by the first. A central problem of neuropsychological assessment has always been the neglect of these essential variables in pursuit of quantifying general intelligence and specific capabilities. When the clinical observations in a neuropsy-chological report include expressions of arousal, agitation, or anxiety, it places all of the objective, empirical results in question. The question then remains, what would someone be capable of if they weren't impaired by ES1 arousal?

After decades of neuropsychologists assessing executive functioning

TABLE 7.2

Second Executive System

Domains	Sustained attention, task focus to completion, problem-solving, abstract reasoning
Indications of deficits	Educational and occupational failure of attention, comprehension, and problem navigation
Situational variables	Head injury, participation in contact sports, time-linked decline in cognitive functioning
Diagnostic aids	Neuropsychological testing, neurological consultation, EEG, brain scan
Possible interventions	Surgery, medication, cognitive, sensory-motor, occupational rehabilitation
Common diagnoses	Brain damage (stroke, lesions, hypoxia, tumors, etc.), neurodevelopmental delays or disorders

through a variety of measures, the new century witnessed the release of a specific set of tests—the Delis-Kaplan Executive Function System (D-KEFS; Delis et al., 2001). Most of the nine subtests of the D-KEFS were adapted from preexisting measures of different aspects of EF. While thought to be a measure of frontal functioning, research supports the idea that all of these tasks rely on a diverse set of neural systems and the development and integration of all three executive systems (Keifer & Tranel, 2013). Table 7.3 contains a list of the D-KEFS subtests and the hypothesized skills they assess.

As you can see, these are tests that depend upon the higher-level functions of the frontal and parietal lobes. Successfully navigating these tasks requires the integration of semantic (left hemisphere), visual (right hemisphere), and conceptual (both hemispheres) processing. Many are also timed tests, so if processing is slowed for any reason, the client will score lower. A process called "testing the limits" during neuropsychological testing can be important. This means that the tester will base their score on the standardized time but still allow the client to finish the task in order to determine how much their performance is hindered by their processing speed. In some situations, it is fair to ask the examiner to test the limits if

TABLE 7.3

Delis-Kaplan Executive Function System (D-KEFS)

Subtest	Executive Functions Being Measured
Trail Making	Flexibility of thinking, visual-motor sequencing
Verbal Fluency	Letter and category fluency, category switching
Design Fluency	Creativity, problem-solving, pattern generation, observing, inhibiting prior responses
Color-Word Interference	Inhibition of dominant responses
Sorting Test	Concept formation, problem-solving, abstract sorting concepts
Twenty Questions	Categorizing, formulating abstract, yes/no questions, and use of feedback
Word Context	Deductive reasoning, integration of information, hypothesis testing, flexibility of thinking
Tower Test	Spatial planning, rule learning, response inhibition, establish and maintain instructional set
Proverbs	Ability to form new verbal abstractions

you feel there may be some reason why your client might perform slowly instead of suffering from cognitive deficits. Reasons can include depression, physical illness, and sensory limitations.

It makes sense to assume that different areas of the frontal lobe participate in tasks that call on higher-level abstract thinking. However, the performance on these tests requires the participation of many areas of the brain for optimal performance. Visual-motor, language, memory, and spatial analysis are needed for successful performance. Thinking about abstract reasoning as being dissociated from the body and other aspects of space-time processing works at a philosophical level, but fails the test of real-world adaptations.

Let's take, for example, the first subtest of the D-KEFS, the trail-making tests (sometimes referred to as "trails"). You may have never seen this test but are likely familiar with the concept if you ever played connect-the-dots as a kid. In most connect-the-dot games, you draw straight lines from 1 upward, and the end result is a drawing of something or other. Trail making works on the same principle and has two parts, A and B. Trails A is the traditional 1-upward process. Trails B alternates from numbers to letters, so you have to follow the sequence 1, A, 2, B, 3, C, and so on. Both Trails A and B require fine motor skills and hand-eye coordination, remembering the task and maintaining attention and focus, and avoiding irrelevant distractions. Trails B is more difficult in that it adds the challenge of remembering to alternate between numbers and letters and not perseverating on whichever one you were working on last.

While this may appear to be a simple child's game, it actually is a long-standing measure of cognitive EF. Clients with various kinds of brain damage may go out of sequence, forget the rules of the task while doing it, or become distracted by inner or outer stimulation. On Trails B, it is common for a client to lose the rules of the task and just connect the numbers or letters. In more severe cases, their choices of numbers or letters may become random, or they may draw across the dots and ignore the numbers and letters. Because it is also a timed task, scores can also decrease due to slow cognitive or motor processing.

If you receive a testing report from a neuropsychologist with results based on these and other empirical measures, it is your job as a clinician to put them in the context of your broader assessment of the other two executive systems, your client's life circumstances, and the other challenges they may be facing. The data gleaned from these tests are only useful if they are well contextualized and translated into interventions that make sense for each client.

Clients vary in how much they are impacted by social context. Some can focus on being tested, and the engagement and warmth of the tester are irrelevant. With others, a transactional approach on the part of the tester or the use of computer-based assessment can cause anxiety and inhibit second executive functioning. Many neuropsychologists are excellent at administering batteries of tests but not necessarily clinically adept. If the tester is not good at establishing a bond with their clients, or the client is hypersensitive to evaluation, criticism, or shame, the results may largely reflect an emotional (first executive) problem masked as a cognitive or intellectual (second executive) deficit.

Another important question is whether the test results are congruent with your experience of the client. For one client, an adolescent girl, neuropsychological testing suggested a deficit in second executive system functioning as an explanation for her failures in school. Her father, a

CEO himself, questioned these findings in light of the fact that his daughter excelled in logical thinking and manipulated others with a high level of sophistication. During sessions, she presented herself as an intelligent, articulate, and perceptive young woman who had a firm grasp on the world around her. She did, however, have a great deal of resentment for her family and all the doctors she had to see and tests she was forced to take. From her perspective, it was her parents' relationship that was the problem and the impact it had on her and her siblings. As I got to know her and her family, I had to agree, and I came to see the test results as her acting out against what she experienced as manipulation, rather than reflecting any real deficit in her cognitive or executive functioning.

We're sure you are aware of the controversies surrounding standardized tests, and neuropsychological testing is no exception. This is why there is sometimes an attempt to establish norms for different ethnic groups and geographical regions. The problem with this is that what we define as a group is usually heterogeneous and ill defined. Because of all these factors, it is not enough for the examiner to come up with scores; they must also contextualize them within a client's life and experiences.

Chapter 8

Assessing the Third Executive System

The key to growth is the introduction of higher dimensions of consciousness into our awareness.

—Lao Tzu

While the functions and failures of ES1 and ES2 have long been explored by psychotherapists and neuropsychologists, respectively, those of ES3 have been largely ignored. With the exception of family therapists and social psychologists, its social and cultural contributions to cognition, decision-making, and EF have remained under the radar. This is not due to a lack of data but to the segregation of academic departments and professional disciplines. Even within the field of neuropsychology, functions beyond cognitive processes are talked about in side discussions but have gained little traction as a focus of study. The challenge of measuring and even thinking about subjective processes doesn't fit the search for standardized and objective measurements. The messy parts of experience are usually pushed to the side or ignored altogether.

In the absence of a diagnostic system or a set of standardized tests to measure third executive functioning, we have to rely on our curiosity, conceptual abilities, and clinical judgment to explore these functions. We also need to rely on our own ES3 to discover, explore, and assess it in others. This leaves us with the very challenge that scientists try to avoid at all costs—using our personal experience and judgment. It also means that we can assess others only to the degree to which we possess the abilities we are assessing. As in psychotherapy, we can't take our clients much beyond the limits of our own development.

It is impressive that so many clients, and even many psychotherapists, have no experience with or comprehension of an inner world. They often grow up in families where all interactions are transactional, and no one is consciously aware of subjective experience. For these people, everything exists outside of themselves, and they are unable to reflect on their experience or think about their thinking. Therapists like this see their work as a set of things you direct a client to learn and do, and rely on checklists and workbooks to organize the important information. When working with a client like this, we ask ourselves (1) are they capable of developing an inner world with the appropriate guidance, and (2) would it be beneficial to them?

The History of Third Executive System Assessment

*Poetry is emotion put in measure. The emotion must come
by nature, but the measure can be acquired by art.*

—Thomas Hardy

Executive function doesn't exist in the abstract, only within a specific context. It is embedded within time, place, and the contextual variables related to specific challenges. Executive function is also not monolithic but a collection of abilities and adaptational skills. What matters is how our clients perform in their lives, not in our office, especially when it comes to the domains of the third executive system.

While no standardized assessment of third executive functions does (or perhaps should) exist, we do have guidance from those who came before us concerning some of the things we should keep in mind. Lezak (1995) provided some clues when she discussed the importance of purposive action, self-awareness, and observing clients in their natural settings. She also stressed the value of gathering personal history, clinical observation, and reports from collaterals. These were all attempts to point beyond the formal testing to a focus on the whole person in their natural environment.

In neuropsychological reports, these informal aspects of the assessment process may be mentioned in a small section or work their way into a treatment suggestion for psychotherapy. But they are by far overshadowed by a lengthy discussion of the statistics, charts, and significance levels of a hundred scales of cognitive functioning. Unfortunately, neuropsychology has become a clerical task done mostly by technicians who speak a different language from the clinicians and clients who need to understand and utilize their testing reports. You could say that the three-system model of EF is largely an effort to rebalance the focus of assessment with its social, emotional, and subjective components.

Subsequent to Lezak, the neuropsychologist Paul Eslinger was especially interested in the impact of dementia on the social and emotional aspects of EF. He repeatedly saw that the social sensitivity required to attune to others and the ability to consider other minds was clearly impaired in his clients. Eslinger (1996) described four "social executors" that he saw repeatedly fail in clients with dementia that fit well into the functions of the third executive system and should be included in our assessment:

1. **Social self-regulation:** processes needed to manage the initiation, rate, intensity, and duration of social interactions. These are often problematic in individuals with spectrum disorders as well as those with anxious attachment, where their anxiety and intrusive memories from the past result in the creation of incoherent narratives.
2. **Social self-awareness:** knowledge and insight about oneself and the impact of one's behavior on others in social settings. This is a level of metacognition, not about ideas, but the ability to interact and observe ourselves interacting for the purpose of monitoring and regulating our social behavior.
3. **Social sensitivity:** the ability to understand another's perspective, point of view, or emotional state. This includes what we call theory of mind, attunement, sympathy, and compassion.
4. **Social salience:** the ability to integrate somatic and emotional states into social interactions that make them connective, meaningful, and specific to an individual or individuals.

When you get to Chapter 14 on attachment, you will notice how Eslinger's observations of patients with dementia align with the assessment of coherent narratives in Mary Main's Adult Attachment Interview (1998).

Our ability to effectively communicate through language requires all of the social and emotional elements organized by the third executive.

In the broadest conceptualization yet proposed, Barkley (2012b) places EF in the context of evolutionary biology as an extensive set of adaptational abilities that have been shaped by natural selection. The most important aspect of his idea, as it relates to the three-system model, is viewing EF as a set of interconnected genetic, developmental, social, and environmental variables that shape our ability to adapt and survive. While the idea of this kind of evolutionary psychology may be controversial, it matches what we are currently learning about EF and brain evolution. His theory of EF includes four levels of interactive and interdependent abilities necessity for the development and integration of all three executive systems.

Across Barkley's four levels of EF, you can see the developmental throughline from early sensory-motor abilities, to cognition, to the social-emotional integration required by complex social animals. You can use this structure with clients of any age, keeping in mind both their chronological and developmental ages. As you can see below, his two higher levels of EF include the ability to connect, cooperate, and work well with others.

1. **Instrumental level:** self-directed attention, restraint, sensory-motor behaviors, and play as means to a specific end
2. **Methodological level:** chains of actions (method) for the near-term goals of adaptive functioning (e.g., time management, delay of gratification, sustenance, care and protection of self and others)
3. **Tactical/interactive level:** hierarchies of behaviors for long-term goals involving others (e.g., taking turns, keeping promises, making contracts, participating in culture)
4. **Strategic/cooperative level:** complex self-organization that allows for successful membership in large groups (e.g., social networks, shared ventures, and shared defense, as well as adherence to the common rules of law, ethics, and social mores)

Barkley also provided us with his thoughts about six components of internal experience, our relationship with our bodies, our experience of self, and their contributions to EF:

1. **Self-restraint:** the ability to inhibit distractions and impulses, and change course based on feedback
2. **Self-directed sensory-motor action:** the use of visualization to rehearse behavior
3. **Self-directed private speech:** the use of internal dialogue to question and problem-solve
4. **Self-directed emotion and motivation:** the ability to perceive, assess, and redirect emotions
5. **Self-directed play:** the use of imagination to stress-test possible actions
6. **Self-directed attention:** self-reflective capacity used for guiding moment-to-moment behavior

While all of these aspects of self-awareness and self-control seem to be related, most are actually separate skills or abilities. Each client will have strengths and weaknesses across these domains, while others may be completely absent. Questioning and assessing each one can provide valuable guidance in creating a plan to build and bolster different aspects of EF.

A common example is a person who is capable of doing any one of the 100 household tasks that may lie before them. Yet, by the end of a busy day, they haven't accomplished any of them. The deficit may be in their ability to follow a task to completion and not be distracted by the other 99 things there are to do. A combination of inhibiting distractions, internal dialogue, and self-reflection are required to keep us on task to completion before we move on to the next. Perseverance to completion connects means-ends relationships and serves as a moment-to-moment navigational map through space and time.

The Functions of the DMN as a Guide to Clinical Assessment

I long, as does every human being, to be at home wherever I find myself.
—Maya Angelou

After a century of searching the frontal lobes for all aspects of EF, the discovery of the DMN provided us with an expanded neural home for social, emotional, and subjective experience. A well-developed and high-functioning ES1 and ES2 frees the third executive system to utilize imagination to build a safe and quiet place within us. This provides us with the ability to feel "at home" wherever we find ourselves.

With the simultaneous expansion of the field of social neuroscience and the mindfulness movement, the central importance of the DMN in clinical practice has become increasingly clear. It also provides a neural platform for the inclusion of other areas of research such as theory of mind, imagination, self-reflection, and empathy in clinical practice. Concepts from psychoanalysis, such as psychological-mindedness, self-reflective capacity, and ego strength also became part of the discussion. See Table 8.1 for an outline of central aspects of the third executive system.

Assessing the third executive system, like all clinical evaluation, relies on us knowing (1) how to listen, (2) what to listen for, and (3) where to search for the information. Learning to listen requires us to know how to remain calm and centered during our interactions with our clients—a good focus for our own therapy, meditation practice, and lifestyle choices. To know what to listen for, we have to study the functions of the DMN and translate that knowledge into language that leads us to the most valuable

TABLE 8.1
Third Executive System

Domains	Theory of mind, empathy, imagination, self-awareness, self-reflective capacity
Indications of deficits	Little understanding of social rules, lack of a mental model of others, inability to articulate emotions or describe inner experience, lack of imagination
Situational variables	Isolation, social withdrawal, ostracism, prejudice, bullying
Diagnostic aids	Behavioral reports from family members, teachers, and colleagues, interpersonal sophistication demonstrated during sessions
Common diagnoses	Spectrum disorder, alexithymia
Possible interventions	Social-skills training, learning to hypothesize about the thoughts, feelings, and intentions of others, family therapy, launching from the family

information. The more you read about the ongoing discoveries connecting the DMN with subjective, social, and emotional experience, the more you will pick up on a range of abilities and absences of subjective experiences in yourself and your clients.

Finding useful information about a client's ES3 rests on our ability to tap into our inner detective, read between the lines, and focus on aspects of our clients' experiences that are usually in the background. In assessing the third executive system, we depend largely on (1) our personal experience of our clients, (2) their description of their subjective experiences, (3) how they think of and interact with others, and (4) collateral information concerning the nature and depth of their social connectedness and interactions. Because the skills and abilities of the third executive are so broad, complex, and context dependent, there is no way to develop an exhaustive list of things to think about. Table 8.2 provides some ideas and questions to consider as you develop an assessment strategy for third executive functioning.

Autobiographical Memory

While many neural networks are involved in autobiographical memory, the ES3 seems to be especially reliant on it when considering aspects of self-identity, mental time travel, and self-reflection. We have learned from attachment research that anxious and avoidant attachment schema correlate with lack of recall for childhood memories. In the Adult Attachment Interview, Mary Main found that the lack of coherence of the narratives of avoidantly attached individuals was due to their lack of supportive evidence from their past for the descriptions of their parents and childhoods. This is likely due to chronic high levels of stress during childhood and inhibition of, or damage to, their hippocampus and its memory functions. This provides solid evidence that a lack of childhood memories may not reflect a resistance to recalling these experiences, but a lack of consolidation of these memories.

Theory of Mind

Theory of mind is a process by which we ascribe thoughts, motivations, and intentions to others. It is believed that this ability was shaped by nat-

TABLE 8.2
A Thumbnail Guide to Third Executive System Assessment

What to Look For	Where to Look
	Social
Connectedness	How does it feel to be in the room with the client? (B)
	Do they feel present and available while interacting with you? (B)
	Do you feel like you have made a human connection with them? (B)
	Does it seem you are getting to know them at an emotional level? (B)
	Do they offer information about their lives, or do they share deep emotional experiences? (B)
	They describe significant others by external characteristics—appearance, occupation, finances—versus aspects of their personality or how others make them feel. (C)
	They say things like, "I must have missed the lecture on how to meet people." (C)
Processing relationships	Are they able to understand and problem-solve interpersonal conflict and moral dilemmas? (A, B)
	Can they take in and make adjustments based on feedback? (A, B, C)
Social skills	What do you observe in session? Are you able to connect? Do they observe usual social interactions? (B)
	Are they able to make and maintain friends? (A, C)
	Do you see them as someone who is sensitive to the feelings and needs of others? (A)
	Do they ever come back after an interaction having reflected on what was discussed? (A)
	How do they describe their friendships? (A)
	Do you feel you can establish an emotional connection with them? (A)
Social self-regulation	How do they manage the rate, intensity, and duration of interactions? (A, B)
	Are they aware of their impact on others? (A, B, C)

Self

Self-awareness	Are they capable of thinking about themselves objectively or from a third-person perspective? (A, B, C)
Self-reflective capacity	Do they have insight into their behavior and how others see them? B
Internal dialogue	Do they have an inner voice? Do they experience an internal dialogue? (C)
	How do they experience it, and how do they use it? (C)
Internal world	Do they have an internal world? Can they use it as a resource for retreat and reflection? (C)
	If you ask a client about their internal world, do they have no clue what you are talking about? (C)
	Do they lack interest in what motivates their emotions, thoughts, or actions? (A, B, C)

Cognitive

Theory of mind	How do they understand and describe the behaviors, emotions, and intentions of others?
	Do they seem to understand your thoughts, motivations, and feelings during sessions? (B)
	Do they report often feeling surprised or confused by the words and actions of others? (C)
	Are they able to read a room? Can they blend in on social occasions? (A)
Empathy	Can they combine their emotional sense of another with thoughts about what they are feeling?
Imagination	Do they daydream? Think about the future? Do they have creative ideas? (C)
	Can they use visualization to practice and stress-test behaviors and interactions? (C)
Mental time travel	Can they imagine their future, and describe their past in reasonable detail? (B)
Contemplation and rest	Can they use their internal space for withdrawal from the world for reflection and recuperation? (C)

A, questions for collaterals; B, in-session observations; C, client direct report.

ural selection to give primates (and other social creatures) the ability to anticipate and predict the actions of others, thereby being better able to compete for resources. It involves taking into account what you know about the other person, the context you are in, and the events that are occurring. Because we share this ability with other primates, it reflects a level of executive functioning that is not necessarily conscious or intentional. It actually has a set of automatic cortical and subcortical processes used to analyze the social environment. Despite this, we placed it in the cognitive category in Table 8.2 because we generally think of it as a cognitive process.

In interacting with a client, we can quickly get the sense if they are including us in their awareness and thoughts or not. We may feel a lack of emotional attunement with them, or notice that we may be talking past or over each other. We may get the sense that we are an anonymous audience to a monologue that is independent of any of our verbal and nonverbal feedback. Some clients on the spectrum, with schizophrenia, or with severe anxiety will give us the feeling that our presence as a separate individual isn't registering for them. In some with spectrum disorder, for instance, both the primitive automatic theory of mind processes and the higher-level cognitive processes may be absent.

Self-Reflective Capacity

Self-reflective capacity can be thought of as an extension of theory of mind applied to the self. In assessing self-reflective capacity, we are listening for an internal dialogue where our clients can shuttle back and forth from being responsive to the external world to considering their own thoughts, feelings, and behaviors. Clients without self-reflective capacity have difficulty making use of reflections and clarification, and may have difficulty in understanding the most basic therapeutic interpretations. Some clients will be completely field-dependent, which means that they are only able to see and consider what is before. They may be unable to consider other ways of reacting to a situation, making them "robotic" in their day-to-day reactions to the world.

Attunement, Resonance, and Emotional Contagion

All three executive systems are involved in our ability to attune to the emotions being experienced by those around us. These abilities evolved long ago for the purposes of group communication and coordination. Emotional contagion is automatic and doesn't require conscious participation. Some individuals with spectrum disorder lack this attunement, as do many with true antisocial personality disorder. On the other hand, individuals with borderline personality disorder and Williams syndrome often show heightened abilities in this area. Our innate abilities to resonate with others provide foundational support for other functions like theory of mind, sympathy, and compassion.

Empathy

At its core, empathy is a high-level executive function that allows us to have a theory about what another person is feeling. It reflects an integration of emotional attunement and a cognitive appreciation for what the other may be experiencing, as well as the ability to express it to them. You can think of empathy as a theory of mind about the subjective environment of the other. Thinking about another person's emotional experience, having an emotional reaction to it, and then testing whether your emotion is congruent with theirs is a good framework for empathy. Attunement, sympathy, compassion, pity—in fact, most positive sentiments about the emotional experience of others—are mislabeled as empathy. Many researchers who have tried to develop scales to assess empathy often overindex on its emotional aspects to the neglect of its cognitive and self-reflective components.

Clinical assessment of empathy is best accomplished by listening for and prompting stories from your client about their interactions with others. Listen for how others feel and react to their behaviors. Do they seem to talk about others as real people with feelings to consider, or do they think of others simply as two-dimensional characters serving their own narrative? This is often the case in those with narcissism, BPD, and antisocial personality disorder. Sharing a personal challenge with a client to assess their reaction can also be helpful. A simple prompt like, "I'm sad today because I lost a family member this week" may provide some insight into their empathy.

Imagination

Assessing imagination can start with listening for content about ideas or plans for the future that show creativity and possibilities. With children, it is easy to see this in their play, drawing, and ability to participate in cocreating stories with you. You can test whether they are capable of considering multiple outcomes to the same storyline. With adult clients, you can test their ability to consider alternative ways of thinking and behavior in situations where their responses have been repetitious or stereotyped. While the DMN may become activated during tasks of imagination, the second executive is likely used as part of its imagination. This is why brain-based deficits of imagination are likely to arise if there are problems with either of these two systems.

More likely, deficits in imagination that we see in our clients will be the result of a hyperactive first executive and the resultant inhibition of the second and third. Anxiety is the enemy of imagination and creativity, precisely because of this inhibition. You will find with many anxious clients that exploring imaginative thought will increase their anxiety. Imagination is inner exploration, paralleling how children explore their environment from a safe base. In the absence of a sense of safety, the child will not explore. In the same way, when adults are frightened, they need the sense of control provided by the familiar, making imagination too dangerous.

Additional Factors to Consider

Family Dynamics and Executive Functioning

> *The family is the crucible of the world's misinformation.*
>   —Don DeLillo

While it is always important to know the current family dynamics when working with children and adolescents, it is just as important to have an understanding of those dynamics with our adult clients. As our brains are shaped during childhood, so are our executive abilities. In families of origin with high levels of conflict, substance abuse, or psychopathology, a child's brain is shaped to deal (and not deal) with these extreme survival challenges. In other words, the developing mind and brain adapt to whatever conditions in which they find themselves. Many children are punished for normal developmental processes such as expressing their emotions, having opinions, or behaving autonomously. Others are discouraged from having trusting relationships, accurate reality testing, or venturing outside of the family for support. All of these strategies, which help them survive childhood, can be maladaptive in their adult personal and professional lives. Recent research in epigenetics strongly suggests that these kinds of environments shape minds and brains that extend into adult life.

Consider a client describing her challenges on a recent vacation who has been referred for EF deficits. She gets to the airport late, lacks the paperwork she needs to enter her country of destination, has a hard time finding her hotel, and didn't acquire any of the proper currency to pay the taxi driver. It would be easy to say that this young woman lacks adequate EF and that she should have thought of, planned for, and taken care of these details weeks before her trip. On the other hand, each of these challenges was faced in a calm, humorous manner and solved as it arose. Despite the glitches, her vacation turns out to be a great success. Another client may plan every detail of a vacation for months in advance but crumble in the face of any unforeseen hiccup and have a miserable time. You may think of these as stylistic differences, but they also reflect different aspects of executive functioning.

In the first scenario, this young lady grew up in a family with two anxious and overcontrolling parents who couldn't tolerate her experiencing any anxiety or failure. They coped with this by doing everything for her, including the planning for most everything in her day-to-day life. While she was emotionally secure, she had never had to plan anything, think about the future, or deal with consequences. She also learned that her autonomy was not acceptable but that her dependency on her parents led to their concern and attention. In essence, what we might call her deficits in EF were functional adaptations to the unconscious needs of her parents. The treatment here would be to help her and her parents to tolerate the anxiety around her independence so she can learn how to plan for herself. If she isn't rescued from the consequences of her poor planning, she may learn to do better. If not, she appears to be great at problem-solving on the fly and regulating her arousal and stress.

In the second scenario, a young man had also been raised by highly anxious parents who tried to keep his life overplanned and organized in order to avoid any unforeseen circumstances. If something couldn't be highly controlled, the family tended to avoid it. What they didn't model or teach (because they lacked it themselves) was the emotional regulation to deal with unexpected challenges. This meant that when things went wrong, they were overwhelmed, disoriented, and unable to quickly recover their emotional equilibrium. Neither of these cases is an example of an organic disorder, but of a developmental adaptation to a particular social-emotional context. They also demonstrate the different aspects of EF and the contribution of each executive system.

Executive Functioning and Gender

Men are governed by lines of intellect—women: by curves of emotion.
                                                    —James Joyce

While Joyce was wrong to make broad gender stereotypes, he was onto something when it comes to the way average masculinized and feminized brains tend to differ in aspects of their focus and functioning. Masculinized clients who have difficulties identifying and articulating their emotions often come to therapy because their partners feel that they have a problem. They question the ability for empathy and relationship, and wonder if they are narcissistic or on the spectrum. This kind of presenting problem from a partner raises the question of a potential challenge within ES3.

In diagnosing men with failures in third executive functioning, a female professional may misread or amplify a male client's disabilities, just as a male professional might overdiagnose borderline personality disorder in female clients. Male professionals might underestimate the social and emotional challenges of male clients if they share the same limitations. These countertransferential biases are everywhere and inescapable. The best we can do is keep them in mind and question our conclusions in light of what we know to be our own biases and misperceptions.

As we know, evolution has biased the average male brain toward action and activity, as it has biased the average female brain toward emotion, communication, and connectivity (Baron-Cohen, 2003). These biases likely stem from long-standing adaptation to the primary roles played by each gender, dating back to prehistory. These biases are also reflected in (and supported by) cultural prejudices about the roles and power dynamics in families and society. The other factor is that gender bias in different occupations often reinforces the very personality dynamics that lead us to choose it. Engineers and accountants—professionals who are traditionally more likely to be men than women—spend their days exercising and expanding their second executive systems while often inhibiting the other two.

Because a hyperaroused first executive system can severely inhibit the activation and functioning of the third, a thorough investigation of a client's arousal and affect regulation should be carried out first. Men are more likely to have habituated to and normalized their anxiety, as well as conformed to cultural mandates that punish men for expressing their emotionality. Because anxiety and fear put us on alert for external threats, they limit our experience of our internal world and thwart our imagination, self-awareness, and empathy. For this reason, assessing third executive functioning in a state of hyperarousal tells you little about its functioning and capabilities, only how it functions in a state of inhibited neural activity.

Male clients suffering from PTSD often report feeling far away from the people around them. Some describe it as looking at others through backward binoculars. Combat veterans—who are disproportionately men—come home to discover that they no longer feel connected to their spouse and children. With minds and emotions filled with images of war, they will isolate themselves from their loved ones out of protectiveness. At the same time, they may feel deeply alone, lost in the past, and disoriented in the present. It is very likely that the high levels of sustained adrenaline, cortisol, and hyperarousal in those with PTSD result in an inhibition of the third executive, leave the pertinent skills and abilities, hindering their connection and attunement with those around them. Thus, the disruptions of social connection seen in many cases of PTSD are likely a direct result of the first executive inhibiting the third.

Assessing Executive Integration and Dissociation

I believe change can only come through collaboration.
—Alain de Botton

After repeated cautions about the first executive's ability to inhibit the other two, let's think about how systems will synergize their abilities to upgrade our performance on certain tasks. When ES3 was first discovered, it was thought that its functioning was anticorrelational with the other two. This means that we initially thought that if ES1 or ES2 were active, ES3 was completely inhibited. While this may be generally true when ES1 is in a hyperaroused state, it appears that the mutual inhibition of the three systems is modulated rather than total. It is also likely that ES2 and ES3 have a more subtle, sophisticated, and synergistic relationship.

For example, some suggest that ES3 provides an experiential framework for the abstract cognitive processes of the ES2. This means that the second relies on the third to ground knowledge in a feeling of the self. Without the participation of ES3, the processing of the ES2 would be solely abstract and unrelated to the experiences of the body, others, or the group mind. We may be seeing this in some forms of autism, where deep interests with a very narrow focus seem disconnected from the social world.

Activation of the second system appears to be able to inhibit or down-modulate the activation of the first. An example of this would be becoming so engrossed in an external activity that you are unaware of your body, emotions, or other human needs. A parallel process can be seen in what can be called manic defenses, where activity and distraction are leveraged to avoid experiencing negative inner emotions. Both of these situations likely demonstrate the learned ability of the second executive to inhibit the first.

Another important set of system interactions is their synergistic relationship during psychotherapy. From the perspective of neural activation, the psychotherapist is usually attempting to (1) downregulate the first executive by creating a safe space and solid therapeutic relationship, (2) activate the third executive to move our clients into a self-reflective and nondefensive place, and then (3) simultaneously activate the second and third executives in order to apply a client's problem-solving abilities to their personal experience and psychological challenges. We will discuss this in more detail when we focus on psychotherapy.

Chapter 9

Assessing Executive Functioning in Children

*The kids who need the most love will ask
for it in the most unloving ways.*

—Russell Barkley

Although we like to think of childhood as innocent and stress-free, most children experience emotional challenges that impact their cognitive functioning at school and at home. Unlike adults, they lack the language and regulatory skills to describe their feelings and cope effectively on their own. When overwhelmed by stress at home, it is unlikely that they will be capable of associating it with their difficulties in the classroom. It is even less likely that they will be able to approach their teacher, articulate their experiences, or explain their situation. Children rely on adults to identify, label, and regulate their emotions, and then to teach them how to do this on their own. If this doesn't occur, it can be extremely difficult for a child to navigate the emotional ups and downs of daily life. This is why it is so important for parents and teachers to identify the source of a child's challenges so that they can be appropriately addressed.

Symptoms commonly seen in childhood, such as impulsivity and difficulties with concentration and distractibility, can all result from stress, amygdala arousal, and emotional dysregulation. The first executive's ability to inhibit the second is common in children struggling at school and in their relationships. All of the things we might expect to cause stress (e.g., family discord, bullying, adjustment to new routines) as well as reactions specific to the child (e.g., private nightmares, specific phobias) can all trigger what appear to be cognitive symptoms. Depending on the help they receive, these children are very vulnerable to receiving a snap diagnosis of ADHD and given a stimulant medication.

While the diagnosis may provide relief to parents, and the medication can help with some of the cognitive symptoms in the classroom, this approach often masks the underlying cause of the stress, which will get worse if neglected. While some children do have actual ADHD based on slowed neurological development and integration, most children who are prescribed stimulants do not. For these cases, the medication masks the child's real social and emotional problems, and may postpone the treatment they actually need for many years. They also never learn to deal with the stress that is causing their cognitive dysfunctions in more appropriate ways, delaying the development of their coping skills, autonomy, and efficacy. In the majority of cases, symptoms related to ADHD are usually better addressed by an assessment of all three executive systems and interventions that address social and emotional as well as cognitive functioning.

Early Assessment of Executive Functioning

You can learn many things from children. How much patience you have, for instance.

—Franklin P. Jones

Assessing EF in children can be especially challenging for a number of reasons. The first is the fact that the three executive systems, as well as the rest of the brain, are in the process of growth and integration. All of our brains differ from one another, just as they differ in their rate and course of maturation. This is the reason why many diagnoses are deferred until later and even after childhood. A second reason is that children are more emotionally labile and sensitive to external circumstances, making their EF more erratic and context dependent. A third reason is that the experience of children is very interwoven with the cognitive and emotional functioning of their families. If a client isn't individuated from their family, at any age, it is difficult to know if you are measuring their innate capacities or the family's level of functioning.

With all of these factors in mind, we approach the assessment of EF in children with more caution and far less certainty. For example, if a five-year-old child is referred to you for possible difficulties with executive functioning, while objective tests show certain measures of cognitive processing, this information must be placed within the context of the child's life circumstances.

Suppose a child is social and intellectually curious and works well independently, but during group activities speaks out of turn and frequently gets into trouble for wandering off during activities outside of the classroom. When the issue is addressed in therapy, there is often concern about the possibility of a serious underlying problem. While this is always possible, it is far more likely that they are having trouble adjusting to the new set of challenges involved in starting school. This may be the first time they've had to cope with institutional structure and groups of new people. It is just as likely that the parents are having difficulty adjusting to their child being away from them and out of their control. In these situations, the therapist's first job is to soothe the anxiety and concern of the parents, avoid jumping to any diagnostic conclusions, and take the necessary time to get to know the child.

The job of the therapist is to learn about the child's home life, family situation, and the parenting style they are being exposed to. It's imperative that a clinician understands the psychology of the child's parents, their level of anxiety, and all of their attachment styles. As she builds a model of her client's experience, she will be able to develop hypotheses about the possible causes of the child's difficulties in adjusting to his new school. For example, she may learn that he was allowed to spend many hours online playing adventure games exploring foreign lands and building civilizations. While these games are designed for older kids, his parents report that the more age-appropriate options don't hold his attention as well. The clinician may also discover that the level of anxiety in both parents is unusually high and that they experience anxiety when separated from one another, and from their child. All of these details are integral to understanding the child's challenges at school.

While there are standardized tests that focus on various aspects of intelligence and cognitive functioning, most of the important information we learn from children comes from our observations during interactions.

And as a client's story unfolds before us, the goal is to continue to ask, "What could be wrong? What am I not considering? How do these pieces fit together?" By using the three-system model, we can generate and test hypotheses both at home and at school to see what interventions could create a positive impact on the child's experience of school. Perhaps we suggest an adjustment to screen time or additional involvement with extracurricular activities, or encourage the parents to consider an emotional support animal. Working with the family to address their shared separation anxiety may also have a positive impact.

What we're driving at is the idea that EF in a five-year-old shouldn't be thought of as a fixed set of abilities within the individual child's brain, but rather a reflection of the family's abilities to manage anxiety and deal with challenges. This doesn't rule out the possibility of there being some nascent underlying problem, it is just difficult to be certain at this age unless it is clearly the result of a brain-based dysfunction. And if it does turn out that these potential signs do indicate some significant challenge in the child, then all of this work will serve as a positive platform for treatment.

Understanding the developmental components of executive functioning is essential when working with children. Although every child is born with innate capacities, the manner in which these systems develop is largely experience dependent. That means that a child's supportive home environment creates the soil for optimal EF development, whereas children who are experiencing chronic stress and parental misattunement may not have the chance to develop to their fullest potential. The quality of the emotional and social conditions of a child's development will either support or hinder their innate developmental trajectory.

The developmental course of each executive system is also unique, creating specific conditions of EF in childhood. For example, anxiety and fear have the biggest impact on a child's EF because the first executive is highly developed at birth, while the second and third executive mature gradually into adulthood. Empathy, social awareness, self-control, and other high-level EF-related abilities are not fully developed in childhood. Our expectations of a child's EF abilities should be matched with developmental stages as well as the unique strengths, weaknesses, and emotional circumstances of the individual. Let's explore how these ideas apply to a slightly older client.

Ollie

Logical activity is not the whole of intelligence. One can
be intelligent without being particularly logical.

—Jean Piaget

Seven-year-old Ollie was referred to me (CD) for what were described as "social and academic challenges." Ollie's parents reported that he was a vibrant, energetic child, who suddenly began having uncharacteristic difficulties at school. According to his teacher, Ollie appeared to be "zoning out" in class and not completing his assignments on time. When his teacher tried to redirect his focus back to his work, he would have emotional outbursts in class. His teacher also reported seeing him arguing with his friends during recess, pushing in line, and crying for no apparent cause. The school psychologist had referred him for neuropsychological testing, which reflected normal cognitive development and ruled out ADHD. Confused and frustrated by the lack of a conclusive diagnosis or successful school-based intervention, Ollie's parents turned to therapy for help.

During the intake process, Ollie's parents reported that they had just finalized the divorce six months earlier, and Ollie had been splitting his time between the two households. Both reported that since that time, he had trouble following directions and that getting to school on time had become impossible. They said that if they didn't monitor him during each step of their morning routine, he would "drift off" or become very upset when time demands were placed on him. Ollie's parents also reported very different approaches to parenting, which was causing stress between them.

His mom was strict and emotionally distant, running the home as a "tight ship" and refusing to talk to Ollie about the divorce and the drastic changes that had occurred in their lives. She was, however, open in expressing her anger with Ollie's father and the lack of respect he showed her, and refused to coparent with him. Ollie's dad was certain that this dynamic was taking a toll on Ollie but felt helpless in knowing how to address it with his son. While he had escaped the pain of his marriage, he feared that he had left Ollie to endure the hurt. His feelings of guilt made it difficult for him to set limits with Ollie, and he felt that his leniency was an attempt to make up for his ex-wife's "cold and authoritarian parenting style."

When Ollie first entered the therapy room, I watched as he quietly took in every detail of the space: the books, the toys, the art supplies, and the paintings on the wall. I sensed the wheels in his mind turning as he nervously tried to figure out what would happen to him next. I could see that Ollie needed some support in entering into our relationship, so I said, "I'd love to show you some of my things. My favorite toy is the alligator! Do you see anything you like?"

A small smile crept across his face as he scanned the array of stuffed animals. Picking up a panda and a walrus, he brought them over to a small kitchen table and sat them down across from one another. He sat quietly with them for a time and volunteered that they were out to dinner at a restaurant. I could see his posture relaxing a bit, so I came over with my alligator, the third customer at his new restaurant. My goal through these initial exchanges was to help Ollie to feel safe as he grew accustomed to the space we would be sharing for our work. By following his lead for the scenario for our play, I hoped to give him a sense of control and show him that his leadership and imagination would be respected. I could feel the comfort he was taking in the toys and could see the muscles of his face relaxing.

Over the following weeks, our sessions included both play and art, as we explored themes of change, separation, fear, and uncertainty. He gradually became comfortable enough to talk about his big feelings about his parents and their family relationships. Prior to therapy, Ollie was alone in coping with his anxiety while also absorbing all of the emotional distress of his parents with little comfort and almost no guidance. His emotional agitation was driving his scattered attention, interpersonal withdrawal, and social impulsivity. In other words, his first executive hyperarousal was inhibiting the cognitive and social processes organized by the other two. This was the cause of his transforming from a normal seven-year-old into a child with much less mature executive abilities.

Therapy provided Ollie with a safe space to express his feelings. Discussing his emotions while feeling safe allowed his first executive to down-regulate, which in turn disinhibited his second and third executives to the point where they could participate in our emotional connection, and access the cognitive abilities to put his feelings into words and make sense of his experiences. The therapeutic relationship is key to the process of downregulating amygdala activation, which allows the cognitive and social aspects of therapy to engender healing. As part of this process, we collaborated on writing a storybook about how his current family structure had changed to help normalize the divorce. We then created another one describing his family and the different experiences and adventures he would have now and in the future. These stories created cortically based narratives in the second executive system, which can be used to regulate amygdala activation, and utilize imagination and a memory for the future in the third. Overall, writing these stories helped to reassure Ollie that he was safe, loved, and supported, regardless of his family situation.

Another important facet of Ollie's therapy was to help his parents to get on the same page about the routines, expectations, and boundaries within and across both of their households. Having a third person as a go-between in these discussions kept the focus on Ollie's well-being and away from the hurt and power struggles that would emerge during direct communication. I reframed his negative behaviors as a cry for help and an indication that his first executive had hijacked his brain and behavior. I explained the neuroscience behind these painful and unproductive dynamics by saying, "Responding to *his* amygdala with *your* amygdala only caused everyone to be out of control and made matters much worse." If they could learn to respond to his being emotionally overwhelmed with understanding, kindness, and support, as often as possible, they could help him learn to integrate his three executives and eventually grow through his current challenges and get back to the level of functioning they saw before the divorce.

I also communicated with Ollie's teacher about the work we were doing and shared the message I gave his parents. With everyone working to help regulate Ollie's stress and distress, and Ollie's parents pursuing their own therapy, my work with him continued to deepen, and our relationship grew stronger. As his first executive became better regulated, we all witnessed the gradual return of the old Ollie along with a new level of sophistication in his understanding of himself and others.

Reflections

If you were shown a closeup picture of a person crying, you might think they were suffering with depression. If the camera zoomed out revealing them at a funeral, you would likely change your diagnosis from depression to grief. You might also say that this is such a normal reaction to loss that a diagnosis isn't even relevant. At first glance, Ollie's behavior displayed aspects of both ADHD and impairments of executive functioning. But when we zoom out and look at the broader context of his life, we can place his symptoms in context and see many of them as natural reactions for a boy his age to the challenges he has been facing.

We can think of Ollie's behavior as a way of communicating his physical and emotional dysregulation, the same dysregulation that his parents were going through. Their world had crumbled around them, and they were all trying to make sense of how to move forward. He was dealing with his own fears as well as resonating with the stress, struggle, and pain his parents were going through. Because our brains are linked together and attuned to one another, the struggles of the people close to us automatically become our struggles. This is especially true for children and adolescents, as well as adults who have been unable to individuate from their families of origin. Our social brains attune to those around us and impact the functioning of each of our executive systems in different ways.

Ollie's First Executive System

Ollie's emotional distress and lack of soothing, attunement, and coregulation with his parents kept him in a chronic state of hyperarousal. His emotional reaction reflected an ongoing sense of anxiety and danger, causing him to feel overwhelmed by the smallest challenge. This made him prone to either agitation or freezing, which made paying attention, being present, cooperating with others, and following directions extremely difficult. When he was in a hyperaroused, fight-or-flight state, he would be emotionally reactive, cry, argue, or run from others. When his behavior was met with anger and frustration from an authority figure, Ollie's symptoms increased and his behaviors worsened.

From a neurobiological perspective, this resulted in an inhibition of both his second and third executive systems, impairing his cognitive capacities, social skills, and self-awareness. These symptoms and behavioral deficits often mimic ADHD. Identifying the underlying cause of these types of symptoms is essential before selecting an approach to treatment. It is our belief that while stimulants might help a child like Ollie attend somewhat better in the classroom, it doesn't address his other challenges, which are likely to grow worse if left untreated. For his therapist, addressing his stress, anxiety, and fears was primary and paramount.

Ollie's Second Executive System

Everyone's cognitive capacities become disrupted during periods of extreme stress. This is especially true for children and adolescents, whose brains are still in the process of development. Moderate to extreme inhibition of ES2 undermines our ability to think, plan, organize, and problem-solve. In light of his age, past school performance, and negative test findings, it is extremely likely that the neural networks and functional abilities of Ollie's second executive were intact. The problem most likely lay in ES1's inhibition of ES2. The clinical strategy was to treat the psychological and emotional issues of the family first to see if Ollie's prior level of cognitive and intellectual functioning reappeared. Once a baseline of regulation was established, the second executive could be leveraged to discuss his parents' divorce to help him process his emotions. From this work, a cohesive narrative about the changes in his family could be created, allowing him to have a new and adaptive picture of his family with which to move forward.

When assessing children and adolescents, it is always important to create a timeline that includes symptoms, medical changes, and life events to search for possible causal connections between increased stress and functional deficits. When there is an abrupt change in functioning, ruling out precipitating medical changes and life events is the logical first step. Children with neurodevelopmental second executive deficits will likely have a history of struggles with one or more areas of cognitive functioning. When the onset seems rapid, rule out life events first. If the symptoms are severe and/or accompanied by changes in consciousness, orientation, and motor behavior, have your client see a neurologist immediately.

Ollie's Third Executive System

Ollie's chronic state of arousal also interfered with the functioning of his third executive system. His uncharacteristic arguments with his friends, pushing into line, and crying in the face of classroom conflict all reflected his lack of insight while navigating interpersonal interactions when under stress. Sharing, perspective taking, and interpersonal flexibility require both emotional equilibrium and an understanding of the intentions and motivations of the minds of others. His teacher reported that he got upset easily and "only wants to do things his way," which was causing his friends to avoid playing with him. His awareness of this rejection created even more stress and made his interactions less adaptive and approachable. He was unable to take in feedback about it being his behavior that was causing the problem, leaving him feeling rejected by his peers and betrayed by his parents.

In the process of therapy with Ollie and his family, his level of arousal gradually decreased to the point where his third executive was once again available for processing information. As his ability to resonate with and understand others got back online, I helped him to reflect on and think through his interactions with his classmates, and he came to see how he had hurt some of their feelings. He came to accept that many of his behaviors, although unintentional, could be hurtful to others. We discussed how he would manage getting back together with his friends and how some apologies might be an important part of reconnecting.

Using the three-system model to treat children like Ollie allows us to identify the relevant components of the difficulties, understand how they interact with one another, and create a sequential treatment plan knowing that we need to focus on affect regulation before trying to address other challenges. EF doesn't only exist solely in the brain of our client but also within the family, school, and broader cultural context it has evolved and developed to adapt to.

The Complexities of Differential Diagnosis of ADHD

Concentrate all your thoughts upon the work at hand.
                        —Alexander Graham Bell

Problems with attention, concentration, and focus can be caused by an array of underlying problems. For example, a study conducted by the Mayo Clinic and Children's Hospital Boston revealed that a diagnosis of childhood ADHD had significant symptom overlap with disorders of adjustment, conduct (ODD), mood, anxiety, and personality, as well as eating and substance abuse disorders during adolescence (Yoshimasu et al., 2012). These findings can be interpreted to mean that childhood ADHD creates a vulnerability to other disorders later in adolescence. In fact, research has shown that children treated with stimulants for ADHD are less likely to develop depression, anxiety disorders, and disruptive behavior (Biederman et al., 2008).

The other possibility is that the child's attentional challenges may have been caused by environmental factors or some underlying disorder that either was missed or doesn't overtly manifest during childhood. Although we tend to think of diagnoses as real entities, they are just theoretical constructs we use to attempt to identify and understand patterns of signs and symptoms. The reason why there are so many editions of the *DSM* is not because new diseases keep popping up but because the way we think about diagnosis is constantly changing. Whether a diagnosis is an accurate description of an underlying illness process or completely misses the mark, a diagnosis is useful in proportion to its accuracy and whether or not it predicts treatment response.

Because many disorders have overlapping symptoms, we engage in what is called differential diagnosis, "the process of differentiating between two or more conditions which share similar signs or symptoms." A symptom is a client's subjective experience that brings them to therapy. A sign is an observation you make about your client's behavior that may be relevant to the challenge they are struggling with. A client may complain of difficulties with completing work assignments, while you notice that they appear agitated; their difficulty at work is a symptom while their physical agitation is a sign.

Diagnostic criteria for ADHD only weakly acknowledge the role of motivation, affective dysregulation, and environmental variables on the expression of inattention and motor agitation. In a study of over 1,000 children, 50% demonstrated mild to moderate levels of emotional lability, and 25% were rated as having severe emotional lability (Sobanski et al., 2010). In another study of 111 children, 36% of the ADHD group were rated as having emotional dysregulation, with 19% rated at a severe level (Biederman et al., 2012). Barkley (2010) describes the emotional self-regulatory problems in ADHD as primarily focused on the inhibition of frustration, anger, and aggression. The comorbidity of ADHD and anxiety during childhood could lead sufferers to be distracted through the hypervigilance to the environment that accompanies heightened amygdala activation. This suggests that ES1 would inhibit ES2, negatively impacting focus, concentration, and working memory.

Problems with mood, anxiety, and sleep can often result in attentional and cognitive deficits easily mistaken for ADHD. These disorders are more easily diagnosed in adults and adolescents than in children, thus they may have been present but masked earlier in life (Pliszka, 1998). Research suggests that during adulthood, 65–89% of all those diagnosed with ADHD suffer from one or more additional psychiatric disorders, including disorders of mood, anxiety, substance abuse, and personality, making differential diagnosis of ADHD especially challenging (Sobanski, 2006). Understanding this challenge, the *DSM-5* presents a six-step algorithm to guide us through possible alternative diagnoses:

Step 1: Rule out malingering and factitious disorder.
Step 2: Rule out substance etiology.
Step 3: Rule out a disorder due to a general medical condition.
Step 4: Determine the specific primary disorder(s).
Step 5: Differentiate adjustment disorders from the residual other specified or unspecified disorders.
Step 6: Establish the boundary with no mental disorder.

If followed, these steps should result in an extensive diagnostic exploration. However, being able to judge whether a client is malingering, engaged in substance abuse, has a chaotic home environment, or has been the victim of trauma or abuse requires an extended and ongoing relationship. Ruling out other medical and psychiatric conditions requires extensive medical

Differential Diagnosis Overview

Biological	Lifestyle	Attachment	Psychological
Underlying medical conditions	Sleep	Chronic relational stress	Depression
Neurodevelopmental differences	Nutrition	Abuse	Anxiety
	Screen time	Neglect	ADHD
	Exercise		Autism
	Caffeine		

ADHD *DSM-5* Symptoms in the Neurodynamic Model of EF

First Executive System	*Overlap with ADHD symptoms*
Emotional center, bodily arousal, fight, flight, and freeze	Impulsivity
	Avoidance of nonpreferred tasks
	Fidgeting
	Difficulty engaging in quiet tasks
	Excessive talking
	Frequent interruptions in conversation
	Difficulty awaiting turn

Second Executive System	*Overlap with ADHD symptoms*
Attentional control, organization and planning, coordination and navigation	Inattention
	Lack of organizational skills
	Difficulty following instructions
	Easily distractible
	Forgetful
	Prone to losing important items

Third Executive System	*Overlap with ADHD symptoms*
Self-awareness, empathy	Emotional dysregulation

workups and psychiatric screening. In reality, the resources for this type of work are often lacking, and the diagnosis of ADHD is often given before many or any of these investigations have been carried out.

There are many differential factors of executive functioning to consider during early assessment. We've narrowed them down to four different categories: biological, lifestyle, attachment, and psychological. Note that there will be some factors that fall into multiple categories, but it's helpful to have a general road map when familiarizing yourself with this process.

Hopefully we've made clear just how complicated executive functioning in children can be. There is no one-size-fits-all pathway to diagnosis when a child is in the midst of development. They live complicated lives just like adults do, and they do it with fewer resources and language capabilities. They're juggling big emotions with limited cognition, in an ever-changing environment, so it's essential that we consider the whole picture. The better we can understand the dynamic balance between our three executive systems, the easier it will be to conceptualize why a child may be struggling before jumping to conclusions about a particular diagnosis.

Part IV

Clinical and Consulting Applications

Chapter 10

Using the Three-System Model With Adolescents

*The chief symptom of adolescence is a state of
expectation, a tendency toward creative work, and
a need for the strengthening of self-confidence.*
—Maria Montessori

The myriad challenges of adolescence play an integral role in facilitating the healthy transition from childhood to adult independence. It is a period of extensive neural reorganization marked by social, emotional, and cognitive changes. Cognition develops from literal to abstract, driving the formation of group membership, belief systems, and worldviews. An adolescent's capacity for metacognition and introspection promotes the emergence of a sense of self. At the same time, the structural and functional changes of the adolescent brain result in an increased vulnerability to stress, impulsivity, and emotional dysregulation. Typical teenage behavior, such as risk-taking, mood swings, social melodrama, and rejection of the status quo, are important aspects of both individuation and finding a place in the tribe. If the hub of social life didn't reorient from the family to peer and romantic relationships, we would never gain the experiences and resulting skills needed for adult life.

Unfortunately, this road to adulthood can be bumpy. The growing pains, social pressures, and emotional challenges involved in this period of development are often associated with psychosocial issues like anxiety, depression, and family conflict. As you know, all of these changes can wreak havoc on an adolescent's ability to plan, focus, and execute tasks at school and in their personal lives. When working with adolescents, we want to (1) be understanding of the importance of this developmental period, (2) match our expectations to what is neurodevelopmentally appropriate, (3) adequately assess situational variables, and (4) take additional factors into account such as drug use, sleep hygiene, internet use, and other lifestyle issues that may have a negative impact on EF.

An adolescent struggling with their sexuality, cyberbullying, or a first heartbreak is navigating these challenges while their frontal lobes are reorganizing. Suffice it to say, they are going to have a different profile of executive abilities than an adult therapist, and it is important that we always keep this top of mind. When proposing interventions, take time to consider whether your adolescent client is actually capable of implementing them given their present cognitive, emotional, and social abilities. As with young children, before accepting a diagnosis of ADHD, take a detailed history of the current family situation and take a few minutes to learn about how the client's parents navigated adolescence. This information can provide clues as to the relative impact of genetic and psychosocial factors on your client's adaptational abilities. Because adolescents are overly self-conscious, take the time to develop a relationship before asking lots of questions. The answers you will get when they feel comfortable are often quite different from those you would receive in a shortened interview.

The World of Today's Adolescence

It is very nearly impossible . . . to become an educated person in a country so distrustful of the independent mind.
—James Baldwin

With the emergence of a new, screen-based world, our youth face a wealth of new challenges. Just a few generations ago, children learned at the knee of their elders within a social-emotional matrix of experience. This allowed the three executive systems to be activated, developed, and integrated during engagement with the analog environment. Today's adolescents, most of whom have grown up on screens, have had far fewer of these neural-integrating experiences during development. Some aspects of their cognitive abilities may have developed (e.g., scanning, multitasking, information management) while others have atrophied (e.g., memory, sustained attention, deep focus). A handful of meaningful face-to-face relationships have been replaced by scores of superficial digital ones, and the development of a social identity has been shaped, and sometimes replaced by, a curated avatar.

While the world of the teenager has gone through a radical change, the mentality of education, the structure of schools, and the idea of the classroom has remained static. We can see this play out in something as trivial as the average school start time, which is typically quite early. While it might work for a lucky few, it's a poor match for the biochemistry and development of many other students. Waking up early and being forced to engage in a rigid curriculum, with little physical movement and social connection, is at odds with the way we evolved to live and learn.

The bias toward cold cognition in the classroom came into focus during the industrialization of our country, during which efficiency and quantifiable measures of success were prioritized above all else. Like a well-oiled machine, our kids would line up on a conveyor belt and work their way through a system that was designed to spit out a perfectly mannered child whose skills could be readily assessed and compared to those of his peers. What this system did not account for was the extraordinary variability in human intelligence. For every genius mathematician, there is a genius musician who speaks a different, equally valuable, language. Unfortunately, not every child will be given the chance to explore their aptitude for subjects such as music, kinesthetics, interpersonal skills, or linguistics, because they're more difficult to standardize and assess, and therefore less of a priority in the classroom. For this population of adolescents, school can become a profoundly stressful experience that leaves them feeling fundamentally broken, misunderstood, and flawed. It's no surprise that many of them will also be diagnosed with disorders such as depression and anxiety.

What we're essentially describing is the deprioritization of social-emotional factors. Our modern education system tells youth that there is one way to be smart, and we undervalue emotional intelligence, creativity, innovation, musical ability, leadership, physical aptitude, interpersonal intelligence, and artistry. When we fail to consider the sheer breadth of our EF, we run the risk of misunderstanding what a particular adolescent may need in order to thrive. In simpler terms, we might become so hyperfocused on the fact that they're not very good at science that we fail to discover that they have phenomenal oratory skills and would make an excellent politician. In order to optimize education and give every student a chance to thrive, it's essential that we consider the basic tenets of executive functioning.

We learn best when learning is:

1. Social
2. Experiential and not purely theoretical
3. Relevant to our lives

If these factors aren't accounted for, second executive functioning may be lessened, and the overall integration of all three systems will be compromised, leading to adolescent struggles that could easily be mistaken for attentional deficits, behavioral issues, or a lack of intelligence. In reality, the first thing we should consider if an adolescent is experiencing challenges at school is whether or not they are learning in an environment that fosters connection to others, hands-on experience, and relevant subject matter. If these needs go unmet, consider the possibility of getting them immersed in another environment such as martial arts or theater, where they are given an alternate outlet to explore interests that are more aligned with the way that we've evolved to learn.

Environmental Factors Impacting EF in Adolescence: Social Media

Being famous on Instagram is basically the same thing as being rich on Monopoly.

—Anonymous

Another layer of the adolescent experience that is likely to compound existing challenges is the use of social media. This digital landscape that so many of our youth use to engage with one another presents new demands and pressures. As time goes on, we're learning more about how this new social world can disrupt the development of healthy EF.

A key element of social media's power is its ability to keep us in a state of autopilot, where we don't realize how much time has passed or even how the experience has made us feel. Scrolling quells our anxiety much like a pacifier calms a baby. It is a comforting lull of visually pleasing content designed to soothe and distract us on demand. For adolescents, whose inhibition has yet to properly develop, this process is even more consuming. Amid the stress and agony of managing schoolwork, family life, and social status, a young person will be especially drawn to the idea of escaping discomfort via social media. However, this existential safety blanket comes with a price. While it may seem harmless enough, an adolescent can quickly become addicted to this coping mechanism. Whenever an unpleasant thought, memory, or emotion enters their minds or bodies, the first executive unconsciously directs them to use their phones (Cozolino, 2020). This distracts a child from stress and simulates a feeling of homeostasis, but it also hinders the development of skills such as true problem-solving and emotional regulation. Unfortunately, the temporary relief it provides is just a quick fix, and the problems they are trying to avoid will eventually catch up to them.

What's more, in-person interactions are a major factor in the shaping of identity, and if an adolescent uses social media as a replacement for friendship and connection, it can impede social development and create unintended anxiety. Social media provides us with an environment where we can acquire validation in the form of likes, comments, views, and shares. Approval acts as a currency that we use to measure our self-worth. Here's the problem: When a person's followers "like" their perfectly curated photos, it subconsciously reinforces the idea that their true self (messy, imperfect, and often contradictory) isn't enough. Rather than boosting confidence, that coveted validation creates an unhealthy expectation for the self and others.

Finally, the nature of social media suggests to the young developing mind that everything they do is meant for public consumption. This belief that life is first and foremost a theatrical display externalizes their view of themselves and makes it difficult to develop a private, meaningful inner world where they can foster the most authentic parts of their identity. This process depends on a teen's ability to self-reflect, daydream, engage in imagination, and explore the inner workings of their mind. It's essential that they're able to develop a sense of themselves in the analog world, apart from the stage that is social media.

First Executive System Development in Adolescence

Love is a battle; love is a war; love is a growing up.
—James Baldwin

The development of the first executive outpaces the development of the second and third executive systems throughout childhood and adolescence. What this means is that emotions reign supreme over logic and rationality until well into our 20s. We observe this bias toward first executive dominance in everyday scenarios like a child throwing a tantrum or the exaggerated emotional reactivity of an adolescent. The teen who storms away from the dinner table and slams the door behind them because they can't go to a concert on a weeknight isn't lacking the cognitive capacity to understand their parent's decision. Rather, these scenes are the result of their underdeveloped ability to think and act rationally, which makes them vulnerable to emotional hijack in the first executive. In moments of heightened emotion, emerging EF capacities such as logical reasoning, sound decision-making, self-awareness, and mindfulness become temporarily less accessible until the first executive is downregulated.

Adolescents also process emotional information differently than children and adults. In particular, they are more sensitive to negative social and emotional input in the first executive. In studies where adolescents are tasked with determining whether a facial expression is positive, negative, or neutral, they are more likely than any other age group to experience amygdala activation and interpret neutral faces as negative (Rosen et al., 2018). This reflects the reactivity of the first executive to negative social evaluation from others and likely serves the developmental goal of the adolescent to create an identity and solidify their social role. As they navigate away from the family unit and toward the greater social world, they are neurologically primed to detect positive and negative input to help guide them in finding their place. This transition is often fraught with anxiety and fears around social rejection because peer acceptance is prioritized during this developmental phase.

The psychosocial factors of adolescence that contribute to increased amygdala activity range from academic pressure to sexuality to social status. Not only are these stressors emotionally charged and foundational to identity, they are also being experienced by the teen for the first time.

As with anything, this means more mistakes and less perspective. Even something like academics, which may seem totally cognitive in nature, has a higher social-emotional salience because it is central in shaping the adolescent's self-esteem and social identity.

The neurobiology of teenage angst can be understood as a function of first executive overdrive inhibiting second and third system integration. The high emotional stakes are not just mental and emotional; they are also reflected in the functioning of the teenage brain. Typically developing adolescents show autonomic nervous system markers such as increased cortisol, pupil activation, startle reflex, and hypervigilance in social situations (Blewitt & Broderick, 2014). This heightened stress reactivity can explain why it is typical for a teenager to struggle with EF tasks like organization, time management, emotional regulation, and empathic behavior.

The neurodynamics of stress that inhibit learning and cognitive abilities often result in academic and EF difficulties. Teens are more likely to experience EF issues like task interference or delayed recall when they are in emotional pain (Harter, 2006). What's happening is that on a biological level, the goal of social acceptance (which is equated with survival) takes priority over finishing a biology report or cleaning their room. It is developmentally appropriate for the teenage brain to delay a cognitive task because of emotional distress. A parent, teacher, or clinician who responds to this behavior with dismissal, shame, or punishment will only increase the first executive system inhibition of the other systems. The focus should instead be on teaching them the necessary coping strategies for emotional regulation and reengaging their cortical problem-solving abilities.

Second Executive System Development in Adolescence

Poetry is when an emotion has found its thought
and the thought has found words.

—Robert Frost

In his stages of cognitive development, developmental theorist Jean Piaget characterized adolescence as a shift from concrete thinking to abstract reasoning. This progression of cognitive development is facilitated by the growth of second executive abilities such as processing speeds, working memory, sustained focus, and cognitive flexibility. Adolescents move from the assumption that the world shapes their reality to the realization that they are an active participant in its construction (Kesselring, 2018). This shift also coincides with the integration of many distinct neural networks that allow ideas to be connected and configured within the mind of the adolescent (Cunningham et al., 2002). These skills are important prerequisites for problem-solving, creativity, and stimulus-independent thought. It is also these changes that give rise to consciousness.

As the mind becomes increasingly aware of its own inner workings, adolescents are faced with the dilemma of having increased awareness and heightened emotions but underdeveloped tools to manage them. Even though there is an increase in neural system integration, our cognitive systems mature at a slower rate than those regulating our emotions (Giedd, 2008).

It is only through a long process of trial and error that adolescents develop the coping skills needed to manage their increased awareness of their thinking, feeling, and behavior. Without the life experience, contextual awareness, and emotional flexibility of an adult brain, they are often unable to manage all that comes with this newfound self-awareness. This is not a character flaw but simply a natural by-product of the uneven development of our executive systems during adolescence.

In the process of the major neural reorganization of the teenage brain, we can expect to witness many fluctuations in these emerging cognitive skills and capacities. An adolescent's EF capacity will change depending on the social and emotional context. The same teenager who can focus and inhibit distractions to complete a task one day may be unable to complete the same task the following day due to stress, lack of sleep, social pressure, or emotional pain.

Executive System Development in Adolescence

Friendships in childhood are usually a matter of chance,
whereas in adolescence, they are a matter of choice.
—David Elkind

A significant number of mental resources during adolescence are dedicated to the development of third executive skills such as establishing social relationships, emotional regulation, and a sense of self. The primary developmental task of adolescence, as defined by Erikson (1994) in his psychosocial stages, is to build an identity and establish our social role. The emerging capacity for social and emotional intelligence and self-awareness supports the carrying out of these important milestones. It also explains why there is an emphasis on social and emotional input during this developmental stage.

Similarly to the second executive, the third executive skills are built stepwise over time, so their initial forms are rudimentary and incomplete. Take the development of a sense of self, which, in its nascent stages, is expressed as egocentrism and a preoccupation with self-perception and peer evaluation. Teens commonly have the perception of an "imaginary audience," which refers to the illusion that people are disproportionately interested and watching their every move (Harter, 2006). These misperceptions can be unpleasant for both the adolescent and those around them, but they serve as building blocks to creating an adult identity.

The capacity for metacognition and introspective thought develops during adolescence, providing the groundwork for the emergence of social and emotional intelligence. Metacognition refers to the ability to think about thinking, and introspection involves thinking critically about the way that one thinks and behaves. Another important cognitive-affective skill that involves the third executive system is mentalizing, which is the ability to infer the mental states of others. The practice of thinking reflectively about oneself and others is something that develops through lived experience. The omnipresence of technology compromises the modern teen's ability to socialize at the same level as previous generations. The frequency of opportunities for quiet self-reflection are also decreased due to the prevalence of handheld media. These environmental changes may impede the development of these important social-emotional EF skills.

A well-developed inner world in the third executive supports the awareness, flexibility, and regulation of the raw emotions of the first executive. This process is only just starting to take shape during adolescence, which is evident in the emotional difficulties that are commonly faced during this phase. While it's important to have developmentally appropriate expectations about an adolescent's limited capacity to be self-actualized, we can still support their ability to identify, express, and cope with their emotions. Journaling, mindfulness, relaxation techniques, and meditation are examples of interventions that provide the experience to learn these foundational social-emotional skills.

Emilia

Adolescence is a time when girls experience social pressure to put aside their authentic selves and to display only a small portion of their gifts.
—Mary Piper

Emilia, a 15-year-old girl, was referred for therapy by her school counselor due to her concerning behavior in the classroom and declining academic performance. Emilia's teachers reported that she struggled to focus and keep up with her assignments, and had difficulty following instructions. She also appeared extremely low energy—even lethargic—during her morning classes. When scheduling her first appointment, Emilia's parents noted that she appeared moody, easily distracted from her chores and homework, and seemed, in their words, to be "checked out." Before the beginning of treatment, Emilia received a comprehensive assessment of cognitive functioning as well as interviews and behavioral rating scales with her parents and teacher.

The results of her assessment revealed difficulties in self-monitoring, impulse control, and cognitive flexibility. Upon evaluation and a preliminary diagnosis of ADHD, Emilia was prescribed stimulant medication and referred to a CBT therapist who specializes in executive coaching strategies such as organizational skills, time management, and impulse control. After six months of CBT treatment, Emilia's parents and teacher agreed that not only had she not gotten better, but she actually seemed worse. After an online search, her parents found Matthew, a therapist who specialized in working with adolescents but focused more on the therapeutic relationship and less on cognitive skill building.

After their initial sessions, Matthew felt that while Emilia did display many of the behavioral symptoms that had led to her original diagnosis and treatment plan, he sensed that something was troubling her at a deeper emotional level. After several sessions of building trust and getting to know one another, Matthew began to get a glimpse into her complex inner world. He could see that she was burdened by a number of emotional challenges but had been unwilling, or unable, to ask for help. She eventually was able to share that around six months earlier, she had told her best friend, in confidence, that she thought that she might be gay.

Soon after, her best friend told some other girls, and the news spread throughout the school in a matter of days. The following week, Emilia began to be cyberbullied about being gay by a couple of girls she never got along with. This created a rift between her and her best friend, and she now felt estranged from her core group of friends. To make matters worse, around the same time Emilia lost her beloved grandmother, who she would often turn to talk about her life and to gain emotional support.

Emilia confided in Matthew that it often felt impossible to clear her mind and pay attention in class because her thoughts raced, and her heart felt heavy with the emotional pain of her grief, betrayal, and ostracism. Emilia reported that academic tasks that used to feel easy and enjoyable now felt difficult, and as the days passed, she was getting more and more behind on her schoolwork. Emilia shared that her parents and younger siblings were struggling with grief about the loss of her grandmother and that she didn't want to add to their stress by asking them for support, nor did she feel comfortable telling them that she had been questioning her sexuality. While she knew they would always love her, she worried that they wouldn't understand her. In a matter of months, she felt like she had lost everyone she could turn to and withdrew into herself.

Her teacher and parents were unaware of Emilia's struggle with her sexual orientation, her estrangement from her friends, or the cyberbullying she was experiencing. In their own grief, Emilia's parents had missed the signs of her emotional pain and the effects on her attention, focus, and concentration at school and at home. Somehow her difficulties in modulating her emotions and controlling her behavior were attributed to teenage rebellion instead of a combination of grief and the other strains she was experiencing. Emilia's teacher was completely unaware of the complex social dynamics causing Emilia to lose focus and shut down in class. The reason that the CBT strategies weren't effective was because they were utilizing solutions for second executive–based problems instead of addressing the underlying social and emotional stressors.

Matthew soon came to realize that there were at least three major issues to address with Emilia: (1) her grief about the loss of her grandmother, (2) the betrayal by her best friend and her estrangement from her social connections, and (3) her confusion and inner conflict about her sexuality. These are three big psychological challenges for anyone at any age, and she had been attempting to navigate them on her own. This emotional overload was putting her in a near constant state of amygdala hijack, turning a difficult season of life into something impossible to manage. Matthew felt confident he would be able to help her with the first two but wasn't sure if he was the right person to help with the third. This was a question that would be answered in time, once Emilia moved through her current crisis mode.

Matthew focused the treatment on the emotional rather than cognitive elements of Emilia's symptoms, creating an environment of emotional safety that was soothing to Emilia's overtaxed first executive. They spent a number of sessions reminiscing about Emilia's grandmother, and Matthew shared stories about his grandmother. Together they grieved both of their losses. Matthew invited Emilia's family into one session to talk about all of their experiences of the loss so they could explore and share their grief as a family. Emilia had to repair her sense of self and her social identity after what had happened with her friends. She needed to develop better boundaries and appreciate the limits of others as opposed to taking responsibility for them. Matthew also helped Emilia identify and express the inner workings of her overwhelming internal world to her parents so that she could receive the understanding and support she needed. As Emilia built internal and external resources to cope with her emotions and stress, her emotional regulation gradually improved, as did her cognitive and behavioral adaptation to the classroom.

As Emilia's story demonstrates, the assessment and treatment of EF difficulties has to be based in all three systems. In particular, clinicians want to assess the stress levels of the first executive, as well as pertinent social and emotional factors in the first and third that might be inhibiting the second. If psychosocial factors are causing symptoms of ADHD, treatment should address the social and emotional components directly. This is especially important with adolescents, since they often lack the ability to identify and label their feelings and ask for the help they need. Standard EF assessment tools will guide clinicians toward cognitive solutions to emotional problems, while the three-system model offers a broader and more comprehensive assessment of the relevant issues.

Chapter 11

Changing Executive Function Throughout the Lifespan

Great works are performed not by strength but by perseverance.

—Samuel Johnson

A general assumption, at least in Western cultures, is that aging is a story of mental decline. As we grow older our memory fades, judgment is impaired, and executive functioning diminishes. A closer look, however, reveals a far more nuanced process. Each neural system has its own functions, evolutionary history, and developmental course. The maturation of the brain and how it changes during our lifetime reveals that some abilities do decline, others stay relatively consistent, while some continue to grow and improve (Anokhin et al., 1996; Tessitore et al., 2005). The pattern of these changes, both positive and negative, appears to be tied to the changing cognitive and social demands that have traditionally gone along with each stage of the lifespan.

As a social organ, the human brain has coevolved with the demands of attachment, caretaking, family relations, tribal life, and culture. This is why many brain changes over the lifespan are tied to social adaptation and the survival of our group. As many as 540 genes, related to brain-based events, have different activation patterns at different times of life (Erraji-Benchekroun et al., 2005). This strongly suggests that evolution has utilized epigenetic processes to reengineer individual brains at each stage of development to optimize group survival.

Based on research on healthy aging brains, it appears that each executive system is impacted by aging in different ways. The headlines are as follows: The first executive system experiences diminished amygdala activation and decreased physiological arousal with age. You could say that it mellows over time, resulting in less focus on immediate survival and decreased inhibition of the second and third executive systems. The second executive system shows a lessened ability for new learning and efficiency (encoding new memories and processing speed) with improvement in the development of complex memories and expert knowledge. The third executive appears to have the potential to thrive during aging, allowing for increased self-awareness, empathy, and wisdom.

As a whole, the healthy aging brain is characterized by more complex brain wave patterns, greater integration across different processing centers, and more holistic processing. These changes allow EF to gradually shift through each era of our lives. During childhood, we are driven to explore, experience, and learn, building our fund of knowledge about the world around us. During adolescence, our goal is to develop an identity within the group, connect with peers, and find a comfortable level of differentiation from our families of origin. Midlife is a time of building home and family as well as creating an identity based on skills and contributions to the community. In our later years, we contribute to the tribe through teaching, child care, and dealing with larger issues that require experience and perspective.

We can think of executive functioning as shifting its strategy and focus across the lifespan in step with our changing contributions to the needs and well-being of the tribe. In contemporary society, this may manifest as retired parents moving to be with and support their children and help with their grandchildren. Those who were in the competitive workforce may find their focus shifting from individual accomplishments to helping younger colleagues attain success. In other words, natural selection may have made the "decision" to continue to develop neural networks dedicated to attachment, affect regulation, and caretaking, while investing less in those focused on individual abilities and accomplishments. This is reflected in the maintenance of networks, such as ES3, that support nurturing others, group involvement, and participation in the social economy.

Despite our culture's pessimistic assumptions about the aging brain, maturation correlates with an increasing fund of knowledge, a deeper comprehension of meaning, and a preservation or even improvement of narrative abilities (Levine et al., 2004). Over the course of our lives, the three executive systems develop in ways that serve us at each developmental stage. As we approach old age, we gradually shift from doing the heavy physical lifting to heavy psychological lifting for the tribe and the family. We face mortality, review our lives, and reevaluate our priorities. The optimal development and integration of our three executive systems, and in fact our entire brains and bodies, provide for this part of life's journey to be a rich, generative, and generous time. Three aspects of development supporting this psychological, emotional, and social process are building a deeper inner world, storytelling, and the emergence of wisdom.

A Mosaic of Brain Development

Biology is the science. Evolution is the concept
that makes biology unique.

—Jared Diamond

As a government of systems from different eras of evolution, brain development is an extremely intricate and complex process. In general, early-evolving brain regions and neural networks tend to mature earlier in development, while later-evolving structures are shaped more by experience in order to adapt to our specific physical and social habitats (Grieve et al., 2005; Whalley, 2004). Although we can think of our three executive systems developing loosely in chronological order (ES1, ES2, ES3), they continue to grow and change their relationship to one another throughout life. Because they share structures and develop interdependently, there are many exceptions to this rule of thumb.

To make things more complicated, each of our brains is made up of two independent half-brains or hemispheres. Each hemisphere has a different set of responsibilities, is wired in different ways, and has its own sequence of critical periods. In addition, the brains and hemispheres of men and women are different and, in many ways, follow divergent developmental paths. The differences created by both laterality and gender reflect the diverse roles men and women have played in the adaptive survival of human tribes. Thus, when we think about executive functioning across the lifespan, we need to keep in mind that certain aspects of EF are influenced by both laterality and gender.

During the first few years of life, the hemispheres operate in a relatively independent manner. As the fibers that connect them mature, they exhibit increasing coordination and integration. During adolescence and into young adulthood, there is more lateral specialization, believed to serve the need for greater speed and efficiency for certain tasks (Liederman & Meehan, 1986). As we age, there is a shift to more bilateral participation in processing strategies supportive of higher-level cognitive and emotional integration during problem-solving (Cabeza et al., 2000). This may be the neural substrate for the maturation of social understanding traditionally required of older adults and tribal elders.

Just as evolution has shaped the right and left hemispheres to play complementary roles in neural processing, the bodies, brains, and biochemistries of males and females have been specialized for gender-specific social roles (Arnold, 2004). For example, women have a greater density of neurons in the planum temporale, a region of the temporal lobes specializing in receptive language (Witelson et al., 2006). Men, on the other hand, process visual-spatial information more directly without the mediation of language and show more activation in the right hippocampus (Frings et al., 2006).

Aging and the First Executive

Pessimism leads to weakness, optimism to power.

—William James

The central role of the first executive system is appraising the environment for safety and danger, and the regulation of physiological arousal. On the one hand, it has to evaluate positive and negative stimuli in order to make approach and avoidance decisions. On the other, it has to work with the medial portions of the frontal lobes to regulate and inhibit these reactions. Signs of a well-functioning first executive system are things like affect regulation, greater impulse control, and the ability to confront challenges and threats with minimal ES2 and ES3 inhibition.

Although the stereotype of older people is that they are cranky and pessimistic, social science research shows that positive emotions tend to endure in healthy older individuals, while negative ones are more likely to decrease (Carstensen et al., 2000; Williams et al., 2006). The neuroscience research also shows that medial frontal areas tend to sustain activation and continue to contribute to amygdala modulation during aging. Older individuals also report having fewer negative experiences and exhibit more affect regulation and emotional control (Gross et al., 1997). In fact, it is earlier in adulthood that negative emotions weigh more heavily in our evaluation of ourselves and others (Ito., 2002).

Sixty- to 80-year-olds demonstrate decreased amygdala activation while analyzing facial expressions, tend to look away from faces with negative expressions and toward those with positive ones, and tend to remember more positive visual images and words than younger subjects (Charles et al., 2003; Iidaka et al., 2002; Leigland et al., 2004; Mather & Carstensen, 2003; Pasupathi & Carstensen, 2003; Tessitore et al., 2005). This shift toward positivity with age has been found to occur between 18 and 60 years of age, at which point it seems to level off (Mroczek & Kolarz, 1998). See Table 11.1 for a summary of research findings on the positivity effect.

Despite this shift, amygdala activation in response to novel fearful faces, a salient social signal of danger for all primates, stays the same into old age. This strongly suggests that the changes are not due to the functional decline of the amygdala but rather to a maturation of orbital-medial PFC–amygdala regulation of fear-based processing (Wright et al., 2006). Older individuals also tend to remember and recount stories from their past with a positive spin. If this has indeed been shaped by evolution, its value may

TABLE 11.1
The Positivity Effect

Compared to young adults, older adults demonstrate:	
Less physiological responsiveness to emotion[1]	Less sensation seeking[5]
	Less emotional lability[6]
Increasing sense of emotional salience[2]	Greater impulse control[7]
Greater understanding of emotional states[3]	
More emotional coping strategies[4]	

[1] Levenson et al., 1991. [2] Carstensen & Turk-Charles, 1994. [3] Labouvie-Vief et al., 1989. [4] Blanchard-Fields & Irion, 1988; Lawton, 1989. [5] Lawton et al., 1992. [6] Lawton et al., 1992. [7] Diehl et al., 1996.

have been to instill optimism in younger people whose primary source of history and cultural information came from their elders (Taylor, 2000).

Based on this research, it appears that the amygdala lessens its grip on how we experience ourselves and the world, which may be why older adults tend to (1) experience fewer negative emotions, (2) pay less attention to negative stimuli, (3) be less likely to remember negative experiences, and (4) spin their histories in ways that make them look more competent, feel better about themselves, and convey an optimistic message to others (Kennedy, 2004; Leigland et al., 2004). All in all, this developmental shift in amygdala activation helps to lessen our focus on external threat and allows the salience network to coordinate the synergistic contributions of ES2 and ES3. As we will discuss later, this may be the neural substrate of the development of wisdom, one of EF's higher accomplishments.

Aging and the Second Executive

The only true wisdom is knowing that you know nothing.
                                                            —Socrates

Through our 20s, the hormonal, neural, and social upheavals of adolescence gradually settle down. During these years we learn to better regulate our emotions in the service of reality-based problem-solving. To this end, the prefrontal cortex continues to develop by pruning less efficient gray matter and increasing white matter connectivity (Sowell et al., 1999, 2001). Overall, we see more streamlined and efficient processing and better performance due to decreasing hormonal and emotional influences. This coincides with improvement on tasks that require planning, spatial memory, and long-term memory (Brown & Sullivan, 2005; Schweinsburg et al., 2005).

Memory is a central contributor to second executive system functioning. And while we generally think of memory as a single function, different forms of memory are processed within different neural networks. Explicit memory is best described as conscious semantic memory for names, places, and events. It is the loss of these forms of explicit memory, with a parallel shrinking of the hippocampus, that is traditionally considered to be the hallmark of aging. In contrast, procedural and emotional memory are relatively untouched by aging (Churchill et al., 2003; Rypma & D'Esposito,

2000). Early attachment, fear conditioning, and other emotional memories fall into this category, as well as procedural memories such as riding a bicycle or playing a musical instrument. With aging, EF shifts its strengths from learning new things in the external world to refining expert skills and caring for the tribe.

Theories of aging that focus on declines of explicit memory and processing speed see executive functioning as declining over time. But what if we see the shift in EF as being in line with our evolutionary history, a shift in the dynamics of the three executive systems, and the needs of the group? Patterns of brain activation across the lifespan show the deployment of alternative neural networks being activated over time. While these shifts result in slower performance, they also reflect more inclusive neural processing, which is better suited to dealing with complex cognitive and social challenges. This would be in line with the traditional role of elders in a tribal living situation. Although the use of brain regions supportive of personal recollection and storytelling are irrelevant to performance on memory tests in the laboratory, they are central to the traditional social requirements of EF throughout evolutionary history.

None of our ancestors depended on their performance on neuropsychological testing for their survival. They did, however, need to employ their emotions and past memories to solve the problems they faced. Tribal organization in the face of new external threats, changing resources, and intertribal disputes would call on their personal memory of prior challenges as well as their abilities to communicate their knowledge in a manner that could be both understandable and influential. If our brains are genetically programmed to shift processing modes over the lifespan, tests of executive functioning need to be tailored to how brains change over time.

Aging and the Third Executive

Everything that irritates us about others can lead
us to an understanding of ourselves.

—Carl Jung

From conception to death, we impact and are impacted by the biology and behavior of those around us, and depend on the scaffolding of others for our survival and sustained well-being. Using evolution as an organizing principle, we can assume that the social brain has been shaped by natural selection because complex relationships, social structures, and culture enhance our survival through adaptation. The third executive system is one of the highest expressions of our sociality. Its functions of understanding others and ourselves greatly expand the scope of our experience, while the cooperation of ES2 and ES3 provides us with the ability to integrate our cognitive abilities with our social and emotional intelligence to address complex social problems.

For most of human history, the lives of children, parents, and grandchildren were unchanging. Older adults had little to learn but much to teach. Prior to the relatively new invention of written language, older individuals were the vessels of knowledge, history, and values. Frontal systems involved in new learning became less vital, and a holistic understanding of situations was far more important than speed. Thus, the way the brain ages has been shaped by the needs of the group within an oral culture (Vaillant et al., 2002). Holding multiple perspectives in mind requires slower and more widespread neural participation that accesses both cognitive and emotional processing, and the weaving together of past learning and present realities.

The retention and even improvement of social judgment and empathy reflect the continued health and development of ES1 and ES3 (Happé et al., 1998). The calming of the amygdala decreases inhibition of the second and third executives and supports its continual development. Solid social judgment relies on the accumulation of experience, slow consideration, and emotional maturity. Although there may be a decreased need for new learning and quick reactions as we age, sustained attachment and emotional stability seem to have been worthy of evolution's continued investment throughout life.

Getting to know ourselves requires many years and overcoming a range of challenges. The development of self-knowledge requires that we turn our attention away from the distractions and demands of the external world and toward our inner experience. As we age, periods of freedom from external demands allow the time for a deeper understanding of the self, reflecting on one's life and reorienting priorities to emerging realities. These reflections can result in an acceptance of being in a new stage of life, accepting changes in physical abilities, and reorienting our time and attention to more age-appropriate or adaptive activities. The ability to turn inward requires the proper neurodynamic relationship among the three executive systems. The salience network (ES1) needs to be free from external and internal threats to allow ES2 and ES3 to function in an unfettered manner. The third executive appears to be the primary hub of inner activity while utilizing the skills of ES2 for the growth of the self.

Adults who are always doing instead of being often forget they have needs, and limitations. The rise of meditation and mindfulness techniques has been a response to a society overindexed on getting things done instead of living life. Because our brains evolved to react to and manage the external environment, we have to be reminded to slow our thinking and look inward. Attention to the experience of self and inner imaginal space creates the possibility for broader perspectives, empathy for others, and deeper self-understanding. You could say that one of the tasks of adulthood is to construct and inhabit this inner space in ways that support executive functioning across changing roles, abilities, and social identity. A denial or avoidance of the realities of aging does not serve late-life adaptation or help us to remain contributing members to our tribe.

The Emergence of Wisdom

Everything comes to us that belongs to us if
we create the capacity to receive it.
—Rabindranath Tagore

Increased neural participation does take more time but provides us with more and better-quality information on which to base our judgments. Consider that stories of young adults usually focus on their immediate personal experiences, while stories from older individuals often integrate both inner and outer realities into a more comprehensive understanding of the world. Wisdom is embodied in considered thought, the inclusion of multiple perspectives, well-balanced conclusions, and care for the audience. All three executive systems need to have developed and integrated properly to reach this level of wisdom.

There are many definitions of wisdom. In fact, each chapter of a popular book on the topic edited by Robert Sternberg (1990) put forth a slightly different definition. In the East, wisdom has traditionally focused on understanding and controlling one's thoughts and passions, as well as the ability to promote social harmony (Takahashi & Bordia, 2000). In Western cultures, wisdom appears as good advice and codes of social behavior, and is more closely associated with knowledge. We tend to think of wisdom as simultaneously grounded in a deep experience of the visceral, emotional, and moral self, and in an abiding awareness of our common humanity. In essence, wisdom is the result of a synthetic or "inclusive way of experiencing the world" (Takahashi & Overton, 2002, p. 275).

While knowledge gives us the capacity to understand what we are doing, wisdom helps us to attain an appropriate application of that knowledge. This is probably why knowledge can be judged against objective standards, while wisdom is recognized in the hearts of listeners and acknowledged through group consensus (Staudinger & Baltes, 1996). Although no specific study has been done measuring brain activation while people are acting wisely, it is safe to assume that we would see more diverse brain activation, slower processing time, and an optimal integration and participation of all three executive systems. This would be especially true for a synergy between the second and third executive systems.

Social science research suggests that wisdom coalesces from a complex pattern of personality variables, life experience, and inner growth (Staudinger, 1999). Those judged as wise in any age group excel in coping with existential issues and grasp the relativism of values (Baltes et al., 1995). They tend to have good social abilities and a rich internal life, and are open to new experiences (Staudinger et al., 1998). Someone with wisdom is capable of sustaining their focus on a problem as they consider its multiple dimensions, meanings, and their personal responsibility in the matter at hand (Holliday & Chandler, 1986).

For adolescents and young adults, learning usually involves gathering information, putting together the pieces, and convincing others of their conclusions. A final solution is sought as soon as possible based on the available information and, once accepted, is energetically defended. Younger people tend to assume the existence of a single valid answer and rarely come to new ways of thinking through disagreement and discussion. This style of executive functioning is likely tied to the challenges historically tied to their stage of development—peer connection, the establishment of an identity, and the transition to a productive and competitive adulthood.

In general, older adults are better able to balance their views with the needs and perspectives of others (Pliske & Mutter, 1996). With maturity, there is an increasing awareness of the complexity of human experience and the limits of our understanding. A reflexive response to obvious solutions gives way to slower deliberation. Time, consideration, and the accumulation of experience also lead to an awareness that not all of the important information may be immediately apparent. Most importantly, experience assures us that solutions to human problems are hardly ever simple or straightforward. The accretion of experience provides us with a framework that allows us to sit with ambiguity while we ponder a complex problem.

Thus, in older age we can expect to see a reduction in information processing speed accompanied by improvement in the practical application of social problem-solving (Tentori et al., 2001). This would reflect a shift from a primary use of ES2 to solve problems to the inclusion of self-awareness and empathy (ES3). Brain processing strategies that make for quick decisions earlier in life gradually give way to the more inclusive and fine-tuned cerebral networks required for wisdom (Mesulam & Weintraub, 1987). It seems almost certain that the potential to become wise depends upon the maturation of thinking and positive emotional development. It is this emotional intelligence that allows us to maximize our intellect in the service of others—a key reason why the attainment of wisdom requires the development and integration of all three executive systems.

To act wisely, we have to simultaneously be aware of our own biases, inhibit impulses that would make us act rashly, and be empathetic toward others, all the while applying our intellectual abilities to complex situations. This framework for executive functioning later in life requires a rebalancing of the dynamic relationships between our three executive systems: less intense emotions and better affect regulation (ES1), relying less on physical skills and abstract problem-solving relating to the physical world (ES2), and a greater emphasis on self-knowledge, empathy for others, and a focus on the well-being of the family (ES3).

Lifelong Executive Functioning

People seldom refuse help, if one offers it in the right way.
　　　　　　　　—A. C. Benson

The changing neurodynamic relationships among the three executive systems over time is an evolutionary strategy to support the adaptation and survival of the group. Slower, more inclusive, and more considered processing as we grow older may serve the increasing synthetic knowledge and problem-solving abilities traditionally ascribed to tribal elders. In fact, when brain activity is measured by the complexity of electrical activity, there is a linear increase from childhood into the 60s, the highest age measured (Anokhin et al., 1996).

By midlife we have usually mated, had a family, and established a foundation for our sustained survival. Given that we evolved in multigenerational tribes where younger people were better fit for hunting and fighting, older adults may have been programmed to take on alternative contributions to the tribe. These tasks would likely be less physically demanding and leverage the accumulated knowledge, experience, and wisdom that come with age. In contrast to declines in ES2 networks dedicated to navigating the physical environment, there appears to be a continued investment in, and development of, the social-emotional networks of ES1 and ES3. An aspect of the new direction of EF is reflected in a decreased ability for new learning and an increased focus on autobiographical memory, storytelling, teaching, and the sharing of wisdom.

Chapter 12

The Executive Brain in Executive Coaching

Leadership is unlocking people's potential to become better.
—Bill Bradley

Executive coaching and psychotherapy are separate but overlapping ways of applying our knowledge of psychology and neuroscience to human experience. Like psychotherapy, coaching occurs within a close, confidential, and safe relationship with the coach in the role of a trusted advisor. The differences between coaching and therapy are often more semantic than actual. While the challenges clients bring to coaching are focused on their professional lives, personal struggles with family, psychological symptoms, problems with addiction, and so on almost always arise. Working as a coach often includes making referrals to other professionals for ancillary treatment and being the coordinator of the treatment team.

There is a range of conceptual models for executive coaching. At one end of the spectrum, there are coaches who are trained in business, finance, and management. These coaches focus on helping their clients build their business platform, improve their supervisory and communication skills, and serve as a thought partner on issues such as hiring, promotion, and succession planning. Others, trained as therapists and counselors, focus more on the psychological aspects of work, such as stress management, work-life balance, and day-to-day survival within the corporate world. In reality, most coaching manifests as some combination of the two.

While our experiences at work and in our private lives may activate different aspects of our personality, there is always some consistency across contexts. Whether you are at work, at home, or wherever you travel, you bring your temperament, strengths, weaknesses, and unresolved emotional and relational issues with you. Different situations may evoke different strengths and weaknesses, and you may perform much better in one than another, but in general, we exhibit patterns of behavior across the context we traverse each day.

The psychological symptoms, difficulties with emotional regulation, and interpersonal problems that manifest in the workplace are usually present in personal relationships. Coaching clients are often surprised to discover how their childhood experience, past traumas, and relationship challenges outside of work reverberate through their work experience and create parallel problems with their colleagues. The goal of psychotherapy, according to Freud, was to diminish or eliminate blocks to a client's ability to love and work. Experience shows that when you focus on one, you also evoke the other. The wide array of challenges that emerge during executive coaching couldn't possibly be covered in a single chapter. There are, however, a number of issues that arise repeatedly across different coaching relationships.

Executive Coaching Is All About Executive Functioning

No matter where you go, there you are.

—Buckaroo Bonzai

Being a good executive at work requires being a good CEO of your own life. Using the three-system model, this means that you have adequate emotional regulation (ES1), bring the necessary skills and intellectual abilities to your life (ES2), and engage in consistent communication, care, and compassion for yourself and those around you (ES3). When one or more of these areas, or executive systems, is underdeveloped or underutilized, we run into challenges that can degrade and even derail our occupational functioning and success.

The topics we focus on in this chapter include (1) the maintenance of work-life balance, (2) understanding the relationship between *good* and *great*, (3) discovering the appropriate pace for optimal success, (4) adjusting work strategies for changing roles and challenges, and (5) any unconscious associations between personal success and a betrayal of our personal identity. Recognizing, processing, and modifying these potentially self-defeating thoughts, feelings, and behaviors requires the buy-in, participation, and realignment of our three executive systems.

Work-Life Balance

In art and dream may you proceed with abandon. In
life may you proceed with balance and stealth.
                                    —Patti Smith

Work-life balance has become a corporate cliché that is talked about far more often than it is actualized. Many companies sing its praises while structuring compensation and advancement plans that punish its practitioners. A successful career is a decades-long marathon, where pacing and work-life balance are essential to build a life of quality. The typical Type A executive believes that success is achieved by a full-frontal assault in a life-or-death battle against their competitors. They love to listen to talks by athletes and Navy SEALs, coming away with images and buzzwords to inspire tomorrow's assault on the next hill. The thought of shutting off their computer, setting their phone aside, and going on vacation triggers the first executive into a state of fight, flight, or freeze.

Living life strictly from the second executive system keeps the first executive in overdrive while inhibiting the third. The result is damage to the body through sustained high levels of stress hormones and undermining our connection with ourselves and others. Instead of having relationships with their spouses and children, their love is expressed by sharing the money they earn, teaching their children to substitute possessions for connections, and engaging in retail therapy. This is the perfect recipe for a family that is addicted to consumerism and social media, and vulnerable to addiction, anxiety, and a loss of meaning.

People can become addicted to work for various reasons. Many clients share that, at some point in their life, their work evolved from a job into a sanctuary from the emotions and relationships failing them at home. Feelings of competence at work serve as a relief from a painful inner world and chaotic personal relationships. Some begin to stay late at the office to avoid the conflict or discomfort that awaits them at home, while others, engrossed in their work, may not realize that their social life has withered and died. By overindexing on the second executive system, they gradually lose the facility of their other executive systems as their life narrows to become a by-product of their job. As you can imagine, these individuals can be quite successful at work, if work is all they do. At the same time, they are at risk for all sorts of social and emotional dysfunctions that may eventually derail their careers. These are the employees who are most at risk for drug and alcohol addiction and having inappropriate or destructive relationships that lead to the loss of family and career.

Most of us are able to sustain a workaholic lifestyle into our 30s or 40s. Adolescent energy, the fear of failure, and caffeine propel us through the necessary long hours and sleep deprivation. With age, we accumulate job pressures and family responsibilities, while our stamina and energy reserves decline. Simultaneously, our adolescent invincibility and other defenses begin to crack, and a growing awareness of time and our own mortality begin to creep in. This is when you have to reindex from a reliance on the abilities of the second executive and call a meeting of all three to come up with a sustainable, long-term plan for survival.

Good Versus Great

The roots of all goodness lie in the soil of appreciation for goodness.
—The Dalai Lama

Most everyone wants to be great; what differs most are the strategies to get there. What seems to work best is forgetting about being great and working hard at being good, perhaps very good. It involves an acceptance of where you are, understanding the steps involved in getting better, and putting in continuous and diligent effort each day. This requires many aspects of EF, including keeping your goals in mind, overcoming challenges, filtering out distractions, and keeping your eye on the prize. Humility is necessary for this stepwise approach to succeed, as well as asking for help and an openness to learning. These are the ballplayers that coaches love to work with, managers that executives commit to mentor and promote, and the students every professor looks for in the sea of faces when giving a lecture.

In contrast, there are those who don't think good is good at all. They actually seem unable to tolerate the good and, if you tell them to shoot for good, take it as a criticism of their capabilities. There are a variety of negative reactions to striving for good such as, "It's a waste of my time, abilities, and potential," or "It's good for average people but I am above average," and so on. They believe that trying to get good at something is shooting too low or isn't a worthy aspiration. Of course, there are those very few extraordinary and lucky people who burst onto the scene and become billionaires in their 20s. These rare individuals are used by others as proof that merely good is a waste of time. This occurs in 50-year-old middle managers who have been waiting a decade for a promotion, people who can't sit through a training session because they can't tolerate an instructor knowing more than they do, and the adolescent who feels that life is over because his YouTube videos didn't hit the desired number of likes by his 16th birthday.

From a psychological perspective, this way of thinking is usually attributed to a grandiose self-image or a narcissistic defense. But let's think for a moment about what is happening (and not happening) at the level of the executive brains. For a number of different reasons, these individuals became anchored in an early stage of development characterized by an egocentric perspective, leading them to disregard objective factors relative to the broader context in which they are operating. This means that their perspectives are limited to themselves and their personal goals versus what is statistically likely; that is, few people become billionaires by 30, and the vast majority of people don't become millionaires during their lifetime.

These individuals usually excel intellectually and academically, and know the workings of their industry very well. There is little doubt that they have an intact second executive system. However, because of their underdeveloped emotional abilities and narrow perspective, they are blocked from focusing their intelligence and problem-solving abilities on developing a realistic strategy for success. Thus, their third executive system is unable to develop a realistic appraisal of their current abilities, while their first executive becomes hyperaroused when faced with realistic limitations. This keeps them in a loop of self-delusion, perpetual underperformance, and waiting for a miracle to happen. This is but one of the many ways in which psychological defenses can undermine EF.

While it does happen on rare occasions, being a legend in your own mind seldom converts into being a legend in anyone else's. For most of us, the good is actually very good, and if we pursue the good, a very small number of us will arrive at being great. Even if most of us never get to be great, we can create a good life by being good at whatever we do. This requires that our first executive allows us to stay calm, our second executive remains focused on our craft, and our third executive stays ever mindful of ourselves and those around us in a humble, considerate, and caring way.

A great definition of the good might be those things which are slightly beyond our reach, attainable through diligent effort, and result in learning and upping our overall game. As in writing a book, it is easy to become overwhelmed and avoid the work if you think of the book as a whole. If, instead, you focus on one chapter, or even one section of one chapter at a time, you may have an easier time getting down to work and writing a good page or two each day. Any writer can stare at a blank page trying to think up a great sentence. But great writers rewrite what they have already written in search of the sentence they are looking for. They have to be able to tolerate living through the bad sentences to find the mediocre ones and occasionally the good and the great. Great may be your final destination, but not necessarily the best place to set your compass for at the beginning of a long career.

Pacing

Slow and steady wins the race.

—Aesop

Many businesspeople come from humble beginnings and overcome a considerable number of obstacles on their way to success. Even they may be surprised by how far they have gotten and find it hard to trust their status and achievements. They have often had to (or believed they had to) give 110% in order to make it. Women and those from marginalized groups also feel this way because not only did they have to do as well as their white male counterparts, they also had to battle stereotypes, exclusion, and microaggressions along the way. An all-out effort to succeed is driven by the positive results of hard work and the terror of falling back into a painful past or negative situation you are trying to escape.

Helping these clients to step back and take an objective look at their lives can be very challenging. They may have learned to avoid self-reflection, put their head down, and just plow ahead. While they may intellectually know that they will never end up back where they began, they may carry the fear of returning to the poverty, depression, or abuse they experienced as a child. These folks are often haunted by the thought of getting fired and ending up on the streets, despite being a valued employee and having all the money they will ever need. These fears, both conscious and unconscious, can turn every work interaction into a life-or-death referendum on their value as a person. They may also spend an inordinate amount of time and energy revisiting work interactions that were less than optimal for hints of their demise. This preoccupation with negative evaluation and the shame it triggers drives them to work harder while diminishing their capacities to work smarter.

This level of all-out focus on work can often be seen in clients with all varieties of anxiety disorders. The anxiety and fear that drives their lives, in a kind of manic defense against their own feelings, often converts into a hyperfocus on work. These clients will experience significant shame when they are given less than stellar feedback from their managers or when they make a mistake in some aspect of their work. Each mistake or imperfection triggers feelings of anxiety, vulnerability, and catastrophic thinking. Instead of celebrating a success at work, their experience is that it was a way of buying a little more time before they get fired.

In cases like these, coaches need to address the cause of their client's unreasonable anxiety and help them get proper psychological treatment. When a lack of proper pacing is driven by conscious and unconscious fears, the first executive needs to be calmed down in order to be able to develop the other two executives for the client's benefit. The significant experiences of anxiety and/or depression in these situations need to be addressed at the beginning of coaching. Once a client establishes a sense of safety, they have the option of stepping back from frantic activity for moments of clarity. As periods of safety and calm are expanded, deeper and more sustained self-awareness and insight can be nurtured. This will eventually allow clients to become the CEOs of their lives with the participation of all three executive systems.

What Got You Here Won't Get You There

Evolution consists of the gradual transformation of
organisms from one condition to another.

—Ernst Mayr

There is a popular phrase in executive coaching that goes, "What got you here, won't get you there." This usually translates to the fact that the technical and interpersonal skills that allowed you to excel as someone else's right-hand assistant or an excellent bench scientist won't necessarily lead to success at the next level of business. This is often the case in successful family businesses and startups when it's time to shift from the early heroic stage of building something from nothing, to organizational charts, legal regulations, and the mountains of paperwork for which no one was prepared. This aspect of executive functioning requires the insight to realize that a change of strategy is required, the emotional regulation to tolerate learning new skills, and the ability to train and trust others to do the things you must move on from.

A half century ago, this problem was labeled the Peter Principle, which asserted that within corporate hierarchies, people tend to rise to their level of incompetence. In other words, people who are recognized for their excellence at specific tasks—financial analysis, engineering, performing surgery—are promoted to positions that require managing people, playing politics, and a high level of emotional intelligence. Put into three-system language, they have succeeded based on their superior second executive functioning, while their new roles require them to put many of those abilities aside in favor of third executive functioning. At this point we find that many have overindexed on their second-executive analytic abilities, and may have underdeveloped first and third executive systems. To complicate matters, their analytic abilities may have served a regulatory function that they lose when separated from the safe haven of technical tasks.

Success as Betrayal

Is it possible to succeed without an act of betrayal?
　　　　　　　　　　　　　　　　—Jean Renoir

There are those in all walks and stages of life that seem to fall short of their potential. As one client described it, "I've never missed an opportunity to miss an opportunity." Chronic underachievement is often confusing to the victim and puzzling to those around them. While there can be many underlying reasons for this flat trajectory, there are many for whom success is bound up in their mind with betrayal. Sometimes this betrayal is related to culture, where business success is experienced as an abandonment of subcultural or family values. A successful individual from a less successful family, or a family with communal cultural values, may experience their rise in professional success as turning their back on their family and culture, experiencing paradoxical feelings of both pride and loss. Sometimes success is a betrayal of some semiconscious pact that someone makes with themselves early in life that continues to undermine their progress.

Success has its obvious surface meaning, but there is usually a deeper narrative, one that revolves around the semiconscious adaptation to past emotional challenges. When the deep narrative is supportive of success, there are few internally generated roadblocks. It is when the deep narrative conflicts with an overt track to success that the symptoms of procrastination, avoidance, and self-sabotage appear. For others, it can be more family specific—a child's academic success is experienced as a betrayal by his father who struggled in school, or a successful career-oriented daughter is perceived by her mother as abandoning the family's traditional values. A darker but altogether common scenario is the parent who is threatened by their child's success, leading them to criticize and thwart their child's progress by undermining their self-esteem.

When coaching someone with an underlying psychological conflict surrounding success, efforts focused on building second-executive abilities—time management, note taking, work structures, and so on—will be met with avoidance and excuses. In order to make progress, unearthing the social-emotional conflict and discovering the feelings driving the self-sabotage will be necessary. This step first requires the downregulation of the first executive through relaxation techniques and perhaps exploring uncovering the deep narrative that pairs success with pain, fear, or loss. This will allow for an increased participation of the third executive via introspection, reflection, and metacognition when the avoidance behaviors are activated. The next step is to have the second and third systems (in conjunction with the coach) collaborate in creating solutions to break up the blockage and create experiments in living that allow insights and strategies to be tested, modified, and permanently implemented. Throughout the process, the first executive will attempt to block progress, so it is also necessary for self-awareness to include the inner voices, habit patterns, and addictions that support the avoidance of confronting the necessary issues.

Monica

> *Virtue is its own punishment.*
> —Aneurin Bevan

Monica was referred to me (LC) from a human resources officer at a large investment firm where she had worked for over a decade. I was told that she had shown an excellent work ethic, dedication to the firm, and success with many of the firm's high-value clients. Through a series of promotions, she had risen from an analyst, to management, to being considered for partnership. Over the past year, partners in the firm had become concerned with the decreasing quality of her work, complaints from some of her direct reports, and an increasing number of days when she was nowhere to be found. Rumors had begun to circulate about problems with substance abuse, mental illness, and a concern that she had "quiet quit."

When a firm hires an executive coach, it usually means that the employee is seen as a person of value that they want to retain, develop, and promote. Firms often like to promote internally because they have a known entity with corporate knowledge, while hiring someone new always entails risk. Although those who do the promoting possess the social and emotional skills to work at a managerial level, they often lack the ability to determine if the promotion is a good fit for their employee. On the other hand, it is difficult for an employee to turn down a promotion due to pay incentives and the negative optics of turning it down. These human and institutional factors, on both sides of the promotion question, are the main drivers of the Peter Principle. The general belief, although often wrong, is that if you are excellent at one thing, you have the potential to do another—if you are a good surgeon, you should be able to run the hospital. If you are an excellent analyst, you should be able to run teams of analysts and be successful in selling consulting work to clients.

During our first meeting, Monica was obviously tense, visibly agitated, and distrustful as she tried to keep a professional demeanor. Like many, she was concerned that the coach wasn't hired to help her succeed but rather as part of the paper trail leading to her being fired. I settled into the gradual process of gaining her trust by sharing about myself and my past coaching experiences. This was all focused on the goal of normalizing what she was going through, instilling optimism, and creating a language of collaboration.

I was sure to share with her all of the positive things her boss had shared about her and the fact that being assigned a coach was a sign of their commitment to her. Over a few sessions, her anxiety gradually lessened as she shared about her professional and personal life. This initial bonding is essential in a successful coaching relationship in the same way it is in psychotherapy. It allows for the downregulating of the first executive so that the second and third can become fully involved in the coaching process.

Monica had grown up in a large, extended family from South America. From an early age, she felt out of place and had a strong desire to escape her family, neighborhood, and culture. She told me, "I grew up feeling suffocated by it all. I knew I had to get out or die." She buried herself in biographies of women who forged their own identities like Frida Kahlo, Amelia Earhart, and Gertrude Stein. She spent as much time as possible at school, taking on every opportunity and challenge presented to her. Recognized as an exceptional student, she won scholarships, admission to prestigious colleges and business schools, and later was recruited by large corporations.

In her early 30s, she moved to her present firm because she thought there might be more opportunities for advancement. After a few sessions, Monica felt comfortable enough to share her recent experiences: "I've been running my whole life with danger snapping at my heels, too afraid to slow down, stop, and face it. It finally caught up with me last year." As she said this, it looked like all of the energy drained from her body. She described her mounting symptoms of anxiety and depression, and the dread that greeted her each morning as she rose into consciousness. In her usual fashion, she dealt with these feelings by working harder, which only made her feel worse. She now felt she was failing on all levels—as a businesswoman, a mother, and a wife. Monica was intense and brilliant, yet extremely fragile, barely making it through the day. The fears and anxieties related to feeling inadequate and out of place as a child were as strong as ever.

Over the first few months of our relationship, it became clear that Monica was struggling with an anxiety disorder and symptoms of OCD. Up until now, these aspects of her biology and personality had contributed to her success. Her ability to sustain focus, pay attention to details, and deny her own needs made her an ace financial analyst and investment strategist. Now in her early 40s, with a husband, two children, a dog, and aging parents to take care of, the abilities of her defenses had been surpassed. She found herself having nightmares of her life falling to pieces, working at a grocery store with girls from her high school, or, as she put it, "falling backwards into hell."

Despite Monica's surface rejection of her roots, she maintained a deep attachment to the idea of being the same kind of matriarch as her mother. She expected herself to do all of the things her mother had done plus a full-time career. "My head understands the absurdity of what I expect of myself," she said, "but my heart can't let go." Although consciously aware of the impossibility of the challenge she had created for herself, her self-esteem had become tied to being a better mom than her mom as well as having the career her mother wasn't allowed to have. Making her job even more difficult was her tendency to defer to those around her and default to a supportive role, especially when working with male colleagues. Living in the shadow of her early developmental struggles and cultural conditioning, she worked herself to exhaustion. At the same time, she felt as if she was failing at everything and doubted her ability to ever succeed.

Monica, like many others, faced her mounting anxiety and depression by turning up the intensity of her work. This strategy allowed her to escape her childhood but was a poor adaptation to her present reality. She had to learn to let go of what made her a success and discover a new strategy for life as an adult. She had a range of responsibilities requiring diverse skills and all of her executive systems. What works at work doesn't necessarily work at home, and the defenses from our early life often fail us in middle age. Fortunately, our brains and minds remain capable of change if we can find the wisdom to let go of the past and develop new ways of navigating our lives. Here is an overview of my initial thoughts about my work with Monica.

Coaching Plan

1. Create the Coaching Contract

Since this was Monica's first coaching experience, we collaborated in establishing an agreement about our work together. We planned on meeting three times a week for the first month to outline her challenges and create a strategy for change. When a client who is used to solving problems feels out of control, it is important to create a clear plan and work on forming a strong connection as soon as possible. High performers need something to do and can easily spin out of control with a "let's wait and see" approach.

2. Downregulate First Executive System Hyperarousal

Getting to know one another, answering questions, and sharing experiences is an important first step in the establishment of confidence and trust. My initial interventions included negotiating a lighter work schedule with her firm and a referral for a medication consult for her symptoms of anxiety and depression. In time, I would add a referral for psychotherapy to address the unresolved issues from her childhood. Those of us who grow up and live in a high state of arousal and stress often don't recognize that this is the case. Helping clients to learn relaxation techniques allows them, perhaps for the first time, to experience relaxation. This is when they can begin to realize just how much stress they live in from moment to moment. Always keep in mind that the regulation of the first executive system is primary if you're going to recruit the other two in the service of change. Creating a safe and secure base in which to do the work is always the first step.

3. Digging Down

Learning as much as you can about a client's life history, experience, culture, the important moments of their life, the metaphoric shorthand they use to describe complex feelings, and their relationships with their parents, spouses, children, and friends all serves in cocreating narratives that can become road maps for learning. As I got to know Monica, it was clear that her difficulties were not related to her cognitive abilities, intelligence, or industry knowledge. However, the skills, abilities, and strategies that got her promoted to her present position were not adequate going forward.

Total control and micromanagement can only work when you have a limited universe of things to deal with. As life expands and our plates get piled high, we all have to learn to be less perfectionist, relinquish some control, and delegate those things we can to others. Monica had already surpassed her ability to cope with her current life, and a promotion would have pushed her over the edge. She eventually confided in me that she lived in fear of the promotion her boss had hinted at because she knew she had reached her limit.

4. Psycho-Neuro-Education

I needed time to learn as much about Monica as I could as well as to teach her about coaching and the partnership we would have to form in order to be successful. I also shared the three executive system model so that we could use it to organize the material that would come up along the way. Being able to have a conceptual handle on her different states of mind, moods, and impulsive reactions within this neurobehavioral framework helps to work with aspects of ourselves that are challenging and unacceptable. Our brain-based model destigmatizes the process while allowing clients to see that they are not dysfunctional; rather, there are certain skills and abilities that need to be upgraded for them to be successful. Being successful requires that we learn to optimize brain functioning while limiting its shortcomings.

5. Targeted Interventions

It soon became clear that Monica needed to step back from hyperfocus on specific tasks to take a look at her life as a whole. She had excellent analytic skills, which she used to great effect at work, but had never thought of using them for her own life. This is where a collaboration between the second and third executives is required. Experience makes it clear that knowing what to do and even giving others advice can be entirely dissociated from our self-awareness. The second executive, focused on the material world and abstract thought, can function independently of personal experiences and self-awareness mediated by the third executive. This is the reason why so many of us are better at giving advice than taking it from ourselves. If we grow up taking care of others and/or are taught that we are not worthy of care, this dissociation serves as an adaptation to our reality while supporting a disconnection between ES2 and ES3. As we worked together, one of my goals was to gradually help Monica learn to apply her intelligence and wisdom to her own life.

Monica came to realize that she had always been driven by fear—fear of failure, abandonment, and ending up back in her childhood. This made her always keep her head down and take on the next challenge while never thinking about her own needs, desires, or the quality of her life. She often became sad as the realities of her life became revealed to her. She did have to fight to escape her childhood but kept fighting even though she had escaped and it was no longer necessary. As she slowly got to know herself and was able to apply her analytic skills to her own life, she found it easy to generate potential solutions for her challenges. Implementing them, however, was an entirely different challenge. Her head knew what to do, but it was difficult for her to convert to a peacetime mentality after so many years in combat.

As I guided Monica through breathing and body awareness exercises, she was surprised to discover that she could create a safe inner space that would always be available to her. Free from the demands of the external world, she could activate her third executive—the experience of self, imagination, and time travel. She could also use this inner space to tap into her second executive to mull over challenges, potential solutions, and imagined consequences. I showed her diagrams of the different executive systems so she could imagine the areas of her brain that were being activated across her various states of mind. This ability to imagine where in the brain things are happening is a strength of the three executive system model, especially with clients who learn better in pictures than words.

Monica slowly discovered layers of survivor guilt over having escaped the neighborhood, leaving her mother and sisters behind. She also began to think fondly about some aspects of her cultural heritage that she had neglected while rejecting other aspects of her past. Reconnecting with cherished aspects of her culture led, over time, to her feeling more grounded and confident. When we eventually got to the notion of work-life balance, she was surprised to find that it made sense, after years of being befuddled when this issue was raised at work. Before coaching, the notion of work-life balance had no place to land, while it now became a touchstone for decisions at work and at home. Progress was slow but the trajectory positive, and she eventually managed to see how much of a success she was across the domains of her life, and that she had to become the CEO of her own life before she could successfully manage her lives at work and home.

Part V

Attachment, Executive Functioning, and Adult Relationships

Chapter 13

Parenting and Executive Functioning

There is no way to be a perfect mother and
a million ways to be a good one.

—Jill Churchill

The quality of our executive functioning relies upon the development and integration of three executive systems. This process is a result of the interaction of genetic inheritance (nature) and experience-driven epigenetic expression (nurture). During the early years of life, our experience is primarily mediated via interactions with our caretakers. This is why the neural structures and behavioral strategies of our executive systems reflect our early relational histories. This is also why early attachment experiences and adverse childhood experiences (ACEs) are correlated with later educational, occupational, and relational success.

In addition to providing for our basic physical needs, the primary function of early parenting is to regulate arousal, stress, and fear. This is necessitated by the fact that we are born with a fully developed amygdala, while the neural networks that modulate it take years to mature. These interactions provide a template for building the neural networks of self-regulation and feeling safe with others. It is within these networks that our first and third executive systems interact and our attachment schema are stored. The robustness of these hierarchical networks provides the foundation for what will become our sense of self, worthiness, and self-esteem.

Attachment research provides us with two windows on the processes of early brain building. The first is reflected in a stressed child's behavior during the Infant Strange Situation test. The second is the coherence of adults' narratives when sharing memories of childhood during the Adult Attachment Interview. In the former, implicit memories of soothing and nonsoothing interactions (the attachment schema) reveal the child's expectations about the parent's ability to soothe them when under stress. In the latter, early experiences influence the development and integration of the three executive systems as measured by the quality of their speech in adulthood. This ability, which we often take for granted, is a high level of abstract functioning that depends upon the fluid collaboration of all three executive systems. The ways in which speech is coherent and incoherent point to different patterns of brain development and impairments of executive functioning.

An adult's style of parenting is significantly influenced by how they were parented and how their parents were parented. This intergenerational influence goes back into every family's history and projects into the future. When studying parenting, attachment, and adult relationships, we take a snapshot in time of this ongoing adaptational process. There is no best place to start, only a choice of where to begin. In the next three chapters we will be looking at the formation of attachment in children, how attachment is assessed in adulthood, and the ways in which our attachment experiences impact the shaping of our EF.

The Epigenetics Matrix

The most powerful force ever known on this planet is human cooperation—a force for construction and destruction.
—Jonathan Haidt

We have a century of research and millennia of literature reflecting our awareness of the connection between childhood experiences and adult functioning. Within the field of psychology, the causal theories of this relationship are described as anything from behavioral modeling, to the cultural shaping of character, to the resolution of the Oedipal complex. Epigenetics provides us with yet another explanation, the translation of experience into neuronal structures and chemical set points during early brain building. This explanation is especially important when thinking of how parenting styles and attachment schema become encoded in our brains and impact the development of executive functioning. The story goes something like this.

From the time of conception, a mother's internal biology is being translated by the fetus into information about the world to which they will soon have to adapt. For example, a mother who is highly anxious sends a message to the baby that it must prepare to be born into a dangerous world. The truth of whether the world is actually dangerous or not is unavailable to the baby; all it knows are the chemical messages it's receiving from its mother's body. The mother's internal chemistry is translated via genetic transcription to build neural structures and neurochemicals best suited to the world to come. This is nature's way of giving the newborn an adaptational advantage.

This epigenetic process continues after birth with the shift in messaging from chemical interactions to social exchanges with caretakers. The centrality of attachment to EF is that the building of our executive systems (like the rest of our brain) is shaped by the information we receive in these early exchanges. Secure attachment appears to stimulate states of brain and mind that optimize brain development and integration, leading to the more robust development of the three executive systems and optimal EF. This is likely the reason for the strong correlations between positive childhood experiences and adult well-being.

Moderate states of arousal, which enhance protein synthesis, brain growth, and neuroplasticity, mediate optimal biological outcomes and secure attachment. This allows children to build the complex web of neurotransmitters and neurohormones needed to support a sense of safety and well-being, and produce the chemical receptors that allow those neurotransmitters and neurohormones to be effective. It downregulates levels of adrenaline and cortisol that inhibit neuroplasticity and result in cell death and diminished neural development. These processes also result in a robust immunological system, the establishment of supportive relationships with others, and greater resilience, grit, and ego strength. In essence, attachment is a workshop for the building of executive functioning.

Good Enough Parenting

Intuition will tell the thinking mind where to look next.

—Jonas Salk

If you were to ask almost any parent—in the midst of juggling groceries and a crying baby—"How do you do it?," they will most likely respond by saying, "I have no idea!" While fumbling with the car seat, they pop a pacifier into the baby's mouth and gently stroke its cheek. Their gaze lingers on their little one, who's settled into a state of calm. "I'm just taking my cues from him." While this may seem like no big deal to a busy mom or dad, it turns out, taking cues from your infant is truly the gold standard of parenting, especially during the first year.

Decades of research have shown that while a child needs basic necessities to survive, they also need emotional care and support to thrive. Affection and comfort are not just a sweet sentiment; rather, they are central to the experience-dependent development of the brain, physical and emotional health, and optimal executive functioning. The field of attachment shows how a sense of safety with our caregivers shapes our ability to regulate our emotions and manage the natural anxiety of life (Schore, 2005). Many psychological disorders are correlated with a lack of attachment security, highlighting how attachment has the power to either set us up for optimal development or hold us back (Set, 2019). It is the quality of these early relationships and their impact on brain development that set the course for optimal EF.

How is secure attachment created within a child? Surprisingly, a major component rests with the executive functioning of the parents. While the parent at the grocery store might feel as if they don't know what they are doing, they are actually engaging in a range of sophisticated cognitive, emotional, and social processes. Taking cues from an infant is a lot more nuanced and precise than it might seem. There are many factors that must converge in order to effectively soothe one's baby in the midst of a chaotic moment. A parent's ability to be aware of their child's needs and respond to them quickly and effectively reflects a combination of her cognitive, social, and emotional intelligence: in other words, the central components of EF. Of course, some basic aspects of parenting are genetically programmed, biologically driven, and instinctually carried out. In the modern world, however, these automatic responses are necessary but far from sufficient.

Hidden in Plain Sight

It is easier to build strong children than to repair broken men.
—Frederick Douglass

If executive functioning is the ability to navigate complex challenges over time, few human activities are as complex, challenging, and prolonged as raising a child. If this is so, why is the relationship among child-rearing, intelligence, and EF never mentioned? Our belief is that this vital relationship has remained hidden in plain sight because of pervasive biases in Western culture. Executive functioning is associated with education, leadership, and control, traditionally thought of as the domain of men. On the other hand, parenting is thought to be basic, instinctual, emotional, and within the realm of women. The history of science, the study of the brain, and notions of intelligence have grown out of the soil of these fundamental cultural biases.

The male-centric narrative of human evolution has focused on the expansion of the human brain and its ability to think abstractly, invent tools, and create weapons. As the story goes, these weapons allowed us to dominate other tribes, kill larger animals, and increase our protein intake, leading to bigger brains and greater intelligence. This narrative, which dominated most of the 20th century, depicted women as passive bystanders of human evolution. It also led scientists to miss the social nature of the brain, neglect the female contribution to brain evolution, and forget that they all had mothers. The broad and synthetic nature of interpersonal neurobiology and the three-system executive model allow us to better integrate the role of both genders in the story of evolution, brain development, and parenting.

The notion that parenting is solely based on "maternal instinct" leads to the idea that it hardly requires thinking or even a cortex. As we will demonstrate, positive parenting involves what is perhaps a higher degree of executive functioning involvement than most tasks. In addition, the EF demonstrated by parents is also central to its development in children. Appropriate parental availability, attention, and attunement correlate not only with a child being securely attached but with neural growth, network connectivity, learning, and emotional regulation necessary for EF in their children. The growing convergence of research in attachment, epigenetics, and developmental neuroscience reflects the interwoven nature of parenting, brain development, and EF.

In this chapter and the next, we will examine two branches of attachment research. The first is the observational work of Mary Ainsworth, who explored the correlations between parental style and attachment security in children. We will then consider Mary Main's linguistic analysis of parents' narratives about their own childhoods to predict the attachment security of their children. We will then deepen our focus to explore (1) how parenting is highly dependent on the development and integration of our three executive systems, and (2) how it predicts these same neurodevelopmental processes in their children. We think in terms of "good enough parenting" to reinforce the idea that there is no perfect or ideal parenting. Rather, parenting is a complex interaction between parents and children which is full of ups and downs, successes and failures, connections and disconnections.

A key notion is the idea of a mother being able to hold her baby in mind. Psychodynamic therapists talk about how, as young children, we learn to "internalize" our caretakers as "inner objects" that serve a soothing function when we are separated from them. In the same way, a mother can create an inner object of her child and hold them in mind. The ability to internalize our child connects us to them when we are separated, but also provides an inner model when we are together. We have a theory of the baby's mind, their perspective, their wants and needs that can guide our caretaking. A mother's internal model of her child allows her to be sensitive, accepting, and understanding of her baby's needs across developmental stages.

Mary Ainsworth: The Exploration of Parent–Child Interaction

Children learn more from what you are than what you teach.
—W. E. B. Du Bois

Inspired by the theoretical work of her mentors William Blatz and John Bowlby, Mary Ainsworth studied parent–child relationships in Uganda and the United States to examine the correlates of parenting behavior and what came to be called *attachment security*. The theoretical foundation of attachment theory was that the parent serves as a secure base from which a child learns to explore and interact with the world. The parent's role is to be available, sensitive to the child's needs, and support their ongoing exploration and development. Ainsworth's cross-cultural experiences provided her with insights into these basic elements of parenting behavior as well as the range of parental styles.

Her research at Johns Hopkins University focused on attachment security and the development of what she called *attachment schema*. Trained observers were sent to the homes of new mothers and their young children to observe, record, and code their interactions. In analyzing these data, Ainsworth came to focus on four components of maternal behavior:

1. Sensitivity versus insensitivity to the baby's signals,
2. cooperation versus interference with their ongoing behavior,
3. physical and psychological availability versus ignoring and neglecting the baby's needs, and
4. acceptance versus rejection of the baby's needs.

These factors were turned into rating scales, which allowed observations to be coded, categorized, and associated with the children's attachment security. An awareness of Ainsworth's observations is clinically useful in that they allow us to make inferences (based on our observations of how our young clients are being treated) about their attachment schema, their neurodevelopmental strengths and weaknesses, and the origins of their difficulties with executive functioning. They also make it very clear how a mother's EF manifests in her interactions with her child.

What follows are general descriptions of Ainsworth's observations across the four components of maternal behavior. We will discuss each in detail with specific references to its likely association with the executive functioning of the mother and its future development in the child. As a side note, the term *mother–child pair* is used throughout these descriptions because Ainsworth's work was done with mothers and their young children. We assume that the same dynamics are at work with all caretaking pairs.

1. Sensitivity Versus Insensitivity

A sensitive mother simultaneously enlists multiple executive functions in order to be aware of their child's signals, accurately interpret them, and respond promptly and appropriately. She has the ability to cope with and manage negative emotions without projecting them onto the child. She also has clear boundaries that protect her from taking on her child's emotions as her own. From a cognitive standpoint, sensitivity also includes keeping in mind the way the child experiences the world as well as their developmental stage. For example, the mother has the ability to recognize that their child's disappointment and anger about having to leave the park is very real to the child. A sensitive caregiver has realistic expectations of the child's ability to regulate their emotions and appropriately supports them through transitions across emotional states. These abilities also require social and self-awareness as well as sensitivity to and empathy for the child. Thus, all three executive systems are involved in interpersonal sensitivity, self-regulation, and attunement to the child.

Ainsworth's rating reflects a number of abilities including availability, emotional attunement, empathy, emotional regulation, and problem-solving abilities. In order to operate at this level, it is necessary for the first executive to have attained a degree of maturity that allows freedom from past trauma and emotional intrusions. This creates the emotional and cognitive space to be fully present and focused on another being—anxiety and arousal are the enemies of empathy and self-awareness. The second executive has to be engaged for the mother to communicate and find alternative solutions to her child's dilemma. Finally, the third executive allows the mother to create an internal model of her child's emotional world to use as information to develop an empathic response. Someone once said that when you have a child, you discover a piece of your heart in another body—this discovery requires our third executive system.

Ainsworth identified four levels of maternal sensitivity: highly sensitive, sensitive, insensitive, and highly insensitive.

> A *highly sensitive* mother demonstrates an exceptional attunement to her baby, perceiving their needs and emotions with clarity and consistency. She is able to see the world from her baby's perspective, allowing her to respond promptly and appropriately to

their signals. Her understanding of the baby's communication is unclouded by her own needs or defenses. When she cannot fulfill her baby's desires, she acknowledges their feelings and offers an acceptable alternative.

A *sensitive* mother's responsiveness is slightly less timely and consistent. While she still recognizes her baby's needs and is able to empathize with their perspective, she demonstrates a lessened ability to pick up on more subtle cues. This mother might find it challenging to balance her baby's needs with other demands on her attention, leading to occasional lapses in her ability to respond promptly.

In an *insensitive* mother, we see frequent failures in responding to her baby's signals in a timely and appropriate manner. She struggles to empathize with her baby's viewpoint, often misinterpreting signals due to her own needs and/or defenses. Even when she understands what her baby wants, she might choose not to respond simply because it is inconvenient or because she is concerned about "spoiling" them. At other times, her responses can be delayed to the point where they no longer align with her baby's immediate needs. She may still manage to respond sensitively when her baby is in distress or when their needs coincide with her own.

A *highly insensitive* mother is primarily focused on her own wishes, moods, and activities. She tends to ignore or misconstrue her baby's signals, responding mainly to her internal cues rather than those of her child. It is only when her baby's needs become intense, repetitive, or prolonged that she may react, highlighting her inability to engage with her baby's emotional world.

High levels of insensitivity to a child's needs are often found with caregivers who struggle with substance abuse, unresolved trauma, and other forms of psychopathology. Extreme examples of empathic failure by the mother can become encoded within the child's brain and mind in the form of anxiety, shame, unlovability, and low self-esteem.

An adult client described how his mother (suffering from OCD) would startle him by barging into his bedroom during the night to vacuum his floor. Another client tells the story of her father (diagnosed with schizophrenia) habitually locking her out of the house in the middle of the desert summer, and her spending the day under their car because it was the only available shade. An elderly client described how her mother (with many symptoms of borderline personality disorder) lifted her up over the coffin at the wake of a classmate who died of scarlet fever and forced her to kiss the corpse. These three cases are clear examples of parents so locked into their own experience that their ability to see the world with empathy had been completely eclipsed.

2. Cooperation Versus Interference

This dimension reflects a mother's ability to support the child's autonomy and exploration of the world. First of all, the mother experiences and interacts with her child as if they are an autonomous being, rather than an extension of themselves. She has baby-proofed her home so as to allow maximum freedom of exploration with minimal danger for the child. She is able to put other things aside and join in activities with them, allowing her child to take the lead, sharing in their discoveries.

A cooperative caregiver sees her baby's wishes and activities as valid. When the baby is involved in play or exploration, she consciously limits her interruptions. Cognitively, this requires putting the baby's needs first and creating supportive strategies when interruptions are necessary. In order to do this, the parent must have the ability to manage anxiety triggered by their child's autonomy and the potential interference with their own schedule. Parental openness and flexibility to a child's expanding needs for autonomy and efficacy are grounded in understanding, perspective-taking, and social intelligence.

Ainsworth separated maternal cooperation into five categories: conspicuously cooperative, cooperative, mildly interfering, interfering, and highly interfering.

> A *conspicuously cooperative* mother recognizes her baby as an autonomous individual and intentionally modifies the environment to minimize the need for her to interfere with her baby's activities and exploration. She joins her baby in their interests, and she engages in reciprocal interactions that foster a sense of

collaboration. When interruptions are necessary, she uses playful and supportive strategies.

A *cooperative* mother is also noninterfering but shows slightly less respect for her baby's autonomy. While she strives to be cooperative, she does not prepare her environment or routines as thoughtfully, leading to more frequent interruptions and control over her baby's activities. Her interactions lack the skillful finesse seen in conspicuously cooperative mothers, resulting in less engaging exchanges during play.

A *mildly interfering* mother exhibits a less considerate approach toward her baby's activities, with frequent interruptions. Most interactions are adult-led and shifts between activities are abrupt and disregard her baby's emotional state.

An *interfering* mother takes this a step further, forcefully interrupting her baby's activities. Her rationale for interference is often tied to adherence to a structured routine and the desire to shape her baby's behavior. She frequently employs physical restraint and commands.

A *highly interfering* mother does not view her baby as a separate individual but interacts with them as if they lack autonomy or a separate will. Her interference with her baby's ongoing activity and exploration are frequent and forceful, lacking any apparent reason.

The imaginal, empathic, and cognitive qualities of the second and third executives cooperate to allow us to create an image of our child's future self that becomes a self-fulfilling prophecy for their future. Despite our child's present dependency on us, we create an inner image of them that embraces the sequence of their future development. We speak to them in words they do not yet understand yet foreshadow their eventual abilities. These imaginative and problem-solving capacities allow us to preemptively protect them from their immature judgments and impulsive behaviors.

These preparations, in turn, support the child's freedom to explore and discover their world. With some minor editing, these could be positive strategies for therapists, friends, managers, and romantic partners.

3. Availability Versus Ignoring and Neglecting

An available parent is one that is accessible and emotionally attentive to their child such that the child is always, at least peripherally, on the parent's mind. The parent is never too absorbed in their own thoughts, feelings, or activities to be unable to shift attention to their child when necessary. In order for this to happen, a parent must be flexible in their attention and alert to the child's whereabouts and needs. Other important executive functions required for this level of attunement include having a selective filter to tune in to the child's sounds, signals, and bodily cues. Like a good CEO, an available parent is strategic in the way that they manage competing needs and responsibilities while remaining present and supportive.

The highly accessible parent can distribute and shift their attention to both their baby and the surrounding world of people and things. They have developed a sweeping radar that allows them to maintain vigilance to their child and still engage with the rest of the world. When they need to, highly accessible parents can quickly shift to an intense focus on their baby. This is perhaps best described as a well-functioning ES2 responding to the world in cooperation with the third executive when the baby needs attunement and connection. As with all three of these parental functions, optimal functioning requires a well-developed first executive to prevent distraction, preoccupation, and a self-protective turning inward.

Ainsworth divided her description of maternal accessibility into five categories: highly accessible, usually accessible, inconsistently inaccessible, often inaccessible (ignoring or neglecting), and highly inaccessible (ignoring or neglecting).

A *highly available* mother takes deliberate steps to ensure that she and her baby can easily reach one another. She remains vigilant, even when her baby is napping in another room, positioning herself close enough to stay aware of their state, signals, and activities. This mother is able to distribute her attention to other things while keeping her baby in mind. She consistently acknowledges her baby's overtures, fostering a secure and responsive environment.

A *usually available* mother is generally tuned in to her child and readily available. However, there are times when she becomes preoccupied, leading to moments when she fails to respond to her child's needs. Despite these occasional lapses, she usually acknowledges her baby's signals, maintaining a fairly attentive relationship.

An *inconsistently available* mother demonstrates stretches of attentive engagement alternating with periods of obliviousness, during which she may become absorbed in other thoughts or activities. While she is more accessible than inaccessible, there are times when she may overlook her baby's attention-seeking behaviors, leading to a less consistent bond.

An *often unavailable* (ignoring or neglecting) mother is more often unavailable than present. She tends to appear preoccupied with her own tasks, often entering and exiting rooms without acknowledging her baby. She is most likely to respond to her baby only in situations of extreme or prolonged protests. On the rare occasions when she does focus on her baby, she may offer intense attention, but such moments are infrequent.

A *highly unavailable* (ignoring or neglecting) mother is so absorbed in her own thoughts or activities that she rarely notices her baby at all. She fails to acknowledge her child's activities or smiles. It appears that the idea of her child feels more real than the child themselves. While she may perform tasks for her baby, she rarely offers attunement or connectedness.

The lack of sustained accessibility to the mother leaves a child to deal with the outside world and inner feelings without a mirror or source of regulation. Development of ES1 suffers due to the absence of stress modulation and assistance with affect regulation. Consistent hyperarousal and distraction interfere with ES2 growth, while maternal inaccessibility thwarts and distorts the personal and interpersonal abilities supported by ES3.

4. Acceptance Versus Rejection of the Baby's Needs

An accepting parent is able to balance positive and negative feelings about parenthood. They do not harbor resentment for the ways that their lives have been turned upside down and wholeheartedly accept the responsibility. The parent is able to tolerate frustration with the baby's behavior without taking it personally. They also support the child's individual sense of self, encouraging them to fully express themselves, even if they find it emotionally triggering. They are not reactive to the child's behavior because their coping skills help them to process difficult emotions in the moment. When there is a rupture, they move swiftly through frustration to repair the bond. They use self-reflection and their inner equilibrium to extend compassion and adjust to the child's emotions and developmental capacity.

Ainsworth created five categories of the acceptance versus rejection of baby's needs: highly accepting, accepting, ambivalent, substantially rejecting, and highly rejecting.

A *highly accepting* mother embraces her baby's behaviors, even those that may be disruptive. She values her baby's will, even when it conflicts with her own, and takes pleasure in their attempts to engage with the world, understanding that these explorations may temporarily draw their attention away from her. When frustration arises, she refrains from directing her irritation toward her baby, instead acknowledging her responsibilities and the limitations that come with caring for them without resentment.

An *accepting* mother exhibits a positive and loving attitude toward her child, though she may show slightly less respect for her baby's autonomy compared to the highly accepting mother. She remains patient and expresses a genuine acceptance of her baby's needs. She is expressive with her baby while accepting the limitations that parenting imposes on her life.

An *ambivalent* mother displays a generally positive demeanor toward her baby and enjoys their company. However, moments of resentment and hurt may occasionally surface, often in inappropriate ways. These feelings can arise when she interprets her baby's behavior, emotions, or attention toward others as opposition or rejection. This can lead to irritability and rejection when she deems her baby's behavior unacceptable.

A *substantially rejecting* mother frequently exhibits negative responses that outweigh her positive feelings. Her anger and resentment manifest through distancing and/or deliberately ignoring her baby. In conversation, she often focuses on her baby's shortcomings and the challenges they present, making critical comments about her child, both to them and in the presence of others.

A *highly rejecting* mother demonstrates overt rejection toward her
baby. Her interactions are marked by frustration and resentment.
She may openly express regret about having her baby, viewing
them as a hindrance in her life. This resentment often translates
into consistent opposition to her baby's wants and needs. Her
approach may involve scolding, physical roughness, and engaging
in power struggles.

As one can clearly see from these descriptions of parenting styles, all three
executive networks are brought to bear in child-rearing. We traditionally
think of suboptimal parenting as the result of a lack of maternal instincts,
psychopathology, or a history of not being properly parented during your
own childhood. While this is true, all of these (and other) challenges to
parenting can be thought of as being mediated by the development, functioning, and cooperation of the three executive systems. In addition, all of
these positive and negative parent–child interactions are translated by the
baby's brain into biochemical signals. These signals, in turn, shape epigenetic processes that guide the building of the anatomy and neurochem-
istry of the child's brain. These epigenetic processes not only influence the
building of the brain's executive networks but the ability to learn, to have
relationships, succeed in school and work, and stay physically healthy. This
is how adverse experiences of childhood become translated to lifelong psychological, social, and physical vulnerabilities to dysfunction.

   If you would like to see these categories in the original scales, please
see "Maternal Sensitivity Scales: The Baltimore Longitudinal Project"
(Ainsworth, 1969).

Chapter 14

Attachment, Coherent Narratives, and Executive Functioning

When little people are overwhelmed with big emotions,
it is our job to share our calm, not join their chaos.

—L. R. Knost

Our brains have coevolved with our capacity for language, a central top-down aspect of executive functioning. This means that most of our communication, abstract thought, and problem-solving are organized and expressed in language—particularly storytelling. Because our ability to learn, remember, and spread culture is grounded in communicating via stories, they are central to understanding how our brains developed into social organs and, more broadly, how we evolved to be a meaning-making species.

For all of these reasons, the ability to use language and tell stories is central to successful EF. Our ES2 organizes the stories we tell, while our ES3 contributes our ability to shape them in a way that is understandable to others. Adequate regulation of ES1 leaves us free from emotional distraction to create and share the stories we tell, while maintaining a theory of the mind of the listener.

We believe that the relationship between insecure attachment schema and failures of coherence reflect the interdependent nature of early caretaking with the neurobiological development of the entire brain, but especially the three executive systems. In other words, varying levels of arousal and specific types of early interactions with caretakers lead the brain to be built and organized in different ways. These differences impact the development of executive functioning and manifest in the construction of our narratives. Our ability to regulate affect, inhibit intrusive emotions, remember our past, and keep the listener in mind shapes how we share our experiences and tell our stories. Because all of these functions are aspects of EF, the coherence of our narratives is a window into how our brains developed.

Creating coherent narratives—telling stories that are linear, understandable, and relatable to the listener—requires the successful early and ongoing development and integration of all three executive systems. Generating coherent narratives is one of the brain's highest achievements and, at the same time, extremely vulnerable to the stresses and strains of everyday life. Given the role that parents play in scaffolding the child as they navigate their world, the nature and quality of the attachment relationship can either enhance, distort, or inhibit the development and integration of our executive systems and our ability to communicate with others.

Mary Main: Narrative Coherence and Executive Functioning

It is not our purpose to become each other; it is to recognize each other, to learn to see the other and honor him for what he is.
—Hermann Hesse

Mary Ainsworth's work with mother-child dyads laid the groundwork for the study of the interactive expression of attachment schema in children. The next logical step was to explore the nature and impact of these schema in adulthood. We know self-report questionnaires about internal emotional experiences are fraught with reporting biases and methodological limitations. We also know from more than a century of experience in psychotherapy that adults reporting about their childhoods yields a mixture of actual and confabulated memories, family mythology, misperceptions, and psychological defenses. In other words, what adults remember of their childhoods is of questionable value when trying to assess their attachment schema. Understanding this challenge, Mary Main and her colleagues developed an innovative and insightful workaround, the Adult Attachment Interview (AAI; Main & Goldwyn, 1998).

The data for the AAI are collected via an interview consisting of open-ended questions about childhood relationships and early experiences. Questions and prompts posed to subjects were similar to these:

Please describe your relationship with your parents when you
    were a child.
What adjectives would you use to describe your mother, your father,
    and your relationships with them?
Did you feel closer to one of your parents? If so, why?

The interview looks similar to questions we might ask a client during
therapy. It also appears to be falling into the trap of collecting unreliable
or even meaningless data. But here is the genius of their approach: On
the surface, the AAI is gathering information about an individual's childhood and family. But instead of analyzing the content of the subject's
reports, it is the linguistic quality and coherence of the narrative itself
that is the focus of analysis. In other words, how do their answers strike
the listener? Are they logical, consistent, understandable, and believable?
Or is the listener left with confusion or skepticism about what they are
being told, such as, "I had a perfect childhood," or "My parents did the
best they could," combined with information that suggests an opposing
reality? Because there is so much room for subjective differences in this
sort of qualitative analysis, raters receive extensive training in what is
called coherence analysis.

Coherence analysis is based on what are called Grice's maxims, which
measure the organization, quality, and understandability of the narrative.
The broad categories of Grice's maxims are:

1. Quality: Be truthful, and have evidence for what you say.
2. Quantity: Be succinct, and yet complete.
3. Relevance: Stick to the topic at hand.
4. Manner: Be clear, orderly, and brief.

Scoring takes into account the integration of thinking and feeling, gaps
in memory and information, and the overall quality of the presentation
(Hesse, 1999). Main and her colleagues found that individuals with different attachment schema could be characterized by the coherence or incoher-
ence of their narratives as well as specific failures to meet Grice's maxims.
They also found that subjects with different attachment schema tended to
have narratives that were coherent and incoherent in similar ways.

Secure Attachment and Executive Functioning

We are only as needy as our unmet needs.
                                        —John Bowlby

Main found that securely attached adults created narratives that satisfy Grice's maxims. Their narratives contained a level of detail that supported the content of their stories, and their emotional descriptions were congruent with the memories being shared. They presented a realistic and balanced perspective of the positive and negative aspects of their parents and childhoods and were able to express negative feelings without being emotionally overwhelmed. This type of coherent presentation in an adult client usually means that their current difficulties are more likely the result of challenges that occurred after the early development and integration of their three executive systems. Their issues in therapy are more often related to relationship challenges, stressful experiences, or specific blind spots related to their defenses and personality style.

Securely attached infants grow into adults who are more likely to engage in self-talk and self-reflection. These processes of mind support the development of ES2 and ES3, allowing for increased affect regulation, cognitive oversight, and coherent discourse. The more these networks integrate, the better able we are to process stressful and traumatic experiences and benefit from psychotherapy. Not surprisingly, parents' emotional insight and availability to themselves appear to parallel their emotional availability to their children. Parents who build secure attachment with their children have all three executive systems online.

Avoidant Attachment and Executive Functioning

It is a joy to be hidden, and a disaster not to be found.
                                        —Donald Winnicott

A second group of adults, categorized as avoidantly attached, had incoherent narratives characterized by significant gaps in memory for important childhood events, referred to as lack of recall. The memories they possess appear to have been retrospectively constructed from family stories and old photographs. Their dismissive attitude toward their children likely parallels experiences with their own parents. They tend to be emotionally distant, to be black and white in their thinking, and to utilize defenses such as denial and intellectualization. Interacting with others creates discomfort, and they tend to experience relationships as a burden.

These are people who weren't adequately scaffolded by their parents and were overwhelmed by stress, which impaired the development and integration of their executive functioning. Their ES2 is usually the most developed while the first and third have been inhibited and dissociated from conscious awareness. Their early stress likely led to high levels of cortisol, hippocampal atrophy, and memory deficits. Inadequate third executive development parallels low levels of imagination, empathy, self-reflective capacity, and psychological mindedness. Transference will focus on a lack of trust of the therapist's motivation, skills, and trustworthiness. Lacking a sense of emotional connection to others, they rely heavily on rules of behavior to evaluate and navigate relationships and are confused by those who rely on their emotions.

Anxious Attachment and Executive Functioning

Parents forgive their children least for the faults
they themselves instilled in them.
                    —Marie von Ebner-Eschenbach

A third group of adults, described as having anxious attachment, tend to produce disjointed narratives driven by intrusive emotions from the past. It is as if they are unsettled by the emotions of what they are saying, which leads them to lose track of the listener. Their narratives are guided by the cascade of emotions and associations that their stories trigger within them. This leads to an absence of self-awareness, monitoring what they are saying, and keeping the perspective and knowledge of the listener in mind. They exhibit a lack of clear boundaries between the past and present, and continue to be preoccupied with their parents later in life.

Anxious attachment reflects a lack of regulation of physiological and emotional arousal, anxiety, and fear. This hyperarousal of ES1 impedes both the development and integration of ES2 and ES3. This leads to deficits in the ability for empathy and theory of mind, making their communication a monologue rather than a vehicle of interpersonal engagement. The inhibition of the second and third executive systems also correlates with lower levels of social and occupational abilities and attainment.

As clients, these individuals have difficulty maintaining interpersonal boundaries and produce a flood of words that can make therapeutic dialogue impossible. The initial challenge facing the therapist is to discover a way to help them decrease their arousal and anxiety. In these cases, your ability to soothe clients' arousal is vital to establishing a therapeutic relationship. Orienting them to the therapeutic process requires teaching them how to talk less and say more, and remember to listen during a discussion. Therapeutic goals are generally to integrate feelings, thinking, and self-awareness, and refocus their attention from the past to the present.

Disorganized Attachment and Executive Functioning

No one ever told me that grief felt so like fear.

—C. S. Lewis

A fourth group of adults, described as having disorganized attachment, produced narratives that contained an abundance of unfiltered content and were difficult to follow and understand. Their narratives were rated as highly incoherent, consistently disrupted by both emotional distractions and bits of fragmented information. Talking of their childhoods resulted in emotional dysregulation, pressured speech, and a fragmentation of their narrative. As an aside to the analysis of coherence, it was reported that the content of their childhood narratives spoke to unresolved trauma, loss, and grief.

Of all of the attachment styles, these individuals demonstrate the most vivid examples of the impact of early stress on the structure of adult narratives and, by association, the development and integration of their EF. Recent research has demonstrated the ability of early stress to negatively impact both the receptive and expressive language systems of the left hemisphere. There is also evidence that high levels of stress actually lead to the inhibition of Broca's area and our ability to produce meaningful speech, resulting in a transient aphasia or the classic "speechless terror" of post-traumatic stress. These data suggest that the fluidity of speech and difficulties in comprehension can be indications of both early stress and trauma as well as a client's current state of arousal.

This may correspond to reports of learning difficulties and impairments of occupational and relationship functioning based on missed cues and distorted communication. It may also lead clients to have difficulties benefiting from talk therapy. With clients like these, you may have to be especially careful in your choice of words, the pacing of your speech, and in monitoring their facial expressions for signs of incomprehension. People with receptive language difficulties often fill in the blanks of what they miss in what others say with their own associations. They may say they understand you when they don't. Having frank process conversations about your ability to track one another in therapy can open the door to deeper disclosure and the opportunity to work together to overcome this challenge to communication.

Clinical Implications of Attachment Research

Children do not need us to shape them. They
need us to respond to who they are.

—Naomi Aldort

The insights offered from these two streams of attachment research are extremely relevant in day-to-day practice. Ainsworth's work provides us with a framework for understanding our observations of mother-child interactions and relating them to the child's social, emotional, and cognitive functioning. Main's work reveals how these early experiences are woven into the development and integration of neural networks and their impact on communication, language, and affect regulation. Looking across three generations of both being parented and parenting reveals a possible mechanism of transmission of social-emotional development and the building of executive functioning.

When we work with couples, the less than positive ways they treat one another are often a reflection of how they themselves were treated as children. Becoming aware of the tendency to repeat these early traumatic experiences in later relationships can provide both increased self-awareness in the clients and a conceptual framework from which to work with couples. Identifying both of their triggers and how they trigger one another allows them to have greater mutual compassion and make different decisions about the ways they interact. For the clinician, an understanding of how the adult client was parented as a child can provide important clues related to defensive structures and transference reactions within therapy. A therapist's understanding of their own attachment history will also provide clues related to countertransference vulnerabilities and can be helpful in their personal therapy.

Main's research helps us to understand that the ways in which a client's speech is coherent or incoherent may reveal information to which they do not have conscious access. Instead of simply being confused by the content of a client's speech or labeling it as defensive, we have a tool to analyze how it is incoherent. This information can lead us to generate hypotheses about not only their attachment security but also how they were parented, their experiences of early stress, and their defense mechanisms, brain organization, and memory capabilities. While the content of explicit memories is highly malleable and vulnerable to distortion, the memories of our early life, embedded within our neurobiology, are highly resistant to change. The nature and quality of our discourse may be one of the best and most accurate retrospective measures of early experience.

Executive Functioning and Parenting

Life is best organized as a series of daring ventures from a secure base.
                                                            —John Bowlby

Families can be closed systems. This means that a family can settle into a set of behaviors, beliefs, and interactions which serve to regulate the anxiety of its more powerful members. This powerful member is usually a parent, the parental relationship, or a child with a functional disability or mental illness. An identified patient often emerges from a rigid family dynamic, but the family typically does not identify itself as having a problem. When children from these families exhibit difficulties in an educational setting, it is easy for teachers and parents to label the children as having attention deficits, executive dysfunctions, learning disabilities, or an impulse control disorder.

Most of the time, children labeled with learning disorders are of normal intelligence, while the diagnosis reflects their difficulties in the classroom.

Many students, especially in disadvantaged regions, are having difficulties learning because they suffer from unresolved trauma, sleep deprivation, hunger, family stress, or domestic or community violence. This toxic stress results in emotional and physical dysregulation that keeps them from being able to regulate their emotions (ES1) and learn in the classroom (ES2). When dysfunction in the family or community becomes the norm, it is the child's reaction that is interpreted as pathological. For example, a child's tantrum may be seen as "will-full" or oppositional, instead of as a cry for help in reaction to fear, dysregulation, or a need for attention.

Consider the case of a family who adopted a sister and brother, now eight and five years old, from an African orphanage. When they were six and three, both parents died of AIDS, leaving them alone in the world. Because no one would take them in for fear of contagion, the six-year-old took her little brother by the hand and walked for a week to the nearest orphanage many miles away. They arrived at the orphanage barely alive due to hunger and exposure. The couple that adopted them was on a mission to Africa and brought them back to the United States.

The problem that brought the adoptive family to therapy was their belief that the girl had a character problem and was growing into a thief. Her sole criminal act was to take two cans of beans from a kitchen cabinet and bring them to her bedroom, where she put one of the cans under her bed and the other under her brother's. Her parents had told her that the entire family shared the food in the kitchen and that she was stealing it by taking it to her room. She told them she understood but was unable to keep herself from taking the two cans of beans. Although the beans were never eaten, finding the unopened cans under the children's beds upset the parents and resulted in them removing privileges from both children and subjecting them to long hours of Bible passages about the evils of stealing.

This child had watched her parents die, was shunned by her community, and barely survived the trek to an orphanage, while near starvation and exposed to the elements. She then had to adapt to an orphanage, new parents, and then a new country, neighborhood, language, and school. It is obvious to most of us that putting a can of beans under her bed was an act of survival and not one of evil. While the parents were aware of all she had been through, as well as her heroic behavior, they were stuck on the belief that it was a reflection of bad character. This case highlights the necessity of empathy, compassion, and theory of mind when parenting, especially with traumatized children.

Children suffer when parents lack the cognitive flexibility to accept that they are separate beings, are at a different stage of development, and have a different perspective than the parents. Parents who can be curious about the meaning of their child's behavior, as opposed to feeling they have to shape that behavior first, are much more likely to develop a positive relationship and have their children accept their authority. Parenting dogma, whether it is from a parent's past, their religious beliefs, or parenting books, reflects a need for certainty that is seldom present in child-rearing. Cognitive flexibility is a sign of mature executive functioning, while the acceptance of dogma is an escape from the anxiety and humiliation of uncertainty and curiosity.

We think it is important for parents to know about the development of the three executive systems as well as the entire brain. While a child begins to use words around their first birthday, it takes many years for them to understand complex concepts like time and the delay of gratification. Because children don't have a developed sense of time, being told that they will be able to do something in a few days may have no meaning to them. This may lead them to ask when it will happen every few hours. They also benefit from warnings 5 or 10 minutes before something is going to happen. Shuttling between an adult's and child's sense of time is an executive skill of good parents. A parent who treats a child as if they have the brain of an adult will have a very difficult time managing the relationship.

Trying to reason with a 16-month-old about why he can't go to school with his five-year-old sibling doesn't work. He is simultaneously experiencing being left behind, a lack of fairness, and jealousy. When a parent launches into a logical explanation about why he can't go to school, all the child hears and feels is "no, no, no, no . . . " As Ainsworth's research demonstrates, good-enough parenting includes showing understanding for these emotions along with offering clever alternatives and distractions. It is a good strategy to redirect the attention of the child, because that is what his 16-month-old brain is capable of responding to. In other words, don't try to enlist the second executive when a child is too immature to understand or use language to regulate emotions or guide behaviors.

Some parents have a natural ability to understand children at different levels of development and how to communicate with them, while others don't. Same thing with teachers. Some teachers will say that they don't care if their students like them, only that they learn the subject they are teaching. This statement shows a deep lack of knowledge of the brain and how humans learn. Children have to know that you care for them before they trust you, and attune their hearts and minds to your teachings. Otherwise, their minds will be closed to information that they intuitively feel might not be in their best interest. Mirror neurons fire less when interacting with those you dislike or don't trust—a kind of safety filter to protect against unhelpful influence. And for children and adolescents, imitation is probably the most powerful avenue of learning.

Carrie

If you want to have a life worth living, a life that expresses your deepest feelings and emotions and cares and dreams, you have to fight for it.
—Alice Walker

Carrie, a 35-year-old businesswoman, came to therapy complaining of long-standing anxiety with the more recent addition of panic attacks occurring about every two weeks. Intelligent, charismatic, and articulate, she reported being very good at regulating her anxiety by working long hours to avoid becoming "upset by life." During the initial session, she exhibited a natural warmth and engaging vulnerability. She shared about her passion for her career, her financial successes, and how rewarding it was to work with her clients and colleagues. Carrie reported having a large group of friends and described many fulfilling and long-standing friendships. The description of her life was so good, one had to wonder how honest she was being with both her therapist and herself.

When asked about her early life, there was an immediate change in her facial expression and tone of voice. She shifted from the type of presentation you might expect from an eager job applicant to what felt like an anxious and frightened adolescent. After a prolonged silence, Carrie began to describe her sister's lifelong struggle with substance abuse, which began when she was 14 and Carrie was nine. She shared her parents' tension and anger as they struggled with trying to help her sister with sobriety, consuming most of their time, attention, and resources until she left for college. Carrie reported that by age nine, she felt emotionally disconnected from her family and essentially invisible. She also pointed out that her parents did the best they could with the heavy burden of caring for her sister while making a living and keeping the house together.

Carrie adapted to her home life by turning her attention away from her family and toward school. She was popular and received the positive attention from her teachers that she craved at home. She also hoped that her successes in academics and extracurricular activities would counter-balance some of the disappointment her parents felt about her sister. While at home, her mom was demanding and critical, her dad withholding and emotionally distant. When asked what a normal day at home was like, she seemed at first to draw a blank. She then described a rather generic day that didn't seem particularly relevant to her or how she described her parents. She had no memories of a family vacation or of any heart-to-heart talks with her sister or either of her parents. When she left for college, a thousand miles from home, Carrie reported strong feelings of liberation and guilt.

Carrie went on to describe her desire to be in love, have a healthy relationship, and build a family. Now that she was well-established in her career, she would have the flexibility to balance work and a family. She said that she could hear her clock ticking. Carrie stated that although she had a few relationships over the years with hopeful starts, they all became emotionally abusive and disappointing. She said, "Regardless of how good they feel at the beginning, I always seem to end up back in my family." She recently began a relationship with a new partner about which she felt hopeful, but was concerned that she had gotten on the same roller coaster, and would only be hurt and disappointed once again. She also feared that the recent onset of her panic attacks was trying to tell her to run away from her current partner before she got hurt yet again.

Although she never took the AAI to assess her attachment schema empirically, a number of factors can lead us to a working hypothesis of Carrie having an avoidant attachment style. These include her isolation and self-sufficiency in childhood, the inability of her parents to connect with or soothe her, and her repeated cycle of approach and avoidance in relationships. An avoidant attachment is also supported by her lack of recall of much of her childhood and the extreme shift in her state of being from talking about her present life to discussing her childhood.

In terms of her three executive systems, it appears that her ES1 has been inadequately shaped to provide emotional regulation and calm. Her ES2 is well-developed and successfully engaged in her professional endeavors but may be inhibited by the stress that becomes activated in intimate relationships. As a result of her early experiences, ES3 is likely underdeveloped due to a lack of supportive emotional connections with her family. It is early interpersonal engagement that shapes the neural networks upon which we rely to create and sustain intimate connections in adulthood. The context and rules of engagement at work likely parallel her well-developed social skills with her teachers and peers at school that she was able to transfer to her workplace. In intimate relationships, however, she is likely bombarded by associations of abandonment that trigger her anxiety and panic. Carrie's interpersonal reactions to her historic fears may be turning into a self-fulfilling prophecy.

In psychotherapy, the first order of business was to work with Carrie to deal with her anxiety via specific relaxation interventions, self-monitoring strategies, breathing techniques, and potentially medication (ES1). The second focus might be an exploration of her relationship patterns to see if there were identifiable situations that exacerbated her anxiety and triggered the need to withdraw from her partner and escape the relationship. Identifying these patterns and developing strategies to counteract them might give her hope in changing this pattern going forward. While she is probably very competent when it comes to interpersonal problem-solving on the job, these skills might be dissociated from awareness in personal relationships. Breaking down these dissociative barriers would also allow her to utilize ES2 in personal relationships.

With traction on these basic emotional and practical issues, the therapy could then move on to exploring neglected or dissociated aspects of ES3 processing such as creating a safe internal space, utilizing imagination for the benefit of potential future relationships, and expanding her theory of mind and empathy abilities, which are often inhibited by the anxiety of proximity and intimacy. The inhibition of ES3 under stress leads those who are frightened to feel alone, even in relationships.

Chapter 15

Executive Functioning in Adult Relationships

You don't have to be interesting; you have to be interested.
                                                    —John Gottman

Navigating relationships is a complicated and ever-changing dance that requires each partner to deal with the competing needs, preferences, and emotions of the other. Simultaneously, we have to develop and maintain a sense of identity as a couple, including sympathy, compassion, and empathy. Success in these complex endeavors requires complex problem-solving, effective communication, and self-awareness. Although EF is seldom mentioned in couples therapy, successful relationships require more executive ability than many of life's other challenges.

To complicate matters, an individual has three executive systems to coordinate but a couple has *six*—each with different developmental histories, problem-solving abilities, and communication styles. In addition, the intimacy, vulnerability, and mutual dependency of romantic relationships makes us more vulnerable to being triggered by attachment trauma and experiencing amygdala hijack. This usually results in the inhibition of the executive systems we need in order to deal with the situation that triggered us in the first place. When both adult partners are triggered, their interactions can devolve into an endless power struggle of two hurt children, each wanting the other to be the understanding adult they've been searching for. These kinds of regressive interactions can go on for days, years, and even a lifetime.

Thinking about relationship challenges from the framework of executive functioning may prove helpful for couples who benefit from having a structured framework to describe, address, and problem-solve around the issues that bring them to treatment. The majority of couples who come to therapy are struggling with insecure attachment in one or both partners. The fearful memories stored in the first executive system lead to mutual regression and an inhibition of their abilities to stay connected, stay attuned, and tackle the problems they are facing. The inhibition of the second and third executive systems sabotages rational problem-solving by limiting the experience of each partner to their own childhood trauma while losing sight of the other's needs. As implicit emotional memories and the physiological arousal they trigger within ES1 take control, we lose the ability to have any metacognition during these painful interactions.

Another common situation is one partner overindexing on second executive functioning to the exclusion of emotional vulnerability, attunement, and intimacy. Think about the engineer, the accountant, or the executive who frames the world in terms of numbers and procedures but struggles to relate to others. This leads their partner to feel lonely, emotionally bereft, and abandoned. Sometimes trauma and first executive hyperarousal inhibit third executive functioning, leading to a withdrawal from connection and self-imposed isolation.

The Need for Safety

Your job is to know what matters to your partner and
how to make him or her feel safe and secure.

—Stan Tatkin

One way that we can determine the health of a relationship is to consider whether each partner feels safe with, and is able to be regulated by, the other. We're not talking about literal safety but a feeling of security within the partnership, that each is held in the mind of the other, and that both parties' opinions and emotions are considered valid and worthy of attention and care. Each partner is willing to listen, take an interest in the other's experience, attune to their emotions, and offer support in difficult times. For many, especially those with problematic attachment histories, the primary association to a feeling of love is the absence of fear.

An adult who is securely attached is able to regulate their own emotions across most situations, has the capacity to be alone, and is free from extreme psychological defenses that distort reality and isolate them. They're able to attune to others, be vulnerable when necessary, and function well in partnership with few emotional intrusions. When two securely attached people enter into an intimate relationship, they come to the table with an ability to create meaningful connection, regulate one another, and communicate in ways that allow them to face and solve problems together. These couples seldom need therapy except for consultation when dealing with situational crises.

An insecurely attached person, on the other hand, can become anxious, afraid, and distrusting of their partner, themselves, and sometimes both. Sustained connection and trust fluctuate from moment to moment, as each interaction is filtered through an unconscious prism of anxiety and fear of abandonment—or worse. They will become suspicious, hypersensitive to lapses of attunement, and always remain vigilant for clues of distraction, disinterest, and infidelity by their partner. Trivial events, such as a partner showing up late for dinner, can affirm a core belief of betrayal and trigger dysregulation and emotional regression. This extreme insecurity, in one or both partners, can turn what feels like a rich, healthy connection one second into a bleak battlefield the next.

A perpetual search for red flags from the beginning of a relationship provides a conceptual escape hatch to cope with the fear of a sense of ever-approaching abandonment. This form of emotional defense leads to serial relationships with consistent patterns of connection, dysregulation, and separation. The insecurely attached couple will come to therapy complaining of the exhausting and repetitive nature of their arguments. What they often fail to understand is that no progress can be made without the participation of all three executive systems: insight into the regressive memories and emotions getting evoked in the relationship (ES3), an application of problem-solving ability to alter ways of interacting (ES2), and the ability to regulate and inhibit negative emotions during interactions (ES1).

First Executive: Contributions and Challenges

Early in life, the neural networks responsible for our emotional regulation and our feelings about others are shaped by our interactions with our caretakers. This ability, commonly described as affect regulation, allows us to feel safe in proximity to, and in states of intimacy with, others. These networks come to serve as a foundation for the psychological, emotional, and behavioral aspects of our attachment schema that influence our subsequent relationships. As our cortex develops, they inform our beliefs about ourselves, the world, and the future. As a result, they influence our perception, expectations, and conscious attitudes, solidifying the intimate connection between emotion and cognition.

Affect regulation and secure attachment allow for warmth, nurturance, and freedom from abandonment anxiety. There is also the expectation of being seen and understood, the ability to trust, and the assumption of being trusted. In secure attachment, partners are innocent until proven guilty and experience one another as the same kind of safe emotional havens as their own parents. This state of brain and mind supports the development and integration of our executive systems in ways that support coherent narratives and effective communication. Individuals who have secure attachment demonstrate lower anxiety levels and a larger window of stress tolerance, and are better able to stay cortical (keep ES2 and ES3 uninhibited) when under stress.

Failures of first executive development combined with an insecure attachment schema result in a sense of fear, uneasiness, and hypervigilance. This chronic emotional dysregulation leads to the use of defenses such as projection, withdrawal, blame, and hostility. Another negative consequence is the ongoing disruption of the development and integration of the second and third systems. This results in deficits in problem-solving, reality testing, social intelligence, and a coherent sense of self.

Remaining vigilant for outside threats leaves these clients to neglect the building of a solid inner world and the development of a sense of safety and autonomy. If one or both individuals in a relationship has this state of brain and mind, there is usually an ongoing power struggle to get the other to be the safe haven. Little progress can be made until the hyperarousal in the first executive system is identified and modulated, so that the second and third executive systems can become part of the therapy.

Second Executive: Contributions and Challenges

The second executive embodies aspects of our conscious identity, intentions, and will. As such, it is the hub of our top-down oversight and control of our social interactions. The primary contributions of the second executive system to relationships center around an understanding and application of the rules of engagement, comprehensible communication, and the ability to think about what is being said, done, and felt by ourselves and our partner. The second executive provides us with the ability to think conceptually, logically, and pragmatically about the challenges we face and the strategies we employ. An important aspect of this is to take an objective look at our expectations of the other and see what is realistic versus a fantasy driven by early unfulfilled attachment needs.

The second executive provides us with the capability of bringing knowledge, judgment, and conscious memoires to bear during social interactions. But without adequate input from the other two systems, we are left to solve problems based on logic alone, a strategy that can leave a partner feeling emotionally distant and invisible. The second executive system is also involved in the recognition and inhibition of unhelpful and negative responses. As we've all experienced, it is important to know what not to say and when to remain silent. Feelings, thoughts, and words may arise in our minds, but monitoring them is essential for effective communication. This gatekeeping function is largely a combined effort of ES2 and ES3, requiring empathy, a theory of mind of the other (ES3), and communication strategies designed to have a specific impact (ES2).

The second system can also learn to identify potentially harmful behaviors, like stonewalling, defensiveness, and contempt, which limit connection. Because our experience is guided by the focus of our attention and the content of our thoughts, it guides our ability to make conscious choices about these internal processes. These choices include focusing on the qualities we appreciate about our partners and what we can do to enhance our connection.

The building blocks of good communication in a relationship include the ability to identify the important facets of our inner world and emotional states. Keeping our partner's feelings and perspective in mind, we then configure ways to express our wants, needs, and fears in a manner that our partner can hear and understand. We also learn the cues and communication style of our partner to ensure they are heard and respected. We also hold our partner's sensitivities and triggers in mind, avoiding them when we can. We then work together to find common ground among two subjective realities. Cognitive flexibility involves the essential skill of adapting to input from your partner and accepting their influence in mutual decision-making.

Failures of second executive development and integration (in addition to first system inhibition) include a lack of successful problem-solving, time management, budgeting, scheduling, and so on, which are involved in the functional aspects of running a household and raising a family. While these deficits are sometimes related to lower levels of intellectual functioning, they are more often tied to psychological defenses and personality traits.

Some clients have been deskilled by overinvolved parents who cannot tolerate the anxiety of separation or their children's failure. As young adults, they never had to learn how to plan a vacation, balance their accounts, or use a washing machine. Others learn that love is never having to do anything and see their partner as a replacement caregiver. In the opposite direction, overindexing on second system functioning—regardless of the cause—can lead to an emotional disconnection from others and turn a romantic relationship into a set of emotionless processes and obligations.

Third Executive: Contributions and Challenges

The third executive system provides us with the awareness and perspective we need to create the simultaneous experience of a separate self and an interdependent connection with a partner. This allows for the possibility of maintaining our own preferences, values, and autonomy while also living within a relationship with shared meanings, rituals, and goals. This is commonly called having and maintaining boundaries. Mental time travel, imagining a joint future, and creating a narrative of the future are other third system contributions to a successful and sustained relationship. These imagined futures scaffold us through time and assist in the many transitions that occur over the course of our lives.

When it comes to relationships, the most important contributions of the third executive are our ability to imagine the mind—our partner's and our own. This allows us to shuttle back and forth between the two and experience a sense of shared presence. These are the golden moments of intimacy that make us feel connected and safe in the relationship and solid within ourselves. The ability to share a resonant state of body and mind with a partner, especially in moments of intensity, is perhaps the strongest glue of a relational bond. The ability to go within, come to know yourself, and share that with a partner can be another powerful element of bonding. The third executive system appears to be a central contributor for many of these deeper aspects of relationships.

Failures of third system development and integration (in addition to first system inhibition) result in deficits in self-awareness, empathic attunement, and imagination. This often results in a person who is externally oriented, rule driven, and fairly unidimensional in their relationship with life. They may notice that they don't have the same reactions as others and don't enjoy many of the things that seem to make others happy. It is difficult for them to identify what is happening in their bodies and to label their feelings. Their relationships will be governed by doing the right things and keeping their agreements. They will often report that they say they love their spouse and children but doubt that they really know what love is. Interventions with these folks, if they are interested and motivated, should focus on learning to pay attention to their bodies, develop language to describe their experience, and, with your guidance, build an inner imaginal space. The more these limitations are based on a lack of experience and practice, the more likely they will be able to be cultivated in adulthood.

Executive System Interactions in Relationships

We love life, not because we are used to living,
but because we are used to loving.

—Friedrich Nietzsche

No couple is immune to conflict or seemingly unsolvable differences, like temperament, parenting styles, or challenging in-laws. What sets successful couples apart is not the number of problems they face but how they respond to them. They rise to these challenges by accessing high-level EF skills such as the ability to find meaning and connection in the challenges they share and the maturity to forgive. During conflict, the dynamic integration of their executive systems allows them to maintain a sense of warmth and levity while communicating hurt feelings or experiencing difficult truths. Although we can discuss the contribution of each executive system separately, successful relationships require the involvement and dynamic balance of all three systems.

There are specific synergies among pairs of our executive systems that allow for the emergence of collaborative abilities. For example, the ability to create a safe inner world relies on the imaginative capacities of the third executive in collaboration with the affect regulation of the first. Storytelling, journaling, and many of the skills we learn in therapy focused on better affect regulation can support and build high-level system integration. This occurs in couples therapy when each person shares their thoughts, feelings, and hopes for the relationship. This shared narrative provides the common ground that both can contribute to, learn from, and refer back to when they lose their way.

When we work in therapy to uncover unhealthy relational patterns and develop ways of altering them, we rely on the self-awareness and autobiographical memories of our third executive system while enlisting the

TABLE 15.1

Three System Neurodynamics

First and Second Executive System Collaboration (Amygdala-P-FIT Integration)
The ability to be conscious of, label, and discuss feelings
The ability to remember and use relaxation techniques to lower arousal
The ability to consciously recognize increases in arousal and remember to employ potential strategies
The ability to receive negative feedback, criticism, and therapeutic interpretations without regression
First and Third System Collaboration (Amygdala-DMN Integration)
The capacity to be alone: creating a safe inner world
The ability to tolerate the natural cycle of rupture and repair in relationships
Wholeheartedness: the ability to be authentic and vulnerable with others
Self-esteem: feeling worthy of loyalty, love, and respect
The ability to maintain a positive attitude when facing specific challenges and to have an optimistic outlook for the future
The ability to make favorable interpretations of partner's undesirable behavior
Second and Third System Collaboration (P-FIT-DMN Integration)
The ability to combine self-awareness with problem-solving abilities to employ new ways of thinking, feeling, and behaving
The ability to combine information and empathy to provide another with wisdom
The ability to combine memories to uncover patterns that lead to insight

DMN, default mode network; Parietal-Frontal Intelligence Theory problem-solving skills of the second. The fact that we are so good at see-ing our partner's problems, and so bad at seeing our own, demonstrates a functional dissociation of ES2 and ES3. Attachment to the projection we use in our relationships is the enemy of both empathy and self-insight. In fact, if we reflect on the complaints about our partners, we can often find truths about ourselves. When couples therapy is successful, we learn to use the collaboration of the second and third executive systems to reframe ourselves from vulnerable individuals to half of a partnership. See Table 15.1 for more examples.

Optimal EF includes our cognitive, emotional, social, and self-reflective capacities. The optimism and positive emotional tone allowed by a well-developed first executive system frees the second to prioritize prosocial thoughts and behaviors, while the third orchestrates the flow of aware-ness, attunement, and interconnectedness. From this state of being, we are able to observe, pause, and respond thoughtfully in high-stress moments because we have optimal access to our cortical processing. It is within this state of mind that we can see and accept our strengths and weaknesses, lapses of care and compassion for others, and achieve the ability to apol-ogize and atone for hurtful behavior.

This high level of neurodynamic integration allows us to turn to our partners for emotional support and share in decision-making while main-taining a sense of our own integrity and identity. Wisdom in a relationship includes an appreciation of the other's perspective, curiosity about their thoughts and feelings, and compassion for their pain. It allows us to man-age conflict while remaining connected, have the vulnerability to express our anger, and keep the rules of engagement in mind even when emotionally activated. And finally, it allows us to keep our own needs in mind while balancing them with the needs of our partners.

Clinical Applications

All happy families are alike; each family is unhappy in its own way.
—Leo Tolstoy

Tolstoy's oft-quoted first line from *Anna Karenina* is as popular as it is wrong. Happy and unhappy families can exhibit many patterns of behavior and a variety of reasons for their satisfaction or discontent. There are some patterns we can detect, but reducing relational dysfunction to categories always ends up glossing over unique qualities of the couple that could be clues to important exploration and greater satisfaction. Many issues that lead couples to seek therapy—explosive anger, emotional withdrawal, workaholism, possessiveness, and so on—can be framed in the context of deficits of development and integration of one or more executive systems. There are countless configurations in which a couple's six executive systems can come together in a relationship. They can also change patterns of interaction based on different situations, states of mind, and stages of life.

The benefit to a case conceptualization from an EF perspective, versus a pathology/diagnosis model, is that it provides neural correlates, historical attachment antecedents, specific skill deficits, and multiple pathways of intervention for both individuals and couples. What we are going to discuss here are some common patterns of behavior that can help you see what areas your couples may be struggling with as individuals and as a unit. Sometimes treatment will require a period of individual therapy to heal some aspects of unresolved attachment trauma. Perhaps both partners may need to develop skills around communication and the establishment of boundaries. Other times, one or both partners need to build a healthy inner world so that they don't overrely on their partner to regulate their emotions for them. Often, there may be a combination of work in all three systems.

The reason the first executive system is the first place to look when it comes to relational problems is because adult relationships rest upon the foundation of childhood relationships, attachment schema, hurtful memories, and abandonment fears. These are all stored in the first executive and lie in wait like land mines to blow up the most mundane interaction into a conflict. This is why couples are so often embarrassed to report that their fights are about nothing; loading the dishwasher wrong, leaving the cap off the toothpaste, or not making the bed. On the surface, these things are nothing. It's what triggers the first executive system that is the problem; memories of being disrespected, disregarded, or abandoned. When the painful memories are substituted for the triggering incident, their emotions make complete sense, and the deep wound they carry becomes revealed.

Gottman's Four Horsemen and Executive Functioning

Admit when you're wrong. Shut up when you're right.

—John Gottman

When working with couples, patterns of negative interactions often reflect the ways in which one or both partners were treated as children. These patterns often contain fragments of both partners' early relationships, sometimes as the child they were, other times as an identification with the parents who caused them anxiety or pain. Many clients specifically express the conscious desire to free themselves from their past and break the cycle of intergenerational conflict they witnessed in their parents' and grandparents' relationships. Unfortunately, the reflexive emotional reactions they experience in intimate relationships lead them to reenact the very interactions they are attempting to escape from.

This paradoxical relationship between our heads and hearts results from a dissociation between the implicit emotional memories that trigger the first executive system and the conscious, rational wishes organized in and articulated by the second and third systems. While our head may know that we are in a safe place with the right person, closeness, intimacy, and dependency may trigger our amygdala and fill us with fear. Early fears of abandonment emerge so intensely that they completely eclipse the realities of our present life. Becoming aware of the tendency to repeat our early experiences in later relationships can provide both partners with increased insight into how they might be contributing to negative interactions.

Unfortunately, our adult relationships are full of opportunities for intrusive thoughts stemming from our early attachment experiences. When these early implicit memories are positive, they serve to make us feel safer, more trusting, and comfortably vulnerable. On the other hand, when unconscious negative emotions are activated, we index on our partner's flaws, negative intentions, and infidelities. Emotions related to shame and abandonment are among the most powerful we ever experience. When they occur, our minds will search for the reasons why we are feeling so threatened. In the absence of real evidence, our minds will create it; humans have a need to know why things happen. Even when we are wrong, we believe we are right.

Based in his clinical research of relational dynamics, John Gottman

(2019) and his associates have identified four interpersonal stances that are statistically correlated with divorce. These dynamics are defensive reactions to the fears of rejection, shame, and abandonment stored in the implicit memory networks of the first executive. They call these predictors the Four Horsemen of the Apocalypse: criticism, defensiveness, stonewalling, and contempt.

Criticism is an attack on a partner's personality or character; *defensiveness* is reflected in reversing blame as a way to avoid accountability; *stonewalling* (or the silent treatment) is a protective withdrawal from conflict, and *contempt* is a deliberate attempt to harm, insult, or shame the other. We can see within these negative interactions the reflections of the insecure attachment that formed them. They embody both the defensive reactions of the child in the adult and the memories of how they were treated by caretakers. In adult relationships, they become both the victim and victimizer.

As an antidote to first executive amygdala activation (which drives the Four Horsemen), Gottman suggests specific coping skills designed to counteract each of them. These methods, which leverage the second and third system capabilities, have been used successfully by clinicians and couples across many forms of relational therapy for the last half-century. Here are examples of each: As an antidote to criticism, use "I" statements to express a positive need instead of a negative statement about a partner. "You never take out the trash—you're lazy!" becomes, "I feel supported when you take out the trash."

As an antidote to defensiveness, take responsibility for your actions, acknowledge your partner's point of view, and apologize for any negative impact it has had on them. As an antidote to stonewalling, be aware of when you are hyperaroused, take a break from the interaction, and engage in self-soothing: "I feel myself shutting down a bit. Can we take a break and plan to talk about this again after we put the kids down?" As an antidote to contempt, work on creating a culture of appreciation and expressing gratitude. Work on increasing the ratio of positive to negative interactions every day.

It is important to note that individuals with disorganized attachment schema, borderline personality disorder, or other severe psychiatric disorders may be unable to employ cortically organized strategies for change. For these clients, first system activation can be too powerful to be counteracted, and the perceptual and cognitive distortions central to these disorders will add to their difficulties in feeling safe with their partner and developing a strong enough therapeutic alliance.

Not all couples will benefit from any or all of these strategies, but many of them will. The deciding factor is the balance of influence between the first executive and the combined strength of the second and third systems. Can you stay present and attuned to one another as tensions rise? Are you able to enlist your imagination and problem-solving abilities, even when the fear of abandonment gets triggered during an argument? This is challenging work even with the most compatible couples, though it does become easier with time, practice, and reflection. The more each of us are able to embrace our minds, hearts, and bodies, the better we become at supporting each of these things in others.

Part VI

Special Topics

Chapter 16

The Impact of Screens on Executive Functioning

We can never attain peace in the outer world
until we make peace with ourselves.

—The Dalai Lama

The human brain is in the process of adapting to a major environmental shift. We aren't referring to climate change, but rather to a rapid change in how we interface with the world and the people around us—digital technology. In just one generation, all aspects of life have been saturated with the presence of screens and global connectivity. Technology, with its unparalleled efficiency and gleaming innovation, has become the preferred landscape for everything from going to work and finding a date, to going to the bank and filing our taxes. These changes have necessitated the collective increasing of our screen time, computer literacy, and the replacement of face-to-face interaction with online platforms. By 2018, a quarter of adults and nearly half of adolescents reported that they were online "almost constantly" (Anderson & Jiang, 2018; Perrin & Jiang, 2018). As a result, our executive functioning has had to adapt to this new digital ecosystem to better meet its demands.

Our goal in this chapter is to explore the impact of screen use on the development and functioning of each of our executive systems as well as the effect it has on the way they communicate, cooperate, and work against one another. As both technology users and clinicians, the ubiquity of screens makes understanding their conscious and subliminal impact on the brain and mind relevant to an understanding of optimal EF. We know that our screens, the content they carry, and the algorithms driving them are designed to keep us clicking, swiping, and liking through our entire waking lives. In our new "attention economy," our screen time is monetized for the benefit of the owners and advertisers of the sites we visit. We also know that a great deal of time has been spent to determine how best to manipulate our attention, emotions, and biochemistry in order to maximize engagement.

Although research into the short- and long-term impact of screens is still in its infancy, we are beginning to see its effects on our emotional regulation, our attentional abilities, and how we engage in relationships. We are witnessing these changes in the consulting room, the classroom, and in our homes. Digital connectivity appears to have benefited some populations, including the elderly, those with limited mobility, and others in remote places who now have access to education, medical care, and previously inaccessible goods and supplies. However, the dark side of this technology is its relationship to higher levels of anxiety, depression, and dissatisfaction, as well as the deliberate spreading of misinformation and propaganda. The reality is, screens aren't going anywhere, and it's up to us to figure out how to use them so they don't use us.

Using the three-system model, we will outline the ways in which each executive system can be impacted by screen use and some of the signs and symptoms of excessive and even detrimental use. We will also explore how the strengths of each system can be leveraged to counterbalance the addictive strategies of the algorithms designed to hijack our attention. Our goal should be to remember to use screens as tools rather than escape strategies, tranquilizers, or distractions from real life.

The Impact of Screens: First Executive System

> *There are only two industries that call their consumers*
> *"users": illegal drugs and software.*
>
> —Edward Tufte

The first executive is our salience network, processing and responding to external and internal stimuli well ahead of our conscious awareness. As we go about our day, our amygdala dutifully maintains its post as our security guard, scanning our inner and outer environments for emotionally relevant information. While this ancient alarm evolved to help our ancestors survive in a harsh and dangerous world, it is now activated by email notifications, salacious headlines, and likes on Instagram. The algorithms know about this primitive alarm system and keep creating new ways to recapture your attention if you happen to look away from your screen. When our phones ring, buzz, or vibrate, ES1 orients our attention to them and away from our social and physical (analog) world.

The constant triggering of our orienting response and amygdala activation stimulates autonomic arousal and activates our flight/fight/freeze system. Of course there is no actual danger to deal with. However, this constant low-level activation of the amygdala and autonomic nervous system increases adrenaline and cortisol while also decreasing other neurochemicals like serotonin that help us to feel safe and calm. This chronic activation can manifest as agitation or anger (fight), distraction and avoidance (flee), emotional shutdown (freeze), and/or excessive social monitoring (fawn). While we consciously know that a notification isn't a threat, many of us are familiar with the anxiety we experience until we're able to check it (What if this call is an emergency, or the email is from our boss?).

Getting sucked into the internet is not a character flaw, but a by-product of ES1's vulnerability to the addictive strategies of the attention economy. If we rely on the internet for our social connection, entertainment, and emotional regulation, the salience network can become hijacked by the algorithms instead of working to serve our well-being. This is likely why consistent screen use is correlated with a decrease in important EF abilities such as inhibition, emotional control, self-monitoring, and task monitoring (Tang et al., 2018). It's important to note that the age of exposure may be an important factor. A longitudinal study found that screen time at the age of two was associated with lower self-regulation at four (Cliff et al., 2018). Another reported that exposure to child-directed screen content was unrelated to EF, while exposure to adult-directed content seemed to impair it (Barr et al., 2010).

When we can't pry ourselves away from mindlessly scrolling, engaging in debates online, or watching an endless stream of YouTube videos, our attention has been hijacked. The amygdala keeps us locked in because it thinks that monitoring these "threats" is keeping us safe. We aren't fully aware of being in this state until we come out on the other side and look at how much time has passed. The term "mindless scrolling" is particularly accurate because ES2 and ES3 are partially inhibited during these times. Our higher-order abilities haven't been lost, but it may feel that way when the salience network is monitoring the environment for threat.

An additional issue is that online content is designed to grab our attention through negative and sensationalistic content. Because our primitive alarm system doesn't distinguish well between real and imagined threats, it is constantly being activated. Seeing images of danger, violence, and war set off a similar sequence of emotions, bodily sensations, and chemical reactions as if we were experiencing it ourselves. To make matters worse, there isn't much we can do about most of it. We're constantly exposed to the pain of the world and left to ruminate about it. A continuous feed of tragedies, crimes, accidents, conspiracies, and propaganda create a blanket of fear. If we don't limit our exposure to distressing content, we can experience vicarious traumatization and compassion fatigue, and develop extremist worldviews. This process has already converted our political discourse into an endless tribal warfare.

The stress resulting from negative media further drives us to seek distraction and numbing from our devices. Feeling overwhelmed compels us to watch kitten videos or play video games to leave the world behind, turning our devices into subpar coping machines. In our modern world, moments of stillness and quiet are a rarity and can trigger anxiety and uncomfortable feelings we have been avoiding. Since our devices are often within reach, we grab them to avoid the possibility that anxiety will invade our consciousness. This cycle of being triggered, distracting ourselves, and avoiding feelings can lead to narrowed focus, isolation, and negative mental health outcomes.

Overall, the impact of screens on ES1 is to decrease our ability to self-regulate, which, in turn, decreases cognitive functioning and behavioral control. We propose that first executive overactivation, and the related inhibition of the second and third executives, are the neurological underpinnings of the depression, anxiety, and perceived stress associated with problematic smartphone usage (Sohn et al., 2019). In order to mitigate these harmful effects, we must downregulate the anxiety responses of the first executive so that our second and third executive stay actively engaged during our screen usage. Keeping the first executive in neurodynamic balance with the other systems makes it possible for us to stay in mindful control of our use of screens.

The Impact of Screens: Second Executive System

Once I was a scuba diver in a sea of words. Now I
zip along the surface like a guy on a jet ski.

—Nicholas Carr

Like the brain as a whole, each of our executive systems evolved to adapt to the people, places, and things around us. From the first days of life, our nervous system is interfacing with all aspects of our environment to learn how to best leverage it for survival. This is how the structures of our brain come to be a reflection of our learning history, from our attachment schema, to the languages we speak, to how we hold a spoon. Screens, as a central focus of our daily lives, are now a ubiquitous presence from early childhood. Those of us born in the previous century have vague memories of things like daydreaming, free time, and boredom. In a purely analog world, things come slower, one at a time, and must be sought out. You had to walk to the store to buy a book or flowers for the garden, and you would have conversations with people along the way. For the past two decades, ES2 has had to adapt to changes in the quality, nature, and delivery of the information we receive, process, and respond to.

The brain's successful adaptation to modern life has allowed us to simultaneously navigate social media, multiple messaging platforms, work and school, gaming, shopping, and keeping up with the news. At the same time, research shows that consistent screen use is correlated with decreases in important EF abilities including initiation, planning, organization, and working memory (Tang et al., 2018). Multitasking has replaced sustained attention, the cloud has replaced the need to store memories, and information is delivered instead of having to actively explore the environment to seek it out. These changes have reshaped ES2 and our mental models of the world and our place with in it.

Information Overload

Before the total penetration of screens into our lives, we had to actively pursue information that might be relevant to us. We would read the newspaper front to back to find out what was happening in the world, go to the library and forage the stacks for needed materials for a paper, or even talk to our neighbors. The bulk of our mental activity was purposeful, self-directed, and goal-driven. Technology has now become the primary tool through which we are fed information. Our devices flood us with content that may or may not be relevant to our lives. When our attention strays away from them, we're signaled by the sounds and vibrations of push notifications to remind us to get back on our screens. The process of being overloaded with information makes it nearly impossible to completely close ourselves off to the digital world. As a consequence, we have less time to both generate and contemplate our own ideas and opinions.

Memory

The infinite memory of the internet is a great boon for those with bad memories and, perhaps, the researchers who benefit from global searches for obscure information. For the rest of us, it is replacing the need to remember much of anything. Why remember information like phone numbers, important dates in history, or the words of a song when they are all available to you in seconds? It must be good to have all of this information at our fingertips—or is it? A heavy internet user may struggle with rote memory due to an atrophy of certain memory networks but develop an exceptional ability to track down the information they need online.

Like most neural systems, we have them on a use-it-or-lose-it contract. If we don't use something, our bodies redirect our metabolic resources to other areas that do get used. For example, when an individual loses their sight, visual areas of the cortex can be rededicated to other sensory and motor activities. Before GPS, taxi drivers in London had significantly larger hippocampi adapted for the navigational demands of their job. We doubt this is any longer the case. At what point does the outsourcing of memory impede our ability to think? After all, memory is the content of our thinking and an in-depth analysis of any subject requires a robust memory of the applicable information, strategies, and structures of thought. A significant question we face is what happens to the content of our thinking if we are outsourcing our memories to our devices? Can we think better with less memory storage, or will we come to rely on artificial intelligence to articulate the thoughts we used to be capable of generating?

Multitasking Versus Sustained Attention

While multitasking has always existed as one aspect of our attentional abilities, it has become the norm, as demonstrated by the frequency of our attention shifting. In a study looking at time spent on different media sources, switching occurred as frequently as every 19 seconds, with 75% of all screen content viewed for less than one minute (Peng et al., 2018). Even short-term activity within a hyperlinked environment has been shown to reduce sustained attentional abilities (Firth et al., 2019). In addition, sustained media multitasking has been associated with decreased gray matter in our prefrontal regions involved in maintaining goals and inhibiting distractions (Loh & Kanai, 2014).

The emerging research suggests that our brains are adapting both structurally and behaviorally to screens. We have exchanged self-directed attention in favor of responding to what the algorithm presents to us. It seems that we also remain ever vigilant for alternative stimuli (previously known as distractions) to orient ourselves to. As evidence of this, the mere presence of our phone decreases our attentional capacity. Research suggests that when our devices are nearby we remain vigilant for a notification that we might be missing something, and it actually requires mental energy to *not* pick it up (Ward et al., 2017). What is called attention deficit disorder in the analog world is actually the most adaptive state of brain and mind within a screen-based ecosystem. When our executive systems are shaped in this way, it becomes extremely difficult for us to focus on a single thing for a sustained amount of time. We become frightened by boredom, and the absence of distraction fills us with anxiety.

The Impact of Screens: Third Executive System

> *We are engaged in a struggle for the center of our lives—*
> *how we think and feel. When you're scrambling all*
> *the time, your inner life becomes scrambled.*
> —William Power

As we have discussed, ES3 provides us with the foundation of a number of skills and abilities essential for successful executive functioning. Its cognitive contributions appear to allow us to synthesize our inner and outer worlds, creating a cohesive and unified experience of self. This creates the potential for building a safe inner world, developing our imagination, and experimenting with invention and creativity. Its social-emotional contributions allow us to link with the group mind via thoughts (theory of mind), emotions (attunement), and our primitive collective instincts. The third executive is built through the experience of face-to-face interactions and during quiet moments of quiescence and reflection. Relationships throughout life regulate our internal chemistry (sociostasis) and provide us with learning through imitation (mirroring), and memories of others (inner objects) provide emotional security when we are alone.

Because so much of the development and maintenance of ES3 is experience dependent, environmental changes that impact our connections with others, level of distraction, and time spent in self-reflection will shape its growth and functional abilities. Living online appears to have resulted in many changes, including (1) fewer face-to-face interactions, (2) distortions of social comparison, and (3) the conflict between distraction, inner experience, and imagination.

Face-to-Face Interactions

The human brain is a social organ, and relationships have been our natural habitat throughout evolution. As social creatures, we rely on our interactions and emotional bonds with others to regulate our biology, support our identity, and reinforce our sense of safety and well-being. One of the most consistent findings in epidemiology research is the positive correlations among the size of our analog social network, our physical health, and longevity. Few would doubt that screens have resulted in less face-to-face interactions and may even compromise the quality of the time we do spend with others. In fact, a study demonstrated that the presence of a mobile phone during an interaction decreased the quality of conversation, lessened empathic concern, and lowered levels of friendliness (Misra et al., 2014). Based on other research, the mere presence of a phone splits our attention with vigilance for what we might be missing. This likely results in at least a partial inhibition of ES3 functioning.

We have yet to learn whether an extended online community has the same beneficial effects as has been found for face-to-face interactions. As the ratio of online to face-to-face interactions has increased, however, we have noticed a number of changes in clients' behaviors and attitudes about social engagement, especially in adolescents and young adults. It may be that as we adapt to the predictability and sense of control we experience in online environments, face-to-face connections become more anxiety provoking.

Research has shown that direct eye contact activates amygdala arousal but this response lessens with time spent together and increased familiarity. Decreased exposure actually increases the likelihood of the amygdala associating face-to-face interactions with threats. This would motivate us to stay within an online environment, causing subsequent declines in social skills and increases in social anxiety. If face-to-face interactions are, in actuality, more beneficial to our psychological and emotional well-being, the shift to online connection may play a role in the current increases in anxiety, depression, and pessimism.

It is likely that the combination of chronic arousal (ES1) and consistent distractions (ES2) inhibits the development and activation of ES3, explaining why "internet addicted" adolescents showed volumetric decreases in some of its neural structures (Wang et al., 2017). Could this contribute to the growing number of online trolls and commenters who act without empathy or compassion? Would these individuals behave the same way in face-to-face interactions, or if their social lives weren't online? On screens, the "other" is reduced to a name, button, or avatar, providing no physiological feedback, bodily cues, or sociostatic information for ES3 to interpret and respond to. The absence of this kind of social-emotional information may make it more difficult to access our humanity and inner feelings, making the internet fertile ground for misplaced anger and cyberbullying.

Distorted Social Comparison

Online versus face-to-face relationships have a number of important differences. When we know someone in real life, we experience them across various moods, situations, and states of mind. They succeed, fail, struggle, and occasionally lose control, just like the rest of us. By contrast, we experience the people we know via social media through filters, constructed narratives, and an array of identity management strategies. Without real-life experiences to balance these online presentations, we are prone to accept them as real people. Much worse, we run the risk of comparing our real life to these curated presentations, resulting in a chronic state of negative self-comparison. The influencers who peddle extravagant lifestyles on social media create the illusion that wealth and beauty are not only attainable, they're the norm (and what we should all aspire to). These unrealistic expectations can result in (or exacerbate) anxiety and depression as well as poor body image, low self-esteem, and pessimism about the future.

For many, the process of identity formation is now played out via posts on social media, with our online profile coming to represent our virtual identity. Each image we choose to share represents a memory or experience we have decided is worthy of who we would like to think we are. These images are then posted for public viewing and appraisal, to be liked or ignored. Seems innocent enough, until you talk to individuals whose moods and self-esteem are shaped by every response to their posts. Further, the popularity of what we post can even affect how our memories of these experiences are reconsolidated in autobiographical memory (Firth et al., 2019). A lack of positive feedback on social media could skew an originally positive memory to a negative one associated with shame and embarrassment. This likely also occurs in face-to-face relationships, but personally shared experiences are far less public and are unavailable for anonymous abusive feedback.

Distraction and Imagination

One of the more interesting and innovative abilities to arise from human evolution is our capacity for self-reflection and imagination. When our executive systems are working properly, they provide us with the possibility of a safe withdrawal from the demands of the external world. When we are daydreaming—traveling through time and space to other eras and places—we become freed from our immediate limitations, and our possibilities are limited only by what we are willing and capable of thinking about. This state is responsible for many of the discoveries and innovations that have marked technological, scientific, and artistic accomplishments through history and across cultures.

The lack of engagement with an external focus can trigger a sense of anxiety and/or boredom. Some run from boredom to avoid the emotional discomfort, while others are able to become absorbed into it, transcend their concerns, and use it as the ground for self-knowledge and using their imagination. The capacity to be alone and the ability to remain in a quiet state are both aspects of emotional development that Donald Winnicott identified as important for a sense of security and centeredness in the self. Addiction to unending stimulation can hinder the development of these important abilities. Without establishing a sense of self that is separate from the external world, we become vulnerable to manipulation and less capable of evaluating the quality of the information that constantly bombards us.

Boredom is a term often used to describe an uncomfortable or negative feeling that occurs in the absence of involvement with an external activity we find interesting or engaging. Intermittent feelings of boredom (state boredom) can trigger the motivation to explore the environment, think of something interesting to do, or engage in creative thought. Recognizing and utilizing states of boredom are aspects of EF that demonstrate affect regulation, self-control, and a sense of personal efficacy. Learning to see opportunity in boredom is an important aspect of self-direction.

For others, boredom, apathy, and a lack of motivation are a consistent experience (trait) and appear to be an aspect of their personality. Some researchers have found a correlation between chronic boredom, often associated with ADHD, and lower than normal dopamine activity, resulting in a diminished experience of the anticipation of reward. These individuals may be significantly more susceptible to internet addiction (IA), where attention shifting is constant with little delay of gratification.

Differential Susceptibility

Nothing vast enters the life of mortals without a curse.

—Sophocles

The power of our devices to attract, engage, and trap us is truly impressive. The social engineers behind the platforms we use have purposefully closed the gap between stimulus and response to the point where there is minimal room for self-reflection, conscious consideration, and the ability to access free will. They have accomplished this by constantly activating ES1, thus inhibiting the power of ES2 and ES3 to pause, reflect, and engage in mindful screen use. The results of three large surveys of adolescents in two countries found that light users of digital media (< 1 hour/day) reported substantially better psychological well-being than heavy users (> 5 hours/

day), who reported higher levels of anxiety, depression, loneliness, and suicidality (Twenge & Campbell, 2019).

While some of us are able to use screens as a tool and maintain our sense of autonomy and self-control, there are many others who are vulnerable to an addictive relationship with the many ways to be online. A reasonable parallel may be drinking alcohol; some of us can drink in moderation for our entire lives and never become alcoholics, while others are not so fortunate. There are many thoughts about what makes for this differential susceptibility to addiction, and we are only at the beginning of an understanding of addiction to the internet. Some individuals do appear to be more vulnerable than others to the negative effects of internet overuse.

Some correlations with screen overuse—sleep disturbance, obesity, and decreasing social contact—could naturally result in decreased cognitive abilities, physical activity, and time spent with others. Other correlations, such as increases in depression, anxiety, and suicidality, are more disturbing and a bit more difficult to understand. As clinicians, we are not only interested in how the internet impacts our clients, but also which of our clients are more susceptible to internet addiction and why.

Variables being discussed in the literature to explain differential susceptibility include psychological constructs such as personality, introversion, developmental stage, ego strength, and resilience. Other possibilities are isolation, lack of social support, transient stressors, and life circumstances. All of these are reasonable and probably apply to some of us and our clients. For others, emotional dysregulation, depression, anxiety, and suicidality may be preexisting risk factors that become exacerbated by excessive or problematic screen use.

Imagine two different adults scrolling the same social media content. Sarah has good coping skills, a strong support system, and a well-developed sense of self. As she scrolls through pictures of happy couples on vacation, she smiles and maintains an objective view of what she sees. After 30 minutes, she decides to close her computer and meet a friend to play tennis. Sam, on the other hand, is struggling with depression and in the midst of a difficult divorce. The same pictures of happy couples remind him of enjoyable times with his soon-to-be ex-wife. He soon gets lost as the algorithms guide him to football gambling sites, new Ford trucks, and a documentary about World War II. The hours go by without him noticing, and he is surprised when he looks up to find that his apartment is now dark. For Sarah, viewing the same images confirms her feeling of being worthy and lovable, while they result in the opposite feelings in Sam. Although the initial content was identical, differing personal traits, life circumstances, and time spent online produced starkly contrasting emotional reactions.

Internet Addiction

None of the most powerful tech companies answer to
what's best for people, only to what's best for them.
                                —Tristan Harris

Internet addiction (IA) may be present when screen time impacts one's thinking, feeling, and behavior to the detriment of their psychosocial well-being. Although IA is not a recognized mental disorder as of this writing, mental health professionals have widely acknowledged the negative consequences of excessive internet use and parallels to the negative consequences of substance abuse (Taherdoost, 2022). Anxiety, depression, loneliness, hostility, and aggression have been associated with IA. Consequences of IA also include sleep disturbance, inattention, and distractibility, as well as decreases in social, academic, and occupational functioning (Chaudhari et al., 2015). In IA, the duration of time spent online detracts from essential analog activities, such as physical activities and face-to-face interactions (Jiang, 2014).

The role of impaired EF in pathological screen use is supported by recent findings which suggest that excessive internet use is associated with an imbalance in interactions among the salience network (ES1), frontal-parietal network (ES2), and default mode network (ES3) (Zhang & Bian, 2021). This evidence suggests that the neural underpinnings of addictive internet use involve a decrease in awareness and self-control provided by ES2 and ES3. Without these systems to modulate the arousal of ES1, we fall victim to the algorithms of the social engineers. It is a form of amygdala hijack where we are fooled into believing that our lives depend on staying connected. The more impulsive a client's online habits are, the more likely they have a preexisting susceptibility to IA, and the more likely they are to suffer its negative mental health outcomes.

Internet Use and Psychotherapy

What is addiction, really? It is a sign, a signal, a symptom of distress.
It is a language that tells us about a plight that must be understood.
                                                              —Alice Miller

We have gotten to the point where clinicians need to inquire about internet use, along with drugs, alcohol, and other potentially harmful behavior. Finding out about time spent on the internet and sites visited is fraught with the same difficulties as other potentially embarrassing activities we ask our clients about. Because the experience of time is easily distorted while online, it may be better to rely on apps that track our time and the sites we spend it on. We also need to assess whether the internet is a source of stress for our client, and if so, what kinds of stress? Are they overloaded by information or unable to resist watching hours of distressing and painful content on their newsfeed? Has this resulted in vicarious anxiety, panic, or trauma? Are they obsessed with curating their social media, hyperfocused on getting likes, or being cyberbullied? Some may feel pressure to be permanently and instantaneously available to respond to every text, message, email, and call.

Another important avenue of investigation is whether they are using screens as a way to cope with stress and regulate their emotions. For example, are they using screens to escape from a difficult home life, ostracism at work, or feelings they are struggling to understand, articulate, and manage? For many clients, screens may be both a source of stress and a means to escape. Both will need to be identified and dealt with accordingly.

Overall, once we have gained a holistic picture of the role that internet use plays in our clients' psychosocial functioning, we can tailor interventions that address the source of their challenges. For many clients who come to therapy, excessive or dysfunctional screen use amplifies deeper emotional issues and poor stress management. Given technology's ability to inhibit healthy EF, screen habits are an important lifestyle factor to consider in assessment. We can view screen-related anxiety, depression, lack of focus, low self-esteem, and relationship problems as disruptions in the development, integration, and functioning of the three executive systems.

First-step interventions for internet addiction can include creating conscious boundaries with devices such as the employment of schedules, time limits, taking apps off the home screen, keeping devices out of the bedroom, and so on. There are books and websites with suggestions for regulating screen use (e.g., Better Screen time, https://www.betterscreentime.com/resources/; and Center for Humane Technology, "Control Your Tech Use," https://www.humanetech.com/take-control). For those who are severely addicted due to entrenched habit patterns and unconscious physiological drives, a detox program or Internet and Technology Addicts Anonymous (https://internetaddictsanonymous.org/) could be beneficial.

Clinicians should also be aware that increasing screen time for some of our clients could have beneficial effects. This may be especially true for individuals who have mobility limitations or are isolated because of geographical factors or psychological challenges. Internet access for older individuals may increase their social connectivity and communication with family. Online games and exposure to news, videos, and entertainment can increase stimulation and may counterbalance some aspects of cognitive decline.

Chapter 17

Executive Dysfunction in Borderline Personality Disorder

We live in a rainbow of chaos.
—Paul Cézanne

The hallmarks of borderline personality disorder (BPD) are extreme and unpredictable emotional reactions along with conflictual and chaotic interpersonal relationships. Clients with BPD are characterized by (1) hypersensitivity to real or imagined abandonment, (2) disturbances of self-identity, (3) intense and unstable relationships, (4) alternating idealization and devaluation of themselves and others, and (5) compulsive, risky, and sometimes self-destructive behaviors. There are many ways in which the brains of those suffering with BPD differ from others', with disruptions across all three executive systems (Bazanis et al., 2002; Johnson et al., 2003). While most researchers and clinicians focus on its emotional and interpersonal symptoms, BPD highlights the interdependency of cognition, emotion, sociality, and self.

Individuals suffering from BPD spend their lives on an emotional roller coaster. They dive into anguish and pain, rising into brief periods of elation, only to plunge into a state of dread. When confronted with even a hint of criticism or rejection, they may experience intense shame, lash out at others, and harm themselves. Many of their symptoms stem from developmental disruptions of the first executive system, which in turn impedes the development and function of the other two. For example, traditional neuropsychological testing of patients with BPD has found deficits of attention, memory, and other aspects of cognitive processes (Coolidge et al., 2000; Dinn et al., 2004; Paris et al., 1999; Posner et al., 2002; Swirsky-Sacchetti et al., 1993; van Reekum et al., 1993). The resulting overall deficits in affect regulation, perception, information processing, and sense of self combine to create crippling deficits in all areas of executive functioning.

The range and severity of BPD symptoms has led it to be a projective test for a century of theorists. It has been alternatively described as a disorder of attachment, a variant of complex PTSD, a character pathology, and a sane reaction to an insane world. The term "borderline" is generally attributed to Freud, who was surprised to discover that clients who seemed neurotic outside of therapy decompensated into what appeared to be psychosis once engaged in the therapeutic process. The term "borderline" comes from his belief that these clients' mental state exists on the border between neurosis and psychosis. This understanding of BPD makes sense in the context of Freudian thought. Despite the many changes in our field and controversy concerning the legitimacy and usefulness of the diagnosis, the label has stuck to this day (Lewis & Grenyer, 2009).

Borderline personality disorder most likely stems from some combination of genetic vulnerabilities, early deficits in emotional regulation, and problematic attachment relationships. There is evidence of altered patterns of brain maturation during childhood, higher levels of childhood trauma, less parental care, and the presence of more dissociative symptoms when compared to other psychiatric diagnoses (Bazanis et al., 2002; Houston et al., 2005; Johnson et al., 2003; Machizawa-Summers, 2007; Sansone et al., 2004; Sar et al., 2006; Watson et al., 2006). A number of clinicians have made the case that what we call BPD is one developmental outcome of early unresolved trauma (Gunderson & Sabo, 1993; Herman, 1992; Hodges, 2003; Wingenfeld et al., 2011).

The Client: Angela

I accept chaos, I'm not sure whether it accepts me.

—Bob Dylan

Referred by her psychiatrist with a diagnosis of major depression, 42-year-old Angela entered therapy with an attitude of exhausted irritability. This presentation is not uncommon in those who have long struggled with a serious affective disorder while trying to navigate the mental health system. She sat down and looked at her therapist with the blank expression of someone who has long since grown weary of dealing with others. Her psychiatrist had reported emotional outbursts during their brief medication consults, which he found unusual among his depressed clients. Angela's therapist, Christine, did her best to make her feel comfortable in the consulting room.

In response to specific questions about her symptoms and day-to-day life, Angela shared brief monotone responses while mostly avoiding eye contact. It was one of those sessions when every minute feels like 10 for the therapist, and the room seems filled with tension and unexpressed emotions. Twenty or so minutes into the session, Angela looked up at Christine and noticed that she was jotting some notes on a pad sitting next to her chair. When Christine looked up, she was surprised to see a radically different Angela. Her slack expression had been replaced by a look of fierce anger—jaw clenched tight, muscles rippling under her reddened skin, Angela's eyes boring through her. Christine's expressions, first of shock, and then of concern, made no impression on Angela's frozen stare.

Attempting to recover her composure, Christine commented on the change in Angela's expression in as neutral a manner as possible. Silence followed her statement as Angela seemed physically and emotionally frozen in place. The therapist, struggling to regulate her own anxiety in the face of this silent confrontation, had an image come to mind. She was standing naked in front of an audience, giving a lecture, as the audience pointed and laughed at her. Her first association was that this image was tied to feeling exposed as incompetent by Angela's stare. She then wondered if this was what Angela might be feeling.

Angela finally burst out, "Do you think I'm a specimen, a bug, something you are studying under your microscope?" Before Christine could respond, she continued, "You are just like the rest of them—just because you have an office and a fancy degree, you look down at the rest of us as if we aren't worthy of your time." At this point Angela stood up and leaned over Christine. "What are you writing on your little pad? How crazy I am? How stupid I am? Well, let me tell you, you don't fool me one bit! I know you don't know what you're doing! You can't hide behind your ferns and your bullshit Crate and Barrel furniture." Angela walked over to the door, grabbed the knob, and opened it. "I've seen it all before, and it's all bullshit. You're all bullshit!" Once in the hall, Angela slammed the door as hard as she could, leaving the therapist alone, watching a painting fall to the floor.

Sitting still in her chair, Christine noticed the tension in her body, and her racing heart, as well as a sense of relief that Angela was gone. This was soon followed by the thoughts, "What just happened?" and "What should I do now?" Given the hyperactivation of the therapist's first executive, she realized that she was not mentally sharp right now and should focus on calming down for her next client. She reasoned that deeper reflections on the interaction should probably wait till the end of the day, after this emotional storm had passed. This is good executive functioning on the therapist's part, but what about Angela? What happens in the brains of clients with BPD that leads them to react to situations like this?

BPD and the Brain

Confusion is a word we have invented for an
order which is not understood.

—Henry Miller

Scores of research studies comparing people with and without BPD have found numerous differences in metabolic levels, size, and activation patterns across the neural networks of all three executive systems. With most clients, one or two of the executive systems are relatively intact, allowing us to leverage them in the service of addressing and working on another. Clients with BPD often lack a part of the self or a state of mind in which they are able to observe the self, making it impossible for the therapist to ally with the healthy part of the self to address the unhealthy impulses, thoughts, and emotions. In the three-system model, they have not experienced the kind of regulation of ES1 that would have allowed ES2 and ES3 to develop a self-reflective capacity and theory of mind. This is why traditional psychodynamic models are unable to enlist these brain systems in treatment. Cognitive behavioral therapy may also fail because of an absence of the observing self, which is needed to explore core beliefs and question irrational thoughts.

The decreased size of brain regions seen in clients with BPD is likely a consequence of a genetic vulnerability interacting with the chronic stress they experience as a result of the constant dysregulation of arousal. This chronic hyperarousal results in higher resting levels of adrenaline, cortisol, and frontal dopamine along with lower levels of serotonin (Hazlett et al., 2007; Lieb et al., 2004; Lyons-Ruth et al., 2011). This biochemical cocktail drives symptoms of anxiety, depression, and impulsivity, while creating a toxic internal environment for the brain, resulting in decreases in neuroplasticity, neuronal loss, and processing compromises (Leyton et al., 2001; Soloff et al., 2000). These neuronal losses are disproportionately concentrated in ES1 and ES2. See Table 17.1 for some of the brain regions found to be smaller in clients with BPD.

The chronic hyperarousal seen in individuals with BPD also results in the same neurodynamic pattern we see in anxiety disorders: first executive system hyperarousal, overactive salience network activation, and inhibited second and third executive system activation (Palaniyappan & Liddle,

TABLE 17.1
BPD and Neural Volume Reduction

Brain Region	Function
Frontal and prefrontal lobes[1]	Executive functioning and affect regulation
Amygdala[2]	Affect recognition and abandonment anxiety
Hippocampus[3]	Reality testing and short-term memory consolidation
Anterior cingulate cortex[4]	Integration of cognitive and emotional processing
Posterior cingulate cortex[5]	Sensory processing
Parietal cortex (right)[6]	Executive processing and somatic awareness
Corpus callosum (women)[7]	Integration of cognition and emotion

[1] Brambilla et al., 2004; Chanen et al., 2008; Lyoo et al., 1998. [2] Driessen et al., 2000; Schmahl et al., 2003; Weniger et al., 2009; Rüsch et al., 2003; Soloff et al., 2008; van Elst et al., 2003; [3] Brambilla et al., 2004; Driessen et al., 2000; Irle et al., 2005; Rodrigues et al., 2011; Schmahl et al., 2003, 2009; Soloff et al., 2008; van Elst et al., 2003; Weniger et al., 2009; Zetzsche et al., 2007. [4] Brambilla et al., 2004; Brunner et al., 2010; Goodman et al., 2011; Hazlett et al., 2005; Minzenberg et al., 2007; Whittle et al., 2009. [5] Hazlett et al., 2005. [6] Irle et al., 2005. [7] Rüsch et al., 2007.

2012; Shin et al., 2008; Thome et al., 2014). Although at rest these individuals are underaroused on measures of heart rate, skin conductance, and pain sensitivity, they show greater activation in the amygdala, prefrontal cortex, motor cortex, and temporal and occipital lobes when exposed to stressful stimuli (Bohus et al., 2000; de la Fuente et al., 1997; Herpertz et al., 2001; Johnson et al., 2003; Juengling et al., 2003; Salavert et al., 2011).

The Therapist: Christine

People seldom refuse help, if one offers it in the right way.
                                            —A. C. Benson

Angela's therapist, Christine, is aware of the neuroscience research on BPD. She knows that what she just experienced is Angela's attempt to navigate the world despite emotional dysregulation, chronic hyperarousal, and pervasive sensory and cognitive distortions. In other words, Angela is living a life with three disrupted and disrupting executive systems. Christine is also aware of the therapeutic approaches, such as dialectical behavior therapy (DBT), that have been developed specifically for BPD clients. Both of these frameworks are helpful in making her client's attack feel less personal. Christine has learned that when her body experiences fight/flight activation in reaction to an attack, she should let enough time pass for her body to return to normal before she moves forward in her work. These are examples of Christine applying each of her three executive systems—first, affect regulation; second, training, knowledge, problem-solving abilities, and experience; and third, theory of mind, perspective taking, self-awareness, and compassion—in her therapeutic role. There is never a good outcome when a therapist with poor EF tries to treat a client with BPD.

Now at the end of the day, Christine has the time and emotional bandwidth to reflect on her session with Angela, go over their interactions, and develop strategies for going forward. The first impulse after a session like this is to find a reason not to see the client again, refer them to another therapist (perhaps one you don't like), or just forget it happened and hope the client never contacts you again. Christine has gone through this before and proceeds through these thoughts in rapid succession, then moves on to hypothesis generation and problem-solving.

It feels apparent to Christine that note taking during the session triggered a strong shame/rage reaction in Angela, which likely activated past memories of rejection, overwhelming her capacity to regulate. Angela went from stimulus to reaction without the intermediate process of reflection, emotional regulation, and communication. Because she lacked the ability to ask Christine to stop taking notes or verbalize how it made her feel, she became full of rage and acted out by trying to shame Christine. This is the rage of the right hemisphere, unregulated and unconstrained by the interactive mediating processes of the left. This was Angela in her most primitive state.

Think for a moment about how differently Angela and Christine reacted to a threatening situation and what it says about each one's executive functioning. Angela reacted to Christine taking notes as a personal affront, which triggered her rage, and a reaction (screaming, criticizing, and slamming the door) designed to create maximum emotional impact and disconnection. Christine reacted to Angela's rage with external calm and quiet in the face of her own physiological and emotional arousal. She realized that she had neither the time nor the presence of mind to react in the moment, so she decided to wait until the end of the day to think it through and make a decision about how best to respond to Angela. The differences in their experience and reactions are almost completely attributable to their different EF capabilities. Let's go through each of the three executive systems as we attempt to understand what in Angela's brain and mind led her to respond the way she did.

First Executive

A man who fears suffering is already suffering from what he fears.
—Michel de Montaigne

Activation of the amygdala is at the heart of both triggering physiological arousal and inhibiting the cortical executive systems capable of regulating them. Individuals with BPD have a highly active amygdala, distorting the proper orchestration of their executive systems by the salience network (ES1). Unfortunately, this leads them to interact with the world in ways that further enhance amygdala activation (Buchheim et al., 2008; Cascio et al., 2014; Minzenberg et al., 2008; Ruocco et al., 2010). You could say that when Angela stood up and began shouting at Christine, her amygdala was in full control while her other two executive systems were largely inhibited.

A fundamental emotional reality for clients with BPD is the experience of the self as defective, bad, and worthy of rejection. To become aware of the self is to feel disgusting, repulsive, and unlovable, launching them into a regressive state of panic. This triggers internal chaos, an inability to accept blame, and the need to project the intense negativity they feel onto others (splitting). Studies have found that women with BPD had higher levels of disgust sensitivity when it came to their self-image, and tended to show disgusted facial expressions when recalling memories of their childhoods (Buchheim et al., 2007; Rüsch et al., 2011).

When Angela noticed that Christine was taking notes, her thought wasn't that Christine was a diligent and responsible therapist, which she is. Rather, it triggered a shame reaction, leading her to compare herself to a crazy person or a bug, and she expressed her rage by attacking Christine. This is not just an exaggerated one-off misperception, but a fairly common interpersonal drama for those suffering with BPD. This type of stimulus-response behavior in the absence of reflection is an aspect of their day-to-day experience. It is easy to imagine how difficult it is to deal with others when your mind leads you to believe that those around you are cruel, hostile, and shaming. You can also imagine how difficult it is for others to sustain connection in the face of such extreme and unpredictable reactions to seemingly neutral or innocuous events.

Second Executive

We live in a fantasy world, a world of illusion.
The great task in life is to find reality.

—Iris Murdoch

As with other disorders that cause chronically high levels of physiological arousal, the primary handicap of the second executive system is caused by being inhibited by the first. Individuals with BPD don't appear to have severe deficits in their general intellectual functioning or their abstract thinking when they aren't triggered. That being said, the frontal and parietal lobes rely on accurate physiological, sensory, and emotional processing to read and navigate the environment. There is considerable evidence that for clients with BPD, the second executive system is reacting to missing and distorted information from their sensory systems, leading them to apply their available executive abilities in idiosyncratic and isolating ways.

For example, in a gambling task, subjects with BPD had difficulties discerning between positive and negative feedback, made riskier choices, and had more difficulty in avoiding adverse consequences (Schuermann et al., 2011). In a game of cooperation and reward sharing, anterior insula activation in those with BPD was correlated only with the magnitude of output to others but not to the magnitude of the offers they received (King-Casas et al., 2008). These studies suggest absent and distorted feedback in different social contexts, which impairs successful problem-solving strategies.

Individuals with BPD tend to read happy faces accurately but misinterpret neutral ones as negative, while exaggerating the intensity of negative ones. They are also more likely to see disgust and surprise in the faces of others while underrecognizing fear (Merkl et al., 2010; Unoka et al., 2011). In combination with higher amygdala and lower medial prefrontal activation, these misinterpretations often trigger antagonism, suspiciousness, and sometimes assaultiveness (Donegan et al., 2003; Hazlett et al., 2007; Minzenberg et al., 2006). The same neurodynamics occur in situations of stress and social exclusion (Buchheim et al., 2008; Minzenberg et al., 2008; Ruocco et al., 2010), a pattern resulting in an inability to regulate negative emotional reactivity. Along with other dysregulated and isolated individuals, those suffering with BPD are more vulnerable to charismatic religious leaders, fringe beliefs, and conspiracy theories, which allow for an abstract sense of connection with others while supporting their ego through the belief that they have insider information about reality.

Third Executive

Create the kind of self you will be happy to live with all your life.
—Golda Meir

Individuals with BPD exhibit either abnormalities or deficits in essentially all of the functions organized within the third executive system, including empathy, self-referential processing, autobiographical memory, and theory of mind (Frewen et al., 2011; Nietlisbach & Maercker, 2009). This leads to both their desperate need for connection and a lack of the necessary resources to attain and maintain stable attachments (Galovski et al., 2004; Nietlisbach & Maercker, 2009; Ray & Vanstone, 2009; Riggs et al., 1998).

Deficits in metabolism are seen in clients with BPD in two key regions of the DMN: the precuneus regions of the parietal lobes and posterior cingulate cortex, both of which contribute to the experience of an inner world, a private sense of self, and access to autobiographical memory (Lange et al., 2005; Philippi, Tranel et al., 2015). Clients with BPD often lack memory across time and emotional states and, when sad or dysregulated, can't remember ever feeling better. This lack of memory leads them to experience their pain in an eternal present where hope for something better is hard to imagine. This pattern of functional activation makes them less able to stop, reflect, and evaluate their situation while more likely to act, react, and be guided by impulse.

Despite their vulnerability to experiencing the pain of others, those with BPD exhibit deficits in both the emotional and cognitive aspects of empathy (Christov-Moore et al., 2014; Dziobek et al., 2011). Like people with depression, borderline clients appear to have deficits in switching modes from self- to other-relevance, which may be why they are unable to convert their high level of sympathy for others into empathy and compassion (Danziger et al., 2009; Schnell et al., 2007). Being empathic requires the ability to put your own perspective and agenda aside, a task that requires both emotional regulation and perspective taking, which they find exceedingly difficult.

Psychotherapy

The self is not something one finds; it is something one creates.
—Thomas Szasz

As Christine experienced firsthand, disruptions in each of the three executive systems individually, and in combination, bring an array of serious challenges to the therapeutic process with clients with BPD. Lacking an understanding and the tools to deal with these clients, Freud simply excluded them from psychoanalysis. While this is still a wise choice a century later (when it comes to psychoanalysis), there are now treatment options that account for and address the challenges posed by borderline pathology. That being said, treatment is still difficult and involved, and is focused more on behavior management and symptom reduction rather than working toward a cure.

The current standard treatment for BPD is DBT. It was developed by psychologist Marsha Linehan, who believed she suffered from the disorder. As a young child, she was a psychiatric inpatient, diagnosed with schizophrenia and treated with electroconvulsive therapy and major tranquilizers. In the 1940s and '50s, this was the standard of care for anyone of any age who was emotionally unstable, behaviorally unpredictable, and considered a danger to others and/or themselves. The DBT treatment she developed was based on things she had discovered during her studies of psychology and Zen Buddhism, which helped her cope with and manage her own symptoms.

Dialectical behavior therapy avoids many of the standard psychotherapeutic methods—a focus on the therapeutic relationship, a nondirective stance, and therapeutic neutrality—which tend to exacerbate the social and emotional dysregulation of BPD. Instead, it focuses on cognitive restructuring, acceptance, mindfulness, and behavioral shaping to create, as the title of Linehan's book describes, "a life worth living" (Linehan, 2021). The structure of DBT has been successful in part because it avoids some of the pitfalls of traditional therapies with BPD clients while addressing and scaffolding dysfunctional perceptual and emotional executive functions, which cause many of the difficulties encountered and created by those with BPD.

Working with borderline clients as individual outpatients requires an understanding of their brains and minds as well as being prepared for the typical challenges that arise in our work. The transference is usually challenging because of failures of attunement and perceived negativity on the part of the therapist. Negative countertransference is also common in reaction to the client's unpredictability, hostility, and attacks on both our professional abilities and who we are as people. When under attack, it is easy for us to forget that these reactions are demonstrations of their own internal pain and usually have little to do with us. However, our bodies feel the threat, and maintaining the proper perspective can be a challenge. Working with clients with BPD requires a high level of executive functioning.

As in their lives, the emotional, physiological, and behavioral impulsivity and instability gets played out in the therapeutic relationship, activating feelings of shame, abandonment, and isolation. Both in and out of the session, they will engage in verbal and physical altercations, suicidal gestures and ideation, promiscuity, substance abuse, recklessness, and road rage. These will be forms of communication to let you know that they are suffering, that you have disappointed them, and that they need more from you than they are receiving. If they feel wronged, which they often do, clients with BPD can become filled with righteous indignation that can propel them on a mission to gain justice for themselves. They will go far out of their way to punish you (and others) for what they feel you have done to them. The need to maintain professional boundaries and good documentation are of primary importance in order to manage your own professional risk.

When working with clients with borderline symptoms, a clear structure and boundary setting combined with flexibility and patience are key. The therapist must provide an external executive scaffolding within which the client can build brain networks of memory, self-organization, and affect regulation. In this way, the therapist serves as an aid for affect regulation, reality testing, and self-reflection. In other words, you have to provide the executive functioning for the both of you.

One of the central tools of the psychotherapist is using interpretations, which is a statement that attempts to make unconscious material conscious. However, benefiting from interpretations requires first executive affect regulation in combination with third executive self-reflection. The reason why interpretations are contraindicated when working with BPD clients is that they lack both of these abilities most of the time. Because of this, borderline clients often demonstrate extreme negative reactions to interpretations. They may become violent, leave the consulting room, and engage in self-injurious behavior.

Accurate interpretations can trigger powerful reactions associated with separation, shame, and abandonment. The most salient indication of whether a client has a borderline pathology is feeling attacked, inadequate, and in danger yourself. This countertransference reaction may be similar to what they feel, and our reactions may be our clearest view into their chaotic and painful emotional world. This is why pragmatic cognitive and behavioral guidance is recommended while avoiding interpretations of unconscious material.

Together, these data suggest that our borderline clients find it difficult or even impossible to find a safe place within themselves. In fact, trying to relax, meditate, or take a yoga class may overwhelm them with internal thoughts and painful feelings that are too difficult to contain. Despite these impediments, clients with BPD are capable of mentalizing their experiences. However, the combination of their anxiety and social information processing distortions leads them to overindex on negative information (Sharp et al., 2011). Thus, while mentalizing may be a positive means of coping for many others, borderline patients are vulnerable to increasingly obsessive and suspicious—even paranoid—ruminations. These patients often report increasingly escalating anxiety and fear to the point where they feel like they are crawling out of their skin.

Angela and Christine

I have three things to teach: simplicity, patience, compassion.

—Lao Tzu

Because Angela refused to engage in any form of group treatment, the local clinic that specialized in DBT was not a possibility. Christine agreed to take Angela as a client knowing that she would have to approximate the approach and techniques of DBT in the context of individual therapy to be successful. Christine realized that Angela was currently unable to verbalize her feelings and needed help to put them into words. One of the long-term goals of therapy would be to help Angela be aware of and express her feelings instead of acting them out. The cognitive/mindfulness aspects of the treatment would have the goal of inserting thinking and self-reflection between Angela's stimulus-response pairing.

A long-term goal of treatment would be to transform the type of alienating interaction that occurred during their first session to an experience of sustained contact. She would need to help Angela make the shift from acting out to acting in—in other words, put her feelings into words, engage in conversation, and stay in the room. This might be reflected in Angela's ability to say, "It makes me feel ignored when you take notes, so could you please wait till after the session?" Christine's response might be, "Absolutely. I wanted to make sure not to forget important points, but I should be able to recall it after our session ends."

Before she left the office for the day, Christine left a voicemail for Angela attempting to bridge the gap between them. She apologized for hurting her feelings by taking notes during the session, saying that while it wasn't an intentional slight, she now realized how painful it was for Angela to see that she wasn't being attended to. "From now on," Christine promised, "I'll only take notes after our sessions are over." Hopefully, this type of response leads to Angela feeling heard, giving her confidence that Christine is able to tolerate her rage without taking revenge, and has the empathic capabilities to read and respect her feelings, even when they are expressed in an exaggerated and attacking manner. The process of therapy will require the repetitive cycle of regulation-dysregulation-reregulation as Angela expands her abilities to regulate her affect, learn to recognize how her brain distorts social information, and develop new levels of cognitive control and relational abilities.

Chapter 18

Executive Functioning and the Practice of Psychotherapy

Love and work are the cornerstones of our humanness.
—Sigmund Freud

Psychotherapists seldom think in terms of executive functioning unless presented with the term by a client, parent, or neuropsychologist. Clinical theory and training have largely ignored the notion of EF and see it as the domain of other disciplines. Yet, despite the lack of specific reference to EF in our theories and techniques, our work relies heavily on the development, integration, and functioning of each executive system. This is true for both our clients and ourselves. The wide range of cognitive, emotional, and interpersonal skills required to be a good therapist require a high level of EF development and integration. This is why an understanding of the functional neurodynamics of how humans navigate relationships should be an essential aspect of training.

As we have seen up until this point, EF is at work across cognitive, social, and emotional domains of life. As Freud often stated, the goal of therapy isn't perfection, but the ability to love and work, which are also the ultimate goals of EF. We have explored the impact of early attachment relationships on the epigenetic development and integration of our EF systems. We have also seen how our attachment schema impacts our affect regulation, social skills, and sense of self. Clients come to therapy because their lives aren't working and, after all, isn't that the job of our executive systems? You could even say the focus of therapy is consulting with our clients' internal CEO to help them be able to run their lives independent from us.

Theoretical Orientation

Work and love; these are the basics.
—Theodore Reich

You may have noticed that there is nothing scientific whatsoever about how therapists choose their theoretical orientation. It largely depends on the teachers we happen to meet, the books we come across, or the conference recommended by a friend. Also crucial is the fit between our choice of orientation and our own personality and defenses. Each of the four basic treatment modalities (CBT, psychodynamic, systems, existential/humanistic) and their countless spinoffs attract many adherents, and each works for some of our clients some of the time. An important question that has not yet been answered is, "Which client would benefit most from which treatments?"

When thinking about which form of therapy might have the greatest chance of helping a particular client, we should consider the strengths and challenges of both client and therapeutic modality. In reality, many clients have a "clinical career" and move from one therapist to another until they either give up or find a good match for their personality, abilities, and needs. We might refer an intellectualizing client to a therapist whose treatment orientation leans toward emotion and somatic experience. On the other hand, a client like this might be so defended against their feelings that a cognitively oriented therapist may be a better choice to help them address specific symptoms. We would hope that the benefits of successful cognitive strategies might eventually help them to open to deeper and broader emotional experiences.

Each orientation to psychotherapy appears to leverage the strengths of one executive system over another or work to integrate systems that have become dissociated from one another. A psychodynamic perspective focuses on uncovering implicit memories stored in networks of ES1, like attachment schema, past traumas, and prior learning, which can inhibit and/or distort executive functions. Cognitive behavioral therapy relies on conscious thoughts (ES2) to regulate symptoms like depression, anxiety, and hopelessness. Mindfulness-based therapy aims to leverage focused attention and self-awareness (ES3) for improved mental well-being.

Somatic therapies tend to leverage the activation and integration of ES1 and ES3 by increasing an awareness of our interwoven physiological and emotional states. These therapies often address developmental or trauma-based defenses stored in ES1, which manifest in the body as defensive postures, physiological arousal, and procedural memory (defensive gestures, fight/flight reactions, etc.). The goal is to express these reactions physically while associating them with the conscious awareness and perspective provided by ES2. While some will find this process helpful in integrating dissociated aspects of experience, others with trauma-based disconnections from their bodies will either flee in fear or be too defended to benefit from this kind of intervention. This is why an understanding of our therapeutic interventions and an appreciation of our client's physiological state are equally important in choosing and implementing orientations and interventions we choose.

Existential-humanistic approaches work to deepen the connections between ES2 and ES3 through the acceptance of death, the search for meaning, and developing a life strategy that allows for the courage to face and accept our own mortality. This type of therapy relies heavily on the abilities of ES2 to create a narrative for the heroic journey of therapy and life in general. At the same time, these forms of therapy are vulnerable to being used as intellectualizing defenses against emotion by overindexing on philosophical discussions while skirting the expression of core emotions. Regardless of how we think about matching clients and therapists, this kind of cost-benefit analysis is important to consider. Ultimately, all we can do is make an educated guess and hope for the best. The complexity of each client and how they match or clash with a particular therapist leads to a wide range of referral failures and successes.

Therapeutic Perspectives and Executive Functioning

When we blindly adopt a religion, a political system,
a literary dogma, we become automatons.

—Anaïs Nin

Our brains create meaning by combining information from within and without, and from the past, present, and an imagined future. This strategy has evolved in the service of survival, which in the past was best served by our ability to predict what is about to happen. As our brains and culture expanded, so did our capacity to think, reason, and remember. Unfortunately, so did our capacity to worry and make up things to be frightened about in the absence of any real threat. What remained at the core, however, was the same drive for prediction in the hope of remaining in control. How this core drive manifests in the contemporary brain and mind is the need for certainty, even when there is none to be found. This drive motivates the creation of false narratives and belief systems that humans will adhere to despite considerable evidence to the contrary. This is why in every war, each side believes that god is on their side.

At a less consequential level, this same need is why psychotherapists become believers in a specific form of treatment over all others. Our faith in our orientation decreases our anxiety by providing an illusion of certainty, and we rely on these beliefs to support our adaptation to the therapeutic role. Each orientation has its own belief system, theory of illness and healing, and jargon that enhances the sense of being a member of a club with special knowledge. The downside is that once we have a belief system, we see the world and other belief systems through the lens of that perspective. We tend to focus on the things our clients say that correspond with our model, and underplay or even completely miss those that don't. We discover what we are looking for and often miss those things in plain sight that don't correspond to our belief system. A central goal of advanced training is to slowly let go of dogmatic beliefs while becoming more oriented to the specific realities and needs of each client.

This understanding is essential when examining the traditional relationship between psychotherapy and executive functioning. Few therapeutic orientations include a focus on EF, which may lead clinicians to think that it is either out of their area of practice or, even worse, that it is irrelevant to their work. What we would like to do in the rest of this final chapter is to take a broad view of some of the challenges that arise in practice that might benefit from the inclusion of the three-system model in conceptualization and treatment. Let's begin with the very important topic of PTSD.

The Impact of Posttraumatic Stress Disorder on Executive Functioning

Trauma is a fact of life. It does not, however, have to be a life sentence.
—Peter Levine

What Freud described as a "surpassing of the stimulus barrier" in PTSD reflects a dramatic shift in the neurodynamic relationships among the three executive systems. Using his term for a moment, our stimulus barrier (or ego) includes our conscious and unconscious mechanisms of defenses. These defenses allow us to modulate or distort incoming stimuli so they do not result in overwhelming anxiety. We can employ different strategies such as directing our attention elsewhere (avoidance), making believe it isn't happening (denial), making a joke (humor), or refocusing our attention and emotions into something else (sublimation). With sufficient bottom-up traumatic arousal (ES1), our cortical mechanisms of defense organized within ES2 and ES3 can be inhibited or completely taken offline.

During highly traumatic experiences, ES1 directs our physiology, behavior, learning, and memory. In this state of amygdala hijack, we regress to a primitive level of functioning with limited cortical involvement, becoming a passive witness to our bodies responding to threat. We might fight, run, freeze, or become subservient to an aggressor with very little ability to make conscious decisions about what we observe ourselves doing. This is why people who experience trauma are, upon reflection, confused about their response, asking themselves, "Why didn't I put up more of a fight, yell, or grab something I could have used as a weapon?" "Was I complicit or did I want this to happen to me?" These are cortical (rational) questions about our subcortical (reflexive) survival responses. But where was our rationality and perspective during the traumatic experience? The answer is that they were unavailable due to ES1 inhibition of ES2 and ES3.

In normal learning situations, novelty, curiosity, or motivation trigger the salience network (ES1) first to orient, and then to focus attention toward whatever we have encountered (a toy, a lesson, or a potential mate). Moderate levels of amygdala arousal stimulate the biochemistry and epigenetics of hippocampal/cortical learning, and we go through the conscious process of engagement, learning, and forming explicit memories. What we learn during normal states of arousal is contextualized within space and time, put on our internal calendar, and woven into our conscious autobiographical memory.

When the amygdala takes over during trauma, there are dramatic shifts in learning, memory, and executive control. It signals the salience network to orient to and focus on the dangerous stimuli and to inhibit ES2 and ES3, while it takes over the processes of learning and memory. Amygdala learning involves basic stimulus-response associations, which don't include information about context (space and time), source attribution, or placement in sequential autobiographical memory. These implicit memories are stored outside of conscious awareness and never get old because they are not stamped for time on our cortical calendar. This is why those who suffer with PTSD are susceptible to stimuli that trigger a physiological, emotional, or sensory response that is outside of their conscious awareness or control. This learning occurred during trauma, when our stimulus barrier was down.

This amygdala hijack results in an interruption of the connection and communication among our executive systems, causing them to function independently, and sometimes at odds. PTSD results if this state of nonintegrated executive functioning becomes a new normal. The core symptoms of PTSD are expressions of this executive dissociation. *Arousal* is the triggering of unmodulated amygdala activation, the inhibition of ES2 and ES3, and the reactivation of a traumatic state of brain and mind. *Intrusions* are the consequences of conscious and unconscious triggers expressed as flashbacks, nightmares, and panic attacks secondary to amygdala activation. *Avoidance* is a behavioral reaction to protect against or limit exposure to potential triggers. Our newer understanding of the inhibition of ES3 (DMN) is helping us to grasp the other socially salient aspects of trauma. The *fragmentation of self* and the *disconnection from others* we witness in trauma victims reflect the inhibition of the self-organizing abilities and social connectivity functions of the DMN, respectively.

Keeping these EF dynamics in mind when treating PTSD can help us to properly curate and sequence interventions for each client. Our inability to access ES2 and ES3 functions should remind us that work needs to focus first on decreasing arousal and establishing a sense of safety. As we sense ES2 and/or ES3 becoming available, we can then shift our focus to interventions that require cortical involvement. These include such diverse techniques as creating coherent narratives about past traumas, attempting to foster habituation to feared stimuli through exposure and response prevention, the use of EMDR, or encouraging vulnerability and trust in the therapeutic relationship. The rule of thumb is that little therapeutic progress can occur when the amygdala and saliency network has taken the cortex offline.

The Effects of THC on Executive Functioning

What a long strange trip it's been.
—Robert Hunter

In addition to the seeming ubiquity of trauma in the clients we see is the legalization and widespread acceptance of THC (tetrahydrocannabinol, an active component of marijuana). Despite its increasing recreational and medical use across all age groups, there is a lack of understanding concerning its impact on cognition, emotion, and executive function. Therapists can play an important role in educating clients about its effects so they are able to make more informed choices about its use. We are born with an abundance of cannabinoid receptors throughout our brain and nervous systems. These receptors (which bind with the THC in marijuana) are especially plentiful in the prefrontal cortex, hippocampus, basal ganglion, and cerebellum (Chayasirisobhon, 2021). Sometimes referred to as "organs of succession," this group of structures is central in the temporal sequencing of our behaviors, thoughts, and communication (Edelman, 1987).

THC receptors are also particularly dense in the hypothalamus, a target of amygdala arousal to activate bodily responses to novelty, threat, and potential danger. The allure of THC is a combination of the diminished vigilance to threat and involvement with external tasks. Inhibiting these abilities provides a respite from an anxiety-provoking fears and demands of the world. Given where and how THC impacts our brains, it is no surprise that it has a significant impact across all three executive systems. Most research has focused on THC's impact on the functional, structural, and developmental aspects of ES2. Recreational users, both current and former, have demonstrated diminished response inhibition, planning abilities, associative memory, and decision-making abilities.

The negative impact of THC on the brain, in many ways, parallels the results of early adverse childhood experiences and trauma. The effects of both appear to be modulated by age of exposure and the degree of use. The earlier and more chronic the use of THC, the greater the long-term impact on brain development and executive functioning (Dahlgren et al., 2016; Sagar et al., 2015). Between 1995 and 2021, the THC levels in marijuana products increased by nearly 200% while the use of vaping resulted in delivery of more concentrated THC (ElSohly et al., 2016; Malouff et al., 2014). It is likely that these trends have continued as marijuana use has been legalized in some states, and its use for medical purposes has increased.

As THC use is becoming increasingly prevalent around the country and across generations, it does not appear at all harmless. Using marijuana as an antianxiety agent to cope with the stress of school, work, or relationships comes with the side effect of having less anxiety tolerance and diminished cognitive skills required to be successful in these contexts. Similar to alcohol addiction, the downward spiral of negative emotions, decreasing functional abilities, and increased marijuana has become a common clinical presentation with younger and younger clients. As clinicians, we should help our clients to discover the emotional and situational factors for which they are using marijuana. We should then search for alternative behavioral, lifestyle, and pharmacological interventions to deal with these challenges that don't have share these negative side effects.

Executive Functioning and Common Therapeutic Concepts

> *A rose is a rose is a rose is a rose.*
> —Gertrude Stein

From the early days of integrating psychotherapy and neuroscience, one of its primary benefits has been to provide a brain-based explanation of psychological functions. This integrated perspective of mind and brain can help both therapists and clients to grasp aspects of their experiences that can be either vague or frightening. Regardless of your orientation to therapy and the language you use to frame your work, you may find it helpful to know how to translate some of them into a three-system framework.

The Therapeutic Relationship

If a therapist has a well-developed and integrated set of executive networks, they are able to identify deficits and imbalances of these networks in their clients. It doesn't take much training to recognize when someone is emotionally dysregulated (ES1), thinking illogically (ES2), or lacking in self-awareness or an understanding of others (ES3). What training can do is to help us to communicate what we see in ways that can be understood, integrated, and used by our clients for positive change. In a way, our clients are able to leverage our executive abilities to develop their own, a process that occurs during early development in the context of good-enough parenting.

Amygdala Whispering

Amygdala whispering is shorthand for the therapist's ability to leverage their relationship with a client to downregulate amygdala activation. Through their words, actions, and other mechanisms of interpersonal regulation, a positive therapeutic relationship fosters a state of mind that allows for decreases in adrenaline and cortisol, and an increase in protein synthesis and other neural mechanisms of learning. At the level of our executive networks, this triggers the amygdala to stand down, allowing the salience network to establish the appropriate cooperation of ES2 and ES3 for proper reality testing, conscious focus on difficult memories, and the reconsolidation of autobiographical memory. Using the therapist for affect regulation parallels how a child uses a parent to comfort them before they develop the systems required to do it themselves.

Core Beliefs

Core beliefs are extrapolated from conscious and semiconscious thoughts, feelings, and patterns of behavior. This means that they likely arise from a combination of all three executive systems. In therapy we activate autobiographical memory in the context of self-reflection (ES3) and build a conscious narrative (ES2) to create a way to understand the emotional background of our day-to-day experiences. Core beliefs that have detrimental impacts on us are generally shame-based, resulting in a variety of negative presuppositions about the self. The most common are not being smart, attractive, or worthy of love.

These are expressions of what Freud thought were the result of a harsh superego, and what Albert Ellis felt resulted in "fundamental votes of no confidence in the self." Some tells for these underlying assumptions are perfectionism, lack of self-care, narcissistic defenses, and high levels of rejection sensitivity. Because the underlying core beliefs operate outside (or just below) conscious awareness, they are most likely organized within the primitive implicit memory systems of ES1. Creating labels and a narrative for them (ES2) allows for conscious examination of their origin and impact (ES3). This is done in the service of counteracting them with new, positive, and more active background emotions.

Interpretations

An interpretation is something said by the therapist that can provide new information for the client to consider. They often focus on connections between two or more pieces of information that the therapist thinks might be related to one another. For example, similar patterns of difficulties across relationships, associating feelings or reactions across situations, or reflecting that when a client talks about a sad or painful situation, they tend to smile. Interpretations require a combination of abstract thinking, autobiographical memory, and self-reflective capacity (ES2 and ES3).

The defenses of psychodynamic theory are believed to arise as a response to overwhelming emotional experiences. Our defenses serve to diminish or fully inhibit the negative emotional impact of negative experiences, and allow us to decrease our anxiety in the service of ongoing functioning. Further, when they are accurately seen, interpreted, and made conscious to the client, they cease to serve the function of protecting them from the emotions they were suppressing. With adequate ego strength (emotional autoregulation) we are able to hear, understand, and begin to incorporate the formerly dissociated material into conscious awareness. In the case of individuals with BPD, accurate interpretations result in a catastrophic reaction because they are flooded with the same overwhelming, primitive emotions that they experienced during early development.

Transference and Countertransference

Transference is the activation of an attachment schema stored in ES1 that influences our conscious experience of our therapist. The ability to observe and work on changing patterns of transference requires the abstract reasoning and self-reflective capacities of ES2 and ES3. All therapists are human, which means we all have our own patterns of neural development, strengths, weaknesses, and blind spots to those things we defend against. Some of these things can change, while others never do. This means that we bring our own biases to every client. The best we can do is try and be as aware of them as we can, and factor them into our perceptions of our clients. An example might be that we rely on intellectual defenses (ES2) and overindex on finding solutions to problems rather than balancing thoughts with feelings. Alternatively, we may rely on specific emotions like fear or depression (ES1) and fail to offer our clients a counterbalance of rationality.

Reality Testing

Reality testing is a metacognitive process that requires multiple separate but interwoven components: the ability to look at both internal and external experience, contrast them, and reflect on their relative saliency to us and those around us. In English this translates into knowing what is real and what isn't, what's a fantasy, and what is actually happening around us. This process requires the collaboration of ES2 and ES3, and for ES1 to tolerate feedback from others and the self-observing functions of ES3. Note that, given that none of us really knows what reality is, reality testing has more to do with shared assumptions and agreed-upon norms. Perhaps a better way to describe reality testing would be "the ability to accept a shared set of assumptions about reality with the therapist."

Helping Clients to Talk Less and Say More

Therapy is the talking cure, and we encourage our clients to speak their mind. On the other hand, continuous pressured speech, incoherent narratives, and tangential stories about external events can serve as a defense against being present and emotionally vulnerable. Clients are usually unaware of when they use sharing as a form of defense, so it requires an interpretation on the part of the therapist to bring the possibility to consciousness. In this case, we try to alert ES2 to this somewhat abstract concept, and then ES3, to reflect on the interactions and emotions involved to test whether the interpretation is relevant. Knowing that narrative coherence is correlated with insecure attachment also provides us with possible theories for the origin of these defenses, which may help a client understand why the defenses exist. The secure attachment we can hopefully create within the relationship may provide the emotional regulation required to enhance and integrate the executive networks needed to create coherent speech.

Inner Child

The notion of an inner child has existed throughout the history of psychoanalysis and was adopted by theorists including Eric Berne, Alice Miller, and John Bradshaw. In transactional analysis, Berne (1961) focused on states of mind (or self-states) that embody and manifest these different aspects of our inner experience. He proposed these three states as adult, parent, and child—a loose parallel to Freud's notion of the ego, the superego, and the id. In terms of EF, the *adult state* reflects the optimal integrating and function of our three executive networks. This includes proper affect regulation, perspective, and an awareness of the self and others.

The *parent state* is guided by our memories and identification with our parents, especially in how we were treated, what values were instilled in us, and how we were disciplined and controlled. This manifests within us in the form of self-esteem, self-care, and the nature of the inner voices that comment on our thoughts, emotions, and actions. These memories are largely implicit but manifest in the narratives we create about ourselves, our core beliefs, and the positive or negative natures of the thoughts and feelings we have about ourselves. The *child state* is also made up primarily of implicit memories of our experiences as a child from our own perspective. Because the internalization of the parent state is dominant when children are abused, neglected, or not attuned to, it can be difficult to find the child state, which is often dissociated in the service of early emotional survival. Inner child work focuses primarily on reassociating the child state to allow those dissociated aspects of the self to be reintegrated into conscious awareness.

The parent and child states both represent an ES1 dominance where memories of identification with the parents and dissociated memories of childhood trigger the amygdala and impair the functioning of ES2 and

ES3. Both states are forms of regression that take us out of the present and reactivate the past. Because they involve the inhibition of ES2 and ES3, we have the experience of "knowing better" while our primitive feelings override our reality testing. These two states are also similar to the intrusions we see in PTSD in that they involve a similar neurodynamic configuration (high ES1 and low ES2/ES3).

Internal family systems (IFS) is an application of traditional psychodynamic treatment for trauma-based dissociation to nontraumatized populations. It utilizes a model where the psyche is broken into a number of parts that serve our adaptation to different situations. The goal of therapy is to increase awareness of nonadaptive and fragmented aspects of experience and work toward integration. The behavior, affect, sensation, knowledge (BASK) model of dissociation is relied on—these different contributors of experiences that rely on separate neural circuits can serve us better when integrated. Working with IFS depends upon a client's abstract and metacognitive abilities to grasp (ES2), accept (ES1), and internalize (ES3) this way of thinking. As always, the therapeutic alliance must establish the safety and affect regulation needed to enable the salience network to incorporate the ES2 and ES3 for active participation .

Being a Biologically Informed Therapist

> *Our world is built on biology and once we begin*
> *to understand it, it becomes a technology.*
> —Ryan Bettencourt

The human nervous system is immensely complex, and there is far more to being a brain-informed therapist than being able to use the words "amygdala" and "vagus" in a sentence. There is a considerable vocabulary to master and a set of brain-behavior associations that need to be learned. Beyond all the definitions, facts, and ideas is the challenge of grasping how the brain works as a broad neurodynamic system. And with so many new findings and ideas emerging on a regular basis, we have to continue to learn new ideas while unlearning old "truths." Always remember that everything we "know" about the brain is a hypothesis waiting to be overturned. Don't get too attached to your knowledge, and be suspicious of certainty.

We encourage all of you to learn as much as possible about neuropsychological assessment, neurology, and psychopharmacology, as you will inevitably become part of a treatment team including these and other professionals. Don't make the mistake of thinking you can remain ignorant of these disciplines because they are outside of your formal training. While you may never prescribe medication or have to read an fMRI, your clients will be dealing with medications, brain scans, and consultations with other professionals and will come to rely on your knowledge to help them interpret, process, and integrate these other aspects of healing into their personal experiences.

As clinicians, we are trained to think in terms of adverse experiences, attachment schema, and the effects of trauma. We are taught to identify, address, and treat the psychological symptoms, core beliefs, and defenses that keep our clients locked into repetitive and maladaptive patterns of behavior. We haven't been taught that there is little separation between our psychology and biology. Most of what we think of as psychological defenses are also reflected in the structures and functions of our brains. Children who experience early emotional conflict around them may show less development in their receptive language systems than adults. Adult women who were sexually abused as children have been shown to have less developed visual and sensory system regions, most likely reflecting the parallel manifestations of their biological and psychological defenses.

During our training, we are provided with metaphors for internal psychological processes like ego, an inner child, or an internal family system, which we hope our clients can relate to. What we aren't taught about are all the relevant aspects of cognition (attention, concentration, focus, distractibility, etc.), memory (short and long term, autobiographical, procedural, sensory, etc.), and learning (motivation, arousal, plasticity, etc.) upon which the successful processes of psychotherapy depend. Therapy is all about memory, from what a client brings into session to how they are able to apply what they learn in therapy to their life outside of the consulting room. Therapy is a classroom where all of the processes of learning come to bear on a range of personal material. If the client is highly aroused, then their attention is spotty, their neuroplastic processes are inhibited, and their ability to learn is greatly limited.

The breakdown of mind–body dualism in our case conceptualizations will lead us to have a more balanced focus on the psychological–somatic interface. For example, a description of depression will include the negative impact on the body of unexpressed anger, the inhibition of cognition, and the downward energetic spiral of social withdrawal and loss of motivation. Working with childhood sexual abuse victims will include an understanding of the impact of sensory-motor functions related to intercourse and physical interventions to address them. Adults who grew up in impoverished and neglectful homes will be recognized as having neurobiological differences that may impair their educational and professional progress, and need to be addressed with cognitive as opposed to psychological interventions.

We can now have some confidence in the fact that the psychological defenses we see in the consulting room parallel biological changes in the neural structures of the brain. This means that, in a manner of speaking, clients with adverse early experiences, trauma, or chronic anxiety also have brains that come to operate in different ways. These differences can impact all aspects of functioning across any and all neural networks that participate in executive functioning and beyond. As a field, we will eventually move past the mind–body dualism that is still pervasive in both our profession and culture. When this happens, we will likely look to the field of rehabilitation medicine, which works with those with physical brain damage, to help us to understand how experience-based brain damage can be better treated and how we can modify psychotherapy to account for the limitations of their particular kind of damage. This is still far off and will rely on the ability of professionals from different fields to work together, something they have not been particularly good at for the past couple of centuries.

Conclusion

> *A classic is a book that has never finished saying what it has to say.*
> —Italo Calvino

We hope that this book has added to your knowledge in ways that will serve both your understanding and clinical practice. Each time you integrate the brain and nervous system into a case conceptualization, you will be on the cutting edge of the integration of mind, body, and brain. You will be going where very few of your teachers and supervisors have successfully trod. Beware of the numerous brain-based theories and treatment orientations that focus on one brain region or neural network that they use to explain and treat all psychological disorders. These are all attempts to oversimplify the complexity of the brain and the heterogeneity of human experience. These cartoon representations and simplistic models of neuroplasticity are why very few neuroscientists take psychotherapy seriously.

The three-neural-network model of executive functioning presented in these pages may appear significantly more complex than other brain-based approaches to clinical treatment you have explored. And yet, many findings, ideas, and theoretical possibilities have been omitted for the sake of brevity, while many others remain to be discovered. Although only weighing in at a few pounds, the human brain is a vast and mostly unexplored territory that will be slow in yielding its secrets. Discovering what has been organized by millions of neurons through trillions of connections, over millions of years, will keep us busy for a long time to come.

As we said at the outset, and wish to remind you at the end, this model and all the findings and theories it rests upon are hypotheses. As is always the case in scientific exploration, we can only hope we are in the right ballpark, or at least in the general vicinity. If not, we hope that the errors of our current thinking will serve as warnings for future theorists to benefit from.

References

Adolphs, R. (2003). Cognitive neuroscience of human social behaviour. *Nature Reviews Neuroscience, 4*(3), 165–178. https://doi.org/10.1038/nrn1056

Adolphs, R., Schul, R., & Tranel, D. (1998). Intact recognition of facial emotion in Parkinson's disease. *Neuropsychology, 12*(2), 253–256. https://doi.org/10.1037//0894 -4105.12.2.253

Akiki, T. J., Averill, C. L., Wrocklage, K. M., Scott, J. C., Averill, L. A., Schweinsburg, B., & Abdallah, C. G. (2018). Default mode network abnormalities in posttraumatic stress disorder: A novel network-restricted topology approach. *NeuroImage, 176*, 489–498. https://doi.org/10.1016/j.neuroimage.2018.05.005

Alexander, G. E., DeLong, M. R., & Strick, P. L. (1986). Parallel organization of functionally segregated circuits linking basal ganglia and cortex. *Annual Review of Neuroscience, 9*, 357–381. https://doi.org/10.1146/annurev.ne.09.030186.002041

Ainsworth, M. D. (1969). Maternal Sensitivity Scales: The Baltimore Longitudinal Project. http://www.psychology.sunysb.edu/attachment/measures/content/maternal%20sensitivity%20scales.pdf

American Psychiatric Association. (2013). *Diagnostic and statistical manual of mental disorders* (5th ed.). American Psychiatric Association.

Andersen, R. A., & Cui, H. (2009). Intention, action planning, and decision making in parietal-frontal circuits. *Neuron, 63*(5), 568–583. https://doi.org/10.1016/j .neuron.2009.08.028

Andersen, R. A., & Mountcastle, V. B. (1983). The influence of the angle of gaze upon the excitability of the light-sensitive neurons of the posterior parietal cortex. *Journal of Neuroscience, 3*(3), 532–548. https://doi.org/10.1523/jneurosci.03-03-00532.1983

Andersen, R. A., Snyder, L. H., Bradley, D. C., & Xing, J. (1997). Multimodal representation of space in the posterior parietal cortex and its use in planning movements. *Annual Review of Neuroscience, 20*(1), 303–330. https://doi.org/10.1146/annurev.neuro.20.1.303

Anderson, M., & Jiang, J. (2018). Teens, social media and technology 2018. Pew Research Center, May 31. https://www.pewinternet.org/2018/05/31/teens-social -media-technology-2018/

Andreasen, N. C., O'Leary, D. S., Cizadlo, T., Arndt, S., Rezai, K., Watkins, G. L., & Hichwa, R. D. (1995). Remembering the past: Two facets of episodic memory explored with positron emission tomography. *American Journal of Psychiatry*, 152(11), 1576–1585. https://doi.org/10.1176/ajp.152.11.1576

Andrews-Hanna, J. (2012). The brain's default mode network and its adaptive role in internal mentation. *Neuroscientist*, 18(3), 251–270. https://doi.org/10 .1177/1073858411403316

Anokhin, A. P., Birbaumer, N., Lutzenberger, W., Nikolaev, A., & Vogel, F. (1996). Age increases brain complexity. *Electroencephalography and Clinical Neurophysiology*, 99(1), 63–68. https://doi.org/10.1016/0921-884x(96)95573-3

Antal, A., Baudewig, J., Paulus, W., & Dechent, P. (2008). The posterior cingulate cortex and planum temporale/parietal operculum are activated by coherent visual motion. *Visual Neuroscience*, 25(1), 17–26. https://doi.org/10.1017/s0952523808080024

Arif, Y., Spooner, R. K., Heinrichs-Graham, E., & Wilson, T. W. (2021). High-definition transcranial direct current stimulation modulates performance and alpha/beta parietal-frontal connectivity serving fluid intelligence. *Journal of Psychophysiology*, 24(10), 5451–5463. https://doi.org/10.1113/jp282387

Arnold, A. P. (2004). Sex chromosomes and brain gender. *Nature Reviews Neuroscience*, 5(9), 701–708. https://doi.org/10.1038/nrn1494

Astafiev, M., Kumra, S., Bhaskar, S. L., Clarke, T., Thaden, E., Cervellione, K. L., Astafiev, S., & Corbetta, M. (2003). Functional organization of human intraparietal and prefrontal cortex for attending, looking and pointing. *Journal of Neuroscience*, 23(11), 4689–4699. https://doi.org/10.1523/jneurosci.23-11-04689.2003

Baars, B. J. (2002). The conscious access hypothesis: Origins and recent evidence. *Trends in Cognitive Sciences*, 6(1), 47–52. https://doi.org/10.1016/s1364-6613(00)01819-2

Baird, B., Smallwood, J., Mrazek, M. D., Kam, J. W., Franklin, M. S., & Schooler, J. W. (2012). Inspired by distraction: Mind wandering facilitates creative incubation. *Psychological Science*, 23(10), 1117–1122. https://doi.org/10.1177/0956797612446024

Baltes, P. B., Staudinger, U. M., Maercker, A., & Smith, J. (1995). People nominated as wise: A comparative study of wisdom-related knowledge. *Psychology and Aging*, 10(2), 155–165. https://doi.org/10.1037//0882-7974.10.2.155

Balthazar, M. L., Campos, B. M., Franco, A. R., Damasceno, B. P., & Cendes, F. (2014). Whole cortical and default mode network mean functional connectivity as potential biomarkers for mild Alzheimer's disease. *Psychiatry Research: Neuroimaging*, 221(1), 37–42. https://doi.org/10.1016/j.pscychresns.2013.10.010

Barbey, A., Colom, R., Paul, E., & Grafman, J. (2012). Architecture of fluid intelligence and working memory revealed by lesion mapping. *Brain Structure and Function*, 219(2), 485–494. https://doi.org/10.1007/s00429-013-0512-z

Barkley, R. A. (2010). Why emotional impulsiveness should be a central feature of ADHD. *ADHD Report*, 18(4), 1–5. https://doi.org/10.1521/adhd.2010.18.4.1

Barkley, R. A. (2012a). *Barkley deficits in executive functioning scale—children and adolescents (BDEFS-CA)*. Guilford.

Barkley, R. A. (2012b). *Executive functions: What they are, how they work, and why they evolved*. Guilford.

Baron-Cohen, S. (2003). *The essential difference: The truth about the male and female brain*. Basic Books.

Barr, R., Danziger, C., Hilliard, M. E., Andolina, C., & Ruskis, J. (2010). Amount, content and context of infant media exposure: A parental questionnaire and diary analysis. *International Journal of Early Years Education, 18*(2), 107–122. https://doi.org/10.1080/09669760.2010.494431

Barrett, L. F., Bliss-Moreau, E., Duncan, S. L., Rausch, S. L., & Wright, C. L. (2007). The amygdala and the experience of affect. *SCAN, 2*(2), 73–83. https://doi.org/10.1093/scan/nsl042

Bartels, A., & Zeki, S. (2000). The neural basis of romantic love. *NeuroReport, 11*(17), 3829–3834. https://doi.org/10.1097/00001756-200011270-00046

Bartolomeo, P. (2006). A parieto-frontal network for spatial awareness in the right hemisphere of the human brain. *Archives of Neurology, 63*(9), 1238–1241. https://doi.org/10.1001/archneur.63.9.1238

Battelli, L., Cavanagh, P., Intrilligator, J., Tramo, M. J., Henaff, M., Michel, F., & Barton, J. J. S. (2001). Unilateral right parietal damage leads to bilateral deficit for high-level motion. *Neuron, 32*(6), 985–995. https://doi.org/10.1016/s0896-6273(01)00536-0

Bauman, M. D., Lavenex, P., Mason, W. A., Capitanio, J. P., & Amaral, D. G. (2004). The development of social behavior following neonatal amygdala lesions in rhesus monkeys. *Journal of Cognitive Neuroscience, 16*(8), 1388–1411. https://doi.org/10.1162/0898929042304741

Bazanis, E., Rogers, R. D., Dowson, J. H., Taylor, P., Meux, C., Staley, C., & Sahakian, B. J. (2002). Neurocognitive deficits in decision-making and planning of patients with DSM-III-R borderline personality disorder. *Psychological Medicine, 32*(8), 1395–1405. https://doi.org/10.1017/s0033291702006657

Beason-Held, L. L., Kraut, M. A., & Resnick, S. M. (2009). Stability of default-mode network activity in the aging brain. *Brain Imaging and Behavior, 3*(2), 123–131. https://doi.org/10.1007/s11682-008-9054-z

Bechara, A., & Damasio, A. R. (2005). The somatic marker hypothesis: A neural theory of economic decision. *Games and Economic Behavior, 52*(2), 336–372. https://doi.org/10.1016/j.geb.2004.06.010

Bechara, A., Damasio, A. R., Damasio, H., & Anderson, S. W. (1994). Insensitivity to future consequences following damage to human prefrontal cortex. *Cognition, 50*(1–3), 7–15. https://doi.org/10.1016/0010-0277(94)90018-3

Bechara, A., Damasio, H., Tranel, D., & Anderson, S. W. (1998). Dissociation of working memory from decision making within the human prefrontal cortex. *Journal of Neuroscience, 18*(1), 428–437. https://doi.org/10.1523/jneurosci.18-01-00428.1998

Bechara, A., & Naqvi, N. (2004). Listening to your heart: Interoceptive awareness

as a gateway to feeling. *Nature Neuroscience, 7*(2), 102–103. https://doi.org/10
.1038/nn0204-102

Beckmann, C. F., DeLuca, M., Devlin, J. T., & Smith, S. M. (2005). Investigations
into resting-state connectivity using independent component analysis. *Philosophical Transactions of the Royal Society: Biological Sciences, 360*(1457),
1001–1013. https://doi.org/10.1098/rstb.2005.1634

Beer, J. S., John, O. P., Scabini, D., & Knight, R. T. (2006). Orbitofrontal cortex and
social behavior: Integrating self-monitoring and emotion-cognition interactions.
Journal of Cognitive Neuroscience, 18(6), 871–879. https://doi.org/10.1162/jocn
.2006.18.6.871

Belfi, A. M., Vessel, E. A., Brielmann, A., Isik, A. I., Chatterjee, A., Leder, H., & Starr, G.
G. (2019). Dynamics of aesthetic experience are reflected in the default-mode network.
NeuroImage, 188, 584–597. https://doi.org/10.1016/j.neuroimage.2018.12.017

Bellana, B., Liu, Z. X., Diamond, N. B., Grady, C. L., & Moscovitch, M.
(2017). Similarities and differences in the default mode network across
rest, retrieval, and future imagining. *Human Brain Mapping, 38*(3),
1155–1171. https://doi.org/10.1002/hbm.23445

Berthoz, S., Armony, J. L., Blair, R. J. R., & Dolan, R. J. (2002). An fMRI study of
intentional and unintentional (embarrassing) violations of social norms. *Brain,
125*(8), 1696–1708. https://doi.org/10.1093/brain/awf190

Berne, E. (1961). *Transactional analysis in psychotherapy: A systematic individual
and social psychiatry.* Grove Press.

Biederman, J., Ball, S. W., Monuteaux, M. C., Mick, E., Spencer, T. J., McCreary,
M., & Faraone, S. V. (2008). New insights into the comorbidity between
ADHD and major depression in adolescent and young adult females. *Journal of the American Academy of Child and Adolescent Psychiatry, 47*(4),
426–434. https://doi.org/10.1097/chi.0b013e31816429d3

Biederman, J., Petty, C. R., Day, H., Goldin, R. L., Spencer, T., Faraone, S. V., Surman, C. B., & Wozniak, J. (2012). Severity of the aggression/anxiety-depression/
attention child behavior checklist profile discriminates between different levels of deficits in emotional regulation in youth with attention-deficit hyperactivity disorder. *Journal of Developmental and Behavioral Pediatrics, 33*(3),
236–243. https://doi.org/10.1097/dbp.0b013e3182475267

Blair, R. J. R. (1995). A cognitive developmental approach to morality: Investigating the
psychopath. *Cognition, 57*(1), 1–29. https://doi.org/10.1016/0010-0277(95)00676-P

Blanchard-Fields, F., & Irion, J. C. (1988). The relation between locus of control and
coping in two contexts: Age as a moderator variable. *Psychology and Aging, 3*(2),
197. https://doi.org/10.1037//0882-7974.3.2.197

Blanke, O., & Arzy, S. (2005). The out-of-body experience: Disturbed self-processing
at the temporo-parietal junction. *Neuroscientist, 11*(1), 11–24. https://doi.org/10
.1177/1073858404270885

Bluhm, R. L., Miller, J., Lanius, R. A., Osuch, E. A., Boksman, K., Neufeld, R., &
Williamson, P. (2007). Spontaneous low-frequency fluctuations in the BOLD sig-

nal in schizophrenic patients: Anomalies in the default network. *Schizophrenia Bulletin*, *33*(4), 1004–1012. https://doi.org/10.1093/schbul/sbm052

Bluhm, R. L., Williamson, P. C., Osuch, E. A., Frewen, P. A., Stevens, T. K., Boksman, K., & Lanius, R. A. (2009). Alterations in default network connectivity in posttraumatic stress disorder related to early-life trauma. *Journal of Psychiatry and Neuroscience*, *34*(3), 187–194.

Bohus, M., Haaf, B., Stiglmayr, C., Pohl, U., Böhme, R., & Linehan, M. (2000). Evaluation of inpatient dialectical-behavioral therapy for borderline personality disorder—a prospective study. *Behaviour Research and Therapy*, *38*(9), 875–887. https://doi.org/10.1016/s0005-7967(99)00103-5

Bonda, E., Petrides, M., Ostry, D., & Evans, A. (1996). Specific involvement of human parietal systems and the amygdala in the perception of biological motion. *Journal of Neuroscience*, *16*(11), 3737–3744. https://doi.org/10.1523/jneurosci.16-11-03737.1996

Brambilla, P., Soloff, P. H., Sala, M., Nicoletti, M. A., Keshavan, M. S., & Soares, J. C. (2004). Anatomical MRI study of borderline personality disorder patients. *Psychiatry Research: Neuroimaging*, *131*(2), 125–133. https://doi.org/10.1016/j.pscychresns.2004.04.003

Brodal, P. (1992). *The central nervous system.* Oxford University Press.

Broderick, P., & Blewitt, P. (2014). *The life span: Human development for helping professionals* (4th ed.). Pearson.

Brothers, L. (1997). *Friday's footprint.* Oxford University Press.

Brown, A. B., Biederman, J., Valera, E., Makris, N., Doyle, A., Whitfield-Gabrieli, S., Mick, E., Spencer, T., Faraone, S., & Seidman, L. (2011). Relationship of DAT1 and adult ADHD to task-positive and task-negative working memory networks. *Psychiatry Research*, *193*(1), 7–16. https://doi.org/10.1016/j.pscychresns.2011.01.006

Brown, H. D., Rosslyn, S. M., Reiter, H. C., Baer, L., & Janice, M. A. (1994). Can patients with obsessive-compulsive disorder discriminate between percepts and mental images? A signal detection analysis. *Journal of Abnormal Psychology*, *103*(3), 445–454. https://doi.org/10.1037//0021-843x.103.3.445

Brown, M. R., & Sullivan, P. G. (2005). Mitochondrial aging and dysfunction in Alzheimer's disease. *Progress in Neuro-Psychopharmacology and Biological Psychiatry*, *29*(3), 407–410. https://doi.org/10.1016/j.pnpbp.2004.12.007

Brozzoli, C., Gentile, G., & Ehrsson, H. (2012). That's near my hand! Parietal and premotor coding of hand-centered space contributes to localization and self-attribution of the hand. *Journal of Neuroscience*, *32*(42), 14573–14582. https://doi.org/10.1523/jneurosci.2660-12.2012

Brunner, M., Keller, U., Dierendonck, C., Reichert, M., Ugen, S., Fischbach, A., & Martin, R. (2010). The structure of academic self-concepts revisited: The nested Marsh/Shavelson model. *Journal of Educational Psychology*, *102*(4), 964. https://doi.org/10.1037/a0019644

Buchheim, A., Erk, S., George, C., Kächele, H., Kircher, T., Martius, P., & Walter, H. (2008). Neural correlates of attachment trauma in borderline personality disorder:

A functional magnetic resonance imaging study. *Psychiatry Research: Neuroimaging, 163*(3), 223–235. https://doi.org/10.1016/j.pscychresns.2007.07.001

Buchheim, A., George, C., Liebl, V., Moser, A., & Benecke, C. (2007). Affective facial behavior of borderline patients during the Adult Attachment Projective [in German]. *Zeitschrift für Psychosomatische Medizin und Psychotherapie, 53*(4), 339–354. https://doi.org/10.13109/zptm.2007.53.4.339

Buckner, R. L., Andrews-Hanna, J. R., & Schacter, D. L. (2008). The brain's default network. *Annals of the New York Academy of Sciences, 1124*(1), 1–38. https://doi.org/10.1196/annals.1440.011

Buneo, C., & Andersen, R. (2006). The posterior parietal cortex: Sensorimotor interface for the planning and online control of visually guided movements. *Neuropsychologia, 44*(13), 2594–2606. https://doi.org/10.1016/j.neuropsychologia.2005.10.011

Bush, G. (2011). Cingulate, frontal, and parietal cortical dysfunction in attention-deficit/hyperactivity disorder. *Biological Psychiatry, 69*(12), 1160–1167. https://doi.org/10.1016/j.biopsych.2011.01.022

Bush, G., Luu, P., & Posner, M. I. (2000). Cognitive and emotional influences in anterior cingulate cortex. *Trends in Cognitive Sciences, 4*(6), 215–222. https://doi.org/10.1016/s1364-6613(00)01483-2

Bush, G., Vogt, B. A., Holmes, J., Dale, A. M., Greve, D., Jenike, M. A., & Rosen, B. R. (2002). Dorsal anterior cingulate cortex: A role in reward-based decision making. *PNAS, 99*(1), 507–512. https://doi.org/10.1073/pnas.012470999

Cabeza, R., Anderson, N. D., Houle, S., Mangels, J. A., & Nyberg, L. (2000). Age-related differences in neural activity during item and temporal-order memory retrieval: A positron emission tomography study. *Journal of Cognitive Neuroscience, 12*(1), 197–206. https://doi.org/10.1162/089892900561832

Cabeza, R., Anderson, N. D., Locantore, J. K., & McIntosh, A. R. (2002). Aging gracefully: Compensatory brain activity in high-performing older adults. *NeuroImage, 17*(3), 1394–1402. https://doi.org/10.1006/nimg.2002.1280

Cabeza, R., Ciaramelli, E., & Moscovitch, M. (2012). Cognitive contributions of the ventral parietal cortex: An integrative theoretical account. *Trends in Cognitive Sciences, 16*(6), 338–352. https://doi.org/10.1016/j.tics.2012.04.008

Calder, A. J., Keane, J., Manly, T., Sprengelmeyer, R., Scott, S., Nimmo-Smith, S., & Young, A. W. (2003). Facial expression recognition across the adult life span. *Neuropsychologia, 41*(2), 195–202. https://doi.org/10.1016/s0028-3932(02)00149-5

Calkins, S. D. (1997). Cardiac vagal tone indices of temperamental reactivity and behavioral regulation in young children. *Journal of the International Society for Developmental Psychobiology, 31*(2), 125–135. https://doi.org/10.1002/(sici)1098-2302(199709)31:2<125::aid-dev5>3.0.co;2-m

Carr, L., Iacoboni, M., Dubeau, M. C., Mazziotta, J. C., & Lenzi, G. L. (2003). Neural mechanisms of empathy in humans: A relay from neural systems for imitation to limbic areas. *PNAS, 100*(9), 5497–5502. https://doi.org/10.1073/pnas.0935845100

Carstensen, L. L., Pasupathi, M., Mayr, U., & Nesselroade, J. R. (2000). Emotional experience in everyday life across the adult life span. *Journal of Personality and Social Psychology, 79*(4), 644–655. https://doi.org/10.1037//0022-3514.79.4.644

Carstensen, L. L., & Turk-Charles, S. (1994). The salience of emotion across the adult life span. *Psychology and Aging, 9*(2), 259–264. https://doi.org/10.1037//0882-7974.9.2.259

Cascio, C. J., Foss-Feig, J. H., Heacock, J., Schauder, K. B., Loring, W. A., Rogers, B. P., & Bolton, S. (2014). Affective neural response to restricted interests in autism spectrum disorders. *Journal of Child Psychology and Psychiatry, 55*(2), 162–171. https://doi.org/10.1111/jcpp.12147

Caspers, S., Schleicher, A., Bacha-Trams, M., Palomero-Gallagher, N., Amunts, K., & Zilles, K. (2012). Organization of the human inferior parietal lobule based on receptor architectonics. *Cerebral Cortex, 23*(3), 615–628. https://doi.org/10.1093/cercor/bhs048

Castelli, F., Glaser, D. E., & Butterworth, B. (2006). Discrete and analogue quantity processing in the parietal lobe: A functional MRI study. *PNAS, 103*(12), 4693–4698. https://doi.org/10.1073/pnas.0600444103

Cavanna, A. E., & Trimble, M. R. (2006). The precuneus: A review of its functional anatomy and behavioural correlates. *Brain, 129*(3), 564–583. https://doi.org/10.1093/brain/awl004

Chai, X. J., Ofen, N., Gabrieli, J. D., & Whitfield-Gabrieli, S. (2014). Development of deactivation of the default-mode network during episodic memory formation. *NeuroImage, 84,* 932–938. https://doi.org/10.1016/j.neuroimage.2013.09.032

Chanen, A. M., Jackson, H. J., McCutcheon, L. K., Jovev, M., Dudgeon, P., Yuen, H. P., Germano, D., Nistico, H., McDougall, E., Weinstein, C., Clarkson, V., & McGorry, P. D. (2008). Early intervention for adolescents with borderline personality disorder using cognitive analytic therapy: Randomised controlled trial. *British Journal of Psychiatry, 193*(6), 477–484. https://doi.org/10.1192/bjp.bp.107.048934

Charles, S. T., Mather, M., & Carstensen, L. L. (2003). Aging and emotional memory: The forgettable nature of negative images for older adults. *Journal of Experimental Psychology, 132*(2), 310–324. https://doi.org/10.1037/0096-3445.132.2.310

Chaudhari, B., Menon, P., Saldanha, D., Tewari, A., & Bhattacharya, L. (2015). Internet addiction and its determinants among medical students. *Industrial Psychiatry Journal, 24*(2), 158–162. https://doi.org/10.4103/0972-6748.181729

Chayasirisobhon, S. (2021). Mechanisms of action and pharmacokinetics of cannabis. *Permanente Journal, 25*(1), 1–3. https://doi.org/10.7812/tpp/19.200

Chen, A. C., Oathes, D. J., Chang, C., Bradley, T., Zhou, Z.-W., Williams, L. M., Glover, G. H., Deisseroth, K., & Etkin, A. (2013). Causal interactions between fronto-parietal central executive and default-mode networks in humans. *PNAS, 110*(49), 19944–19949. https://doi.org/10.1073/pnas.1311772110

Chen, X., Chen, N.-X., Shen, Y.-Q., Li, H.-X., Li, L., Lu, B., Zhu, Z. C., Fan, Z., & Yan, C. G. (2020). The subsystem mechanism of default mode network underlying rumination: A reproducible neuroimaging study. *NeuroImage, 221,* 117185. https://doi.org/10.1016/j.neuroimage.2020.117185

Chochon, F., Cohen, L., Demoortele, S., & Dehaene, S. (1999). Differential contributions of the left and right parietal lobules to number processing. *Journal of Cognitive Neuroscience, 11*(6), 617–630. https://doi.org/10.1162/089892999563689

Christov-Moore, L., Simpson, E. A., Coudé, G., Grigaityte, K., Iacoboni, M., & Ferrari, P. F. (2014). Empathy: Gender effects in brain and behavior. *Neuroscience and Biobehavioral Reviews, 46*, 604–627. https://doi.org/10.1016/j.neubiorev.2014.09.001

Chugani, H. T., Phelps, M. E., & Mazziotta, J. C. (1987). Positron emission tomography study of human brain functional development. *Annals of Neurology, 22*(4), 487–497. https://doi.org/10.1002/ana.410220408

Churchill, J. D., Stanis, J. J., Press, C., Kushelev, M., & Greenough, W. T. (2003). Is procedural memory relatively spared from age effects? *Neurobiology of Aging, 24*(6), 883–892. https://doi.org/10.1016/s0197-4580(02)00194-x

Claeys, K. G., Lindsey, D. T., De Schutter, E., & Orban, G. A. (2003). A higher order motion region in human inferior parietal lobule: Evidence from fMRI. *Neuron, 40*(3), 631–642. https://doi.org/10.1016/s0896-6273(03)00590-7

Cliff, D. P., Howard, S. J., Radesky, J. S., McNeill, J., & Vella, S. A. (2018). Early childhood media exposure and self-regulation: Bidirectional longitudinal associations. *Academic Pediatrics, 18*(7), 813–819. https://doi.org/10.1016/j.acap.2018.04.012

Colby, C. L. (1998). Action-oriented spatial reference frames in cortex. *Neuron, 20*(1), 15–24. https://doi.org/10.1016/s0896-6273(00)80429-8

Colby, C. L., & Goldberg, M. E. (1999). Space and attention in parietal cortex. *Annual Review of Neuroscience, 22*, 319–349. https://doi.org/10.1146/annurev.neuro.22.1.319

Colom, R., Haier, R. J., Head, K., Álvarez-Linera, J., Quiroga, M. Á., Shih, P. C., & Jung, R. E. (2009). Gray matter correlates of fluid, crystallized, and spatial intelligence: Testing the P-FIT model. *Intelligence, 37*(2), 124–135. https://doi.org/10.1016/j.intell.2008.07.007

Coolidge, F. L., Thede, L. L., & Young, S. E. (2000). Heritability and the comorbidity of attention deficit hyperactivity disorder with behavioral disorders and executive function deficits: A preliminary investigation. *Developmental Neuropsychology, 17*(3), 273–287. https://doi.org/10.1207/s15326942dn1703_1

Corballis, M. C. (2013). Wandering tales: Evolutionary origins of mental time travel and language. *Frontiers in Psychology, 4*, 485. https://doi.org/10.3389/fpsyg.2013.00485

Corbetta, M., & Shulman, G. (2002). Control of goal-directed and stimulus-driven attention in the brain. *Nature Reviews Neuroscience, 3*(3), 201–215. https://doi.org/10.1038/nrn755

Cornette, L., Dupont, P., Salmon, E., & Orban, G. (2001). The neural substrate of orientation working memory. *Journal of Cognitive Neuroscience, 13*(6), 813–828. https://doi.org/10.1162/08989290152541476

Costa, V. D., & Averbeck, B. B. (2013). Frontal-parietal and limbic-striatal activity underlies information sampling in the best choice problem. *Cerebral Cortex, 25*(4), 972–982. https://doi.org/10.1093/cercor/bht286

Coull, J., Cotti, J., & Vidal, F. (2014). Increasing activity in left inferior parietal cortex and right prefrontal cortex with increasing temporal predictability: An fMRI study of the hazard function. *Procedia-Social and Behavioral Sciences, 126,* 41–44. https://doi.org/10.1016/j.sbspro.2014.02.311

Courtney, A. L., & Meyer, M. L. (2020). Self-other representation in the social brain reflects social connection. *Journal of Neuroscience, 40*(29), 5616–5627. https://doi.org/10.1523/jneurosci.2826-19.2020

Cozolino, L. (2020). *The pocket guide to neuroscience for clinicians.* Norton.

Critchley, H. D., Wiens, S., Rotshtein, P., Öhman, A., & Dolan, R. J. (2004). Neural systems supporting interoceptive awareness. *Nature Neuroscience, 7*(2), 189–195. https://doi.org/10.1038/nn1176

Crittenden, B. M., Mitchell, D. J., & Duncan, J. (2015). Recruitment of the default mode network during a demanding act of executive control. *eLIFE, 4,* e06481. https://doi.org/10.7554/elife.06481

Crowe, D. A., Goodwin, S. J., Blackman, R. K., Sakellaridi, S., Sponheim, S. R., MacDonald, A. W., & Chafee, M. V. (2013). Prefrontal neurons transmit signals to parietal neurons that reflect executive control of cognition. *Nature Neuroscience, 16*(10), 1484–1491. https://doi.org/10.1038/nn.3509

Csikszentmihalyi, M. (2008). *Flow: The psychology of optimal experience.* Harper.

Culham, J. C., & Kanwisher, N. G. (2001). Neuroimaging of cognitive functions in human parietal cortex. *Current Opinion in Neurobiology, 11*(2), 157–163. https://doi.org/10.1016/s0959-4388(00)00191-4

Cunningham, C. E., Woodward, C. A., Shannon, H. S., MacIntosh, J., Lendrum, B., Rosenbloom, D., & Brown, J. (2002). Readiness for organizational change: A longitudinal study of workplace, psychological and behavioural correlates. *Journal of Occupational and Organizational Psychology, 75*(4), 377–392. https://doi.org/10.1348/096317902321119637

Dahlgren, M. K., Sagar, K. A., Racine, M. T., Dreman, M. W., & Gruber, S. A. (2016). Marijuana use predicts cognitive performance on tasks of executive function. *Journal of Studies on Alcohol and Drugs, 77*(2), 298–308. https://doi.org/10.15288/jsad.2016.77.298

Damasio, A. R. (1994). *Descartes' error: Emotion, reason and the human brain.* Putnam and Sons.

Daniels, J., Frewen, P., McKinnon, M. C., & Lanius, R. A. (2011). Default mode alterations in posttraumatic stress disorder related to early-life trauma: A developmental perspective. *Journal of Psychiatry and Neuroscience, 36*(1), 56–59. https://doi.org/10.1503/jpn.100050

Daniels, J. K., McFarlane, A. C., Bluhm, R. L., Moores, K. A., Clark, C. R., Shaw, M. E., Williamson, P. C., Densmore, M., & Lanius, R. A. (2010). Switching between executive and default mode networks in posttraumatic stress disorder: Alterations in functional connectivity. *Journal of Psychiatry and Neuroscience, 35*(4), 258–266. https://doi.org/10.1503/jpn.090175

Danziger, N., Faillenot, I., & Peyron, R. (2009). Can we share a pain we never felt? Neural correlates of empathy in patients with congenital insensitivity to pain. *Neuron, 61*(2), 203–212. https://doi.org/10.1016/j.neuron.2008.11.023

D'Argembeau, A., Renaud, O., & Van der Linden, M. (2011). Frequency, characteristics and functions of future-oriented thoughts in daily life. *Applied Cognitive Psychology, 25*(1), 96–103. https://doi.org/10.1002/acp.1647

Davey, C. G., Pujol, J., & Harrison, B. J. (2016). Mapping the self in the brain's default mode network. *NeuroImage, 132,* 390–397. https://doi.org/10.1016/j.neuroimage .2016.02.022

Davis, M. (1992). The role of the amygdala in fear and anxiety. *Annual Review of Neuroscience, 15*(1), 353–375. https://doi.org/10.1146/annurev.neuro.15.1.353

Davis, M. (1997). Neurobiology of fear responses: The role of the amygdala. *Journal of Neuropsychiatry and Clinical Neurosciences, 9*(3), 382–402. https://doi.org/10.1176/jnp.9.3.382

Davis, M., & Whalen, P. J. (2001). The amygdala: Vigilance and emotion. *Molecular Psychiatry, 6*(1), 13–34. https://doi.org/10.1038/sj.mp.4000812

Dehaene, S., Molko, N., Cohen, L., & Wilson, A. J. (2004). Arithmetic and the brain. *Current Opinion in Neurobiology, 14*(2), 218–224. https://doi.org/10.1016/j.conb .2004.03.008

Dehaene, S., Piazza, M., Pinel, P., & Cohen, L. (2003). Three parietal circuits for number processing. *Cognitive Neuropsychology, 20*(3), 487–506. https://doi.org/10 .1080/02643290244000239

de la Fuente, J., Goldman, S., Stanus, E., Vizuete, C., Morlán, I., Bobes, J., & Mendlewicz, J. (1997). Brain glucose metabolism in borderline personality disorder. *Journal of Psychiatric Research, 31*(5), 531–541. https://doi.org/10.1016/s0022-3956(97)00001-0

Delis, D. C., Kaplan, E., & Kramer, J. H. (2001). *Delis-Kaplan executive function system* [Dataset]. PsycTESTS Dataset. American Psychological Association. https:// doi.org/10.1037/t15082-000

D'Esposito, M. (2007). From cognitive to neural models of working memory. *Philosophical Transactions of the Royal Society B: Biological Sciences, 362*(1481), 761–772. https://doi.org/10.1098/rstb.2007.2086

Diamond, M. C., Law, F., Rhodes, H., Lindner, B., Rosenweig, M. R., Krech, D., & Bennett, E. L. (1966). Increases of cortical depth and glia numbers in rats subjected to enriched environment. *Journal of Comparative Neurology, 128*(1), 117–126. https://doi.org/10.1002/cne.901280110

Diamond, M. C., Scheibel, A. B., Murphy, G. M., & Harvey, T. (1985). On the brain of a scientist: Albert Einstein. *Experimental Neurology, 88*(1), 198–204. https://doi.org/10.1016/0014-4886(85)90123-2

Dias, R., Robbins, T. W., & Roberts, A. C. (1996). Dissociation in prefrontal cortex of affective and attentional shifts. *Nature, 380*(6569), 69–72. https://doi.org/10.1038/380069a0

Diehl, M., Coyle, N., & Labouvie-Vief, G. (1996). Age and sex differences in strategies of coping and defense across the life span. *Psychology and Aging, 11*(1), 127–139. https://doi.org/10.1037//0882-7974.11.1.127

Dinn, W. M., Harris, C. L., Aycicegi, A., Greene, P. B., Kirkley, S. M., & Reilly, C. (2004). Neurocognitive function in borderline personality disorder. *Prog-

ress in Neuro-Psychopharmacology and Biological Psychiatry, 28(2), 329–341. https://doi.org/10.1016/j.pnpbp.2003.10.012

Dolan, R. J. (1999). On the neurology of morals. *Nature Neuroscience*, 2(11), 927–929. https://doi.org/10.1038/14707

Dolan, R. J., & Vuilleumier, P. (2003). Amygdala automaticity in emotional processing. *Annals of the New York Academy of Sciences*, 985(1), 348–355. https://doi.org/10.1111/j.1749-6632.2003.tb07093.x

Donegan, N. H., Sanislow, C. A., Blumberg, H. P., Fulbright, R. K., Lacadie, C., Skudlarski, P., Gore, J. C., Olson, I. R., McGlashan, T. H., & Wexler, B. E. (2003). Amygdala hyperreactivity in borderline personality disorder: Implications for emotional dysregulation. *Biological Psychiatry*, 54(11), 1284–1293. https://doi.org/10.1016/s0006-3223(03)00636-x

Driessen, M., Herrmann, J., Stahl, K., Zwaan, M., Meier, S., Hill, A., & Petersen, D. (2000). Magnetic resonance imaging volumes of the hippocampus and the amygdala in women with borderline personality disorder and early traumatization. *Archives of General Psychiatry*, 57(12), 1115–1122. https://doi.org/10.1001/archpsyc.57.12.1115

Driver, J., & Mattingley, J. B. (1998). Parietal neglect and visual awareness. *Nature Neuroscience*, 1(1), 17–22. https://doi.org/10.1038/217

Duffy, K. A., Rosch, K. S., Nebel, M. B., Seymour, K. E., Lindquist, M. A., Pekar, J. J., Mostofsky, S. H., & Cohen, J. R. (2021). Increased integration between default mode and task-relevant networks in children with ADHD is associated with impaired response control. *Developmental Cognitive Neuroscience*, 50, 1–12. https://doi.org/10.1016/j.dcn.2021.100980

Dziobek, I., Preißler, S., Grozdanovic, Z., Heuser, I., Heekeren, H. R., & Roepke, S. (2011). Neuronal correlates of altered empathy and social cognition in borderline personality disorder. *NeuroImage*, 57(2), 539–548. https://doi.org/10.1016/j.neuroimage.2011.05.005

Edelman, M. W. (1987). *Families in peril: An agenda for social change* (Vol. 2). Harvard University Press.

Edin, F., Macoveanu, J., Olesen, P., Tegner, J., & Klingberg, T. (2007). Stronger synaptic connectivity as a mechanism behind development of working memory-related brain activity during childhood. *Journal of Cognitive Neuroscience*, 19(5), 750–760. https://doi.org/10.1162/jocn.2007.19.5.750

El-Sheikh, M., & Buckhalt, J. A. (2005). Vagal regulation and emotional intensity predict children's sleep problems. *Journal of the International Society for Developmental Psychobiology*, 46(4), 307–317. https://doi.org/10.1002/dev.20066

ElSohly, M. A., Mehmedic, Z., Foster, S., Gon, C., Chandra, S., & Church, J. C. (2016). Changes in cannabis potency over the last 2 decades (1995–2014): Analysis of current data in the United States. *Biological Psychiatry*, 79(7), 613–619. https://doi.org/10.1016/j.biopsych.2016.01.004

Erikson, E. H. (1994). *Identity and the life cycle*. Norton.

Erraji-Benchekroun, L., Underwood, M. D., Arango, V., Galfalvy, H., Pavlidis, P.,

Smyrniotopoulos, P., & Sibille, E. (2005). Molecular aging in human prefrontal cortex is selective and continuous throughout adult life. *Biological Psychiatry*, *57*(5), 549–558. https://doi.org/10.1016/j.biopsych.2004.10.034

Eslinger, P. J. (1996). Conceptualizing, describing, and measuring components of executive function: A summary. In G. R. Lyons & N. A. Krasnegor (Eds.), *Attention, memory, and executive function* (pp. 233–248). Paul H. Brooks.

Eslinger, P. J., Moore, P., Antani, S., Anderson, C., & Grossman, M. (2012). Apathy in frontotemporal dementia: Behavioral and neuroimaging correlates. *Behavioural Neurology*, *25*(2), 127–136. https://doi.org/10.1155/2012/286427

Esménio, S., Soares, J. M., Oliveira-Silva, P., Zeidman, P., Razi, A., Gonçalves, Ó. F., & Coutinho, J. (2019). Using resting-state DMN effective connectivity to characterize the neurofunctional architecture of empathy. *Scientific Reports*, *9*(1), 1–9. https://doi.org/10.1038/s41598-019-38801-6

Estrada, E., Ferrer, E., Román, F. J., Karama, S., & Colom, R. (2019). Time-lagged associations between cognitive and cortical development from childhood to early adulthood. *Developmental Psychology*, *55*(6), 1338. https://doi.org/10.1037/dev0000716

Etkin, A., Prater, K. E., Hoeft, F., Menon, V., & Schatzberg, A. F. (2010). Failure of anterior cingulate activation and connectivity with the amygdala during implicit regulation of emotional processing in generalized anxiety disorder. *American Journal of Psychiatry*, *167*(5), 545–554. https://doi.org/10.1176/appi.ajp.2009.09070931

Fan, F., Liao, X., Lei, T., Zhao, T., Xia, M., Men, W., Wang, Y., Hu, M., Liu, J., Qin, S., Tan, S., Gao, J.-H., Dong, Q., Tao, S., & He, Y. (2021). Development of the default-mode network during childhood and adolescence: A longitudinal resting-state fMRI study. *NeuroImage*, *226*, 117581. https://doi.org/10.1016/j.neuroimage.2020.117581

Fedorenko, E., Duncan, J., & Kanwisher, N. (2013). Broad domain generality in focal regions of frontal and parietal cortex. *PNAS*, *110*(41), 16616–16621. https://doi.org/10.1073/pnas.1315235110

Fias, W., Lamartine, J., Caessens, B., & Orban, G. (2007). Processing of abstract knowledge in the horizontal segment of the intraparietal sulcus. *Journal of Neuroscience*, *27*(33), 8952–8957. https://doi.org/10.1523/jneurosci.2076-07.2007

Fias, W., Lammertyn, J., Reynvoet, B., Dupont, P., & Orban, G. (2003). Parietal representation of symbolic and nonsymbolic magnitude. *Journal of Cognitive Neuroscience*, *15*(1), 47–56. https://doi.org/10.1162/089892903321107819

Firth, J., Torous, J., Stubbs, B., Firth, J. A., Steiner, G. Z., Smith, L., Alvarez-Jimenez, M., Gleeson, J., Vancampfort, D., Armitage, C. J., & Sarris, J. (2019). The "online brain": How the internet may be changing our cognition. *World Psychiatry*, *18*(2), 119–129. https://doi.org/10.1002/wps.20617

Fiset, P., Paus, T., Daloze, T., Plourde, G., Meuret, P., Bonhomme, V., Hajj-Ali, N., Backman, S. B., & Evans, A. C. (1999). Brain mechanisms of propofol-induced loss of consciousness in humans: A positron emission tomographic study. *Journal of Neuroscience*, *19*(13), 5506–5513. https://doi.org/10.1523/jneurosci.19-13-05506.1999

Fraenz, C., Schlüter, C., Friedrich, P., Jung, R. E., Güntürkün, O., & Genç, E. (2021). Interindividual differences in matrix reasoning are linked to functional connectivity between brain regions nominated by parieto-frontal integration theory. *Intelligence, 87*, 101545. https://doi.org/10.1016/j.intell.2021.101545

Fransson, P. (2005). Spontaneous low-frequency BOLD signal fluctuations: An fMRI investigation of the resting-state default mode of brain function hypothesis. *Human Brain Mapping, 26*(1), 15–29. https://doi.org/10.1002/hbm.20113

Frewen, P. A., Dozois, D. J., Neufeld, R. W., Lane, R. D., Densmore, M., Stevens, T. K., & Lanius, R. A. (2011). Emotional numbing in posttraumatic stress disorder: A functional magnetic resonance imaging study. *Journal of Clinical Psychiatry, 72*(4), 6425. https://doi.org/10.4088/jcp.10m06477

Frey, S., & Petrides, M. (2000). Orbitofrontal cortex: A key prefrontal region for encoding information. *PNAS, 97*(15), 8723–8727. https://doi.org/10.1073/pnas.140543497

Frick, R. B. (1982). The ego and the vestibulocerebellar system: Some theoretical perspectives. *Psychoanalytic Quarterly, 51*(1), 93–122. https://doi.org/10.1080/21674086.1982.11926986

Frings, L., Wagner, K., Unterrainer, J., Spreer, J., Halsband, U., & Schulze-Bonhage, A. (2006). Gender-related differences in lateralization of hippocampal activation and cognitive strategy. *NeuroReport, 17*(4), 417–421. https://doi.org/10.1097/01.wnr.0000203623.02082.e3

Fuster, J. M. (1997). *The prefrontal cortex: Anatomy, physiology, and neuropsychology of the frontal lobe* (3rd ed.). Lippincott-Raven.

Fuster, J. M. (2000). Executive frontal functions. *Experimental Brain Research, 133*(1), 66–70. https://doi.org/10.1007/s002210000401

Gallagher, M., McMahon, R. W., & Schoenbaum, G. (1999). Orbitofrontal cortex and representation of incentive value in associative learning. *Journal of Neuroscience, 19*(15), 6610–6614. https://doi.org/10.1523/jneurosci.19-15-06610.1999

Galovski, T., & Lyons, J. A. (2004). Psychological sequelae of combat violence: A review of the impact of PTSD on the veteran's family and possible interventions. *Aggression and Violent Behavior, 9*(5), 477–501. https://doi.org/10.1016/s1359-1789(03)00045-4

Gao, T., Newman, G. E., & Scholl, B. J. (2009). The psychophysics of chasing: A case study in the perception of animacy. *Cognitive Psychology, 59*(2), 154–179. https://doi.org/10.1016/j.cogpsych.2009.03.001

Garavan, H., Pendergrass, J. C., Ross, T. J., Stein, E. A., & Risinger, R. C. (2001). Amygdala response to both positively and negatively valenced stimuli. *NeuroReport, 12*(12), 2779–2783. https://doi.org/10.1097/00001756-200108280-00036

Garrity, A. (2007). Aberrant "default mode" functional connectivity in schizophrenia. *American Journal of Psychiatry, 164*(3), 450. https://doi.org/10.1176/appi.ajp.164.3.450

Gehring, W. J., & Willoughby, A. R. (2002). The medial prefrontal cortex and the rapid processing of monetary gains and losses. *Science, 295*(5563), 2279–2282. https://doi.org/10.1126/science.1066893

Genovesio, A., Wise, S., & Passingham, R. (2014). Prefrontal-parietal function: From foraging to foresight. *Trends in Cognitive Sciences, 18*(2), 72–81. https://doi.org/10.1016/j.tics.2013.11.007

Gentili, C., Ricciardi, E., Gobbini, M. I., Santarelli, M. F., Haxby, J. V., Pietrini, P., & Guzzelli, M. (2009). Beyond amygdala: Default mode network activity differs between patients with social phobia and healthy controls. *Brain Research Bulletin, 79*(6), 409–413. https://doi.org/10.1016/j.brainresbull.2009.02.002

Ghashghaei, H. T., Hilgetag, C. C., & Barbas, H. (2007). Sequence of information processing for emotions based on the anatomic dialogue between prefrontal cortex and amygdala. *NeuroImage, 34*(3), 905–923. https://doi.org/10.1016/j.neuroimage.2006.09.046

Giedd, J. N. (2008). The teen brain: Insights from neuroimaging. *Journal of Adolescent Health, 42*(4), 335–343. https://doi.org/10.1016/j.jadohealth.2008.01.007

Glascher, J., Hampton, A. N., & O'Doherty, J. P. (2009). Determining a role for ventromedial prefrontal cortex in encoding action-based value signals during reward-related decision making. *Cerebral Cortex, 19*(2), 483–495. https://doi.org/10.1093/cercor/bhn098

Goel, V., & Dolan, R. J. (2001). The functional anatomy of humor: Segregating cognitive and affective components. *Nature Neuroscience, 4*(3), 237–238. https://doi.org/10.1038/85076

Goodman, M., Hazlett, E. A., Avedon, J. B., Siever, D. R., Chu, K., & New, A. S. (2011). Anterior cingulate volume reduction in adolescents with borderline personality disorder and co-morbid major depression. *Journal of Psychiatric Research, 45*(6), 803–807. https://doi.org/10.1016/j.jpsychires.2010.11.011

Goodwin, S., Blackman, R., Sakellaridi, S., & Chafee, M. (2012). Executive control over cognition: Stronger and earlier rule-based modulation of spatial category signals in prefrontal cortex relative to parietal cortex. *Journal of Neuroscience, 32*(10), 3499–3515. https://doi.org/10.1523/jneurosci.3585-11.2012

Gordon, E. M., Laumann, T. O., Marek, S., Raut, R. V., Gratton, C., Newbold, D. J., Greene, D. J., Coalson, R. S., Snyder, A. Z., Schlaggar, B. L., Petersen, S. E., Dosenbach, N. U. F., & Nelson, S. M. (2020). Default-mode network streams for coupling to language and control systems. *PNAS, 117*(29), 17308–17319. https://doi.org/10.1073/pnas.2005238117

Gottman, J. M., Cole, C., Cole, D. L. (2019). Four horsemen in couple and family Therapy. In: J. L. Lebow, A. L. Chambers, D. C. Breunlin. (Eds.) *Encyclopedia of couple and family therapy.* Springer. https://doi.org/10.1007/978-3-319-49425-8_179

Gray, J. R., Braver, T. S., & Raichle, M. E. (2002). Integration of emotion and cognition in the lateral prefrontal cortex. *PNAS, USA, 99*(6), 4115–4120. https://doi.org/10.1073/pnas.062381899

Gray, J. R., Chabris, C. F., & Braver, T. S. (2003). Neural mechanisms of general fluid intelligence. *Nature Neuroscience, 6*(3), 316–322. https://doi.org/10.1038/nn1014

Grefkes, C., & Fink, G. R. (2005). The functional organization of the intraparietal sulcus in humans and monkeys. *Journal of Anatomy, 207*(1), 3–17. https://doi.org/10.1111/j.1469-7580.2005.00426.x

Gregory, M. D., Kippenhan, J. S., Dickinson, D., Carrasco, J., Mattay, V. S., Weinberger, D. R., & Berman, K. F. (2016). Regional variations in brain gyrification are associated with general cognitive ability in humans. *Current Biology, 26*(10), 1301–1305. https://doi.org/10.1016/j.cub.2016.03.021

Greicius, M. D., Krasnow, B., Reiss, A. L., & Menon, V. (2003). Functional connectivity in the resting brain: A network analysis of the default mode hypothesis. *PNAS, 100*(1), 253–258. https://doi.org/10.1073/pnas.0135058100

Greicius, M. D., & Menon, V. (2004). Default-mode activity during a passive sensory task: Uncoupled from deactivation but impacting activation. *Journal of Cognitive Neuroscience, 16*(9), 1484–1492. https://doi.org/10.1162/0898929042568532

Greicius, M. D., Supekar, K., Menon, V., & Dougherty, R. F. (2009). Resting-state functional connectivity reflects structural connectivity in the default mode network. *Cerebral Cortex, 19*(1), 72–78. https://doi.org/10.1093/cercor/bhn059

Grieve, S. M., Clark, C. R., Williams, L. M., Peduto, A. J., & Gordon, E. (2005). Preservation of limbic and paralimbic structures in aging. *Human Brain Mapping, 25*(4), 391–401. https://doi.org/10.1002/hbm.20115

Griffiths, T. D., Rees, G., Rees, A., Green, G. G. R., Witton, C., Rowe, D., Büchel, C., Turner, R., & Frackowiak, R. S. J. (1998). Right parietal cortex is involved in the perception of sound movement in humans. *Nature Neuroscience, 1*(1), 74–79. https://doi.org/10.1038/276

Grimm, S., Ernst, J., Boesiger, P., Schuepbach, D., Boeker, H., & Northoff, G. (2011). Reduced negative BOLD responses in the default-mode network and increased self-focus in depression. *World Journal of Biological Psychiatry, 12*(8), 627–637. https://doi.org/10.3109/15622975.2010.545145

Grinband, J., Savitskaya, J., Wager, T. D., Teichert, T., Ferrera, V. P., & Hirsch, J. (2011). The dorsal medial prefrontal cortex is sensitive to time on task, not response conflict or error likelihood. *NeuroImage, 57*(2), 303–311. https://doi.org/10.1016/j.neuroimage.2010.12.027

Gross, J. J., Carstensen, L. L., Pasupathi, M., Tsai, J., Götestam Skorpen, C., & Hsu, A. Y. (1997). Emotion and aging: Experience, expression, and control. *Psychology and Aging, 12*(4), 590. https://doi.org/10.1037//0882-7974.12.4.590

Gündel, H., López-Sala, A., Ceballos-Baumann, A. O., Deus, J., Cardoner, N., Marten-Mittag, B., Soriano-Mas, C., & Pujol, J. (2004). Alexithymia correlates with the size of the right anterior cingulate. *Psychosomatic Medicine, 66*(1), 132–140. https://doi.org/10.1097/01.psy.0000097348.45087.96

Gunderson, J. G., & Sabo, A. N. (1993). The phenomenological and conceptual interface between borderline personality disorder and PTSD. *American Journal of Psychiatry, 150*(1), 19–27. https://doi.org/10.1176/ajp.150.1.19

Gur, R. C., Sara, R., Hagendoorn, M., Marom, O., Hughett, P., Macy, L., Turner, T., Bajcsy, R., Posner, A., & Gur, R. E. (2002). A method for obtaining 3-dimensional facial expressions and its standardization for use in neurocognitive studies. *Journal of Neuroscience Methods, 115*(2), 137–143. https://doi.org/10.1016/s0165-0270(02)00006-7

Gusnard, D. A., Akbudak, E., Shulman, G. L., & Raichle, M. E. (2001). Medial pre-frontal cortex and self-referential mental activity: Relation to a default mode of brain function. *PNAS, 98*(7), 4259–4264. https://doi.org/10.1073/pnas.071043098

Haier, R., Jung, R., Yeo, R., Head, K., & Alkire, M. (2004). Structural brain variation and general intelligence. *NeuroImage, 23*(1), 425–433. https://doi.org/10.1016/j.neuroimage.2004.04.025

Hamilton, J. P., Farmer, M., Fogelman, P., & Gotlib, I. H. (2015). Depressive rumination, the default-mode network, and the dark matter of clinical neuroscience. *Biological Psychiatry, 78*(4), 224–230. https://doi.org/10.1016/j.biopsych.2015.02.020

Hammack, S. E., Cooper, M. A., & Lezak, K. R. (2012). Overlapping neurobiology of learned helplessness and conditioned defeat: Implications for PTSD and mood disorders. *Neuropharmacology, 62*(2), 565–575. https://doi.org/10.1016/j.neuropharm.2011.02.024

Hampson, M., Driesen, N. R., Skudlarski, P., Gore, J. C., & Constable, R. T. (2006). Brain connectivity related to working memory performance. *Journal of Neuroscience, 26*(51), 13338–13343. https://doi.org/10.1523/jneurosci.3408-06.2006

Happé, F. G., Winner, E., & Brownell, H. (1998). The getting of wisdom: Theory of mind in old age. *Developmental Psychology, 34*(2), 358. https://doi.org/10.1037//0012-1649.34.2.358

Hariri, A. R., Bookheimer, S. Y., & Mazziotta, J. C. (2000). Modulating emotional responses: Effects of a neocortical network on the limbic system. *NeuroReport, 11*(1), 43–48. https://doi.org/10.1097/00001756-200001170-00009

Harlow, J. M. (1848). Passage of an iron rod through the head. *Boston Medical and Surgical Journal, 39*(20), 389–393. https://doi.org/10.1056/nejm184812130392001

Harrison, B. J., Pujol, J., López-Solà, M., Hernández-Ribas, R., Deus, J., Ortiz, H., Soriano-Mas, C., Yücel, M., Pantelis, C., & Cardoner, N. (2008). Consistency and functional specialization in the default mode brain network. *PNAS, 105*(28), 9781–9786. https://doi.org/10.1073/pnas.0711791105

Harter, S. (2006). The developing self. In W. Damon & R. M. Lerner (Eds.), *Child and adolescent development: An advanced course* (pp. 216–262). Wiley.

Hassabis, D., & Maguire, E. A. (2007). Deconstructing episodic memory with construction. *Trends in Cognitive Sciences, 11*(7), 299–306. https://doi.org/10.1016/j.tics.2007.05.001

Hauser, M. D., Carey, S., & Hauser, L. B. (2000). Spontaneous number representation in semi-free-ranging rhesus monkeys. *Proceedings of the Royal Society of London, Series B: Biological Sciences, 267*(1445), 829–833. https://doi.org/10.1098/rspb.2000.1078

Hazlett, E. A., New, A. S., Newmark, R., Haznedar, M. M., Lo, J. N., Speiser, L. J., Chen, A. D., Mitropoulou, V., Minzenberg, M., Siever, L. J., & Buchsbaum, M. S. (2005). Reduced anterior and posterior cingulate gray matter in borderline personality disorder. *Biological Psychiatry, 58*(8), 614–623. https://doi.org/10.1016/j.biopsych.2005.04.029

Hazlett, E. A., Speiser, L. J., Goodman, M., Roy, M., Carrizal, M., Wynn, J. K., Williams, W. C., Romero, M., Minzenberg, M. J., Siever, L. J., & New, A. S. (2007). Exaggerated affect-modulated startle during unpleasant stimuli in borderline personality disorder. *Biological Psychiatry, 62*(3), 250–255. https://doi.org/10.1016/j.biopsych.2006.10.028

Henson, R. N. A., Shallice, T., & Dolan, R. J. (1999). Right prefrontal cortex and episodic memory retrieval: A functional MRI test of the monitoring hypothesis. *Brain, 122*(7), 1367–1381. https://doi.org/10.1093/brain/122.7.1367

Herman, J. L. (1992). Complex PTSD: A syndrome in survivors of prolonged and repeated trauma. *Journal of Traumatic Stress, 5*(3), 377–391. https://doi.org/10.1007/bf00977235

Herpertz, S. C., Dietrich, T. M., Wenning, B., Krings, T., Erberich, S. G., Willmes, K., Thron, A., & Sass, H. (2001). Evidence of abnormal amygdala functioning in borderline personality disorder: A functional MRI study. *Biological Psychiatry, 50*(4), 292–298. https://doi.org/10.1016/s0006-3223(01)01075-7

Hesse, E. (1999). The adult attachment interview: Historical and current perspectives. In J. Cassidy & P. R. Shaver (Eds.), *Handbook of attachment: Theory, research, and clinical applications* (2nd ed., pp. 395–415). Guilford.

Hodges, S. (2003). Borderline personality disorder and posttraumatic stress disorder: Time for integration? *Journal of Counseling and Development, 81*(4), 409–417. https://doi.org/10.1002/j.1556-6678.2003.tb00267.x

Hoekzema, E., Carmona, S., Ramos-Quiroga, J. A., Richarte Fernández, V., Bosch, R., Soliva, J. C., Rovira, M., Bulbena, A., Tobeña, A., Casas, M., & Vilarroya, O. (2014). An independent components and functional connectivity analysis of resting state fMRI data points to neural network dysregulation in adult ADHD. *Human Brain Mapping, 35*(3), 1261–1272. https://doi.org/10.1002/hbm.22250

Holliday, S. G., & Chandler, M. J. (1986). The secular, religious, and philosophic wisdom traditions: A historical reconstruction. In *Wisdom: Explorations in Adult Competence* (pp. 10–22). Karger.

Horn, A., Ostwald, D., Reisert, M., & Blankenburg, F. (2013). The structural-functional connectome and the default mode network of the human brain. *NeuroImage, 102*, 142–151. https://doi.org/10.1016/j.neuroimage.2013.09.069

Horovitz, S. G., Braun, A. R., Carr, W. S., Picchioni, D., Balkin, T. J., Fukunaga, M., & Duyn, J. H. (2009). Decoupling of the brain's default mode network during deep sleep. *PNAS, 106*(27), 11376–11381. https://doi.org/10.1073/pnas.0901435106

Houston, R. J., Ceballos, N. A., Hesselbrock, V. M., & Bauer, L. O. (2005). Borderline personality disorder features in adolescent girls: P300 evidence of altered brain maturation. *Clinical Neurophysiology, 116*(6), 1424–1432. https://doi.org/10.1016/j.clinph.2005.01.013

Husain, M., & Nachev, P. (2007). Space and the parietal cortex. *Trends in Cognitive Sciences, 11*(1), 30–36. https://doi.org/10.1016/j.tics.2006.10.011

Iacoboni, M., Lieberman, M. D., Knowlton, B. J., Molnar-Szakacs, I., Moritz, M., Throop, C. J., & Fiske, A. P. (2004). Watching social interactions produces dorsomedial prefrontal and medial parietal BOLD fMRI signal increases compared to a resting baseline. *NeuroImage, 21*(3), 1167–1173. https://doi.org/10.1016/j.neuroimage.2003.11.013

Iidaka, T., Okada, T., Murata, T., Omori, M., Kosaka, H., Sadato, N., & Yonekura, Y. (2002). Age-related differences in the medial temporal lobe responses to emotional faces as revealed by fMRI. *Hippocampus, 12*(3), 352–362. https://doi.org/10.1002/hipo.1113

Irle, E., Lange, C., & Sachsse, U. (2005). Reduced size and abnormal asymmetry of parietal cortex in women with borderline personality disorder. *Biological Psychiatry, 57*(2), 173–182. https://doi.org/10.1016/j.biopsych.2004.10.004

Ito, M. (2002). The molecular organization of cerebellar long-term depression. *Nature Reviews Neuroscience, 3*(11), 896–902. https://doi.org/10.1038/nrn962

Jackson, P. L., & Decety, J. (2004). Motor cognition: A new paradigm to study self-other interactions. *Current Opinion in Neurobiology, 14*(2), 259–263. https://doi.org/10.1016/j.conb.2004.01.020

Jacob, Y., Morris, L. S., Huang, K.-H., Schneider, M., Rutter, S., Verma, G., Murrough, J. W., & Balchandani, P. (2020). Neural correlates of rumination in major depressive disorder: A brain network analysis. *NeuroImage: Clinical, 25*, 102142. https://doi.org/10.1016/j.nicl.2019.102142

Jang, J. H., Jung, W. H., Choi, J.-S., Choi, C.-H., Kang, D.-H., Shin, N. Y., Hong, K. S., & Kwon, J. S. (2011). Reduced prefrontal functional connectivity in the default mode network is related to greater psychopathology in subjects with high genetic loading for schizophrenia. *Schizophrenia Research, 127*(1–3), 58–65. https://doi.org/10.1016/j.schres.2010.12.022

Jardri, R., Pins, D., Bubrovszky, M., Despretz, P., Pruvo, J., Steinling, M., & Thomas, P. (2007). Self-awareness and speech processing: An fMRI study. *NeuroImage, 35*(4), 1645–1653. https://doi.org/10.1016/j.neuroimage.2007.02.002

Jenkins, A. C., & Mitchell, J. P. (2011). Medial prefrontal cortex subserves diverse forms of self-reflection. *Social Neuroscience, 6*(3), 211–218. https://doi.org/10.1080/17470919.2010.507948

Jiang, Q. (2014). Internet addiction among young people in China: Internet connectedness, online gaming, and academic performance decrement. *Internet Research, 24*(1), 2–20. https://doi.org/10.1108/intr-01-2013-0004

Jilka, S., Scott, G., Ham, T., Pickering, A., Bonnelle, V., Braga, R., Sharp, D. (2014). Damage to the salience network and interactions with the default mode network. *Journal of Neuroscience, 34*(33), 10798–10807. https://doi.org/10.1523/jneurosci.0518-14.2014

Johnson, A. (2006). Healing shame. *Humanistic Psychologist, 34*(3), 223–242. https://doi.org/10.1207/s15473333thp3403_2

Johnson, E. S., & Meade, A. C. (1987). Developmental patterns of spatial ability: An early sex difference. *Child Development, 58*(3), 725–740. https://doi.org/10.1111/j.1467-8624.1987.tb01413.x

Johnson, M. (1987). *The body in the mind.* University of Chicago Press.

Johnson, P. A., Hurley, R. A., Benkelfat, C., Herpertz, S. C., & Taber, K. H. (2003).

Understanding emotion regulation in borderline personality disorder: Contributions of neuroimaging. *Journal of Neuropsychiatry of Clinical Neuroscience*, 15(4), 397–402. https://doi.org/10.1176/jnp.15.4.397

Jonides, J., Schumacher, E. H., Smith, E. E., Koeppe, R. A., Awh, E., Reuter-Lorenz, P. A., Marshuetz, C., & Willis, C. R. (1998). The role of parietal cortex in verbal working memory. *Journal of Neuroscience*, 18(13), 5026–5034. https://doi.org/10.1523/jneurosci.18-13-05026.1998

Joseph, R. (1996). *Neuropsychiatry, neuropsychology, and clinical neuroscience*. Williams and Wilkins.

Juengling, F. D., Schmahl, C., Hesslinger, B., Ebert, D., Bremner, J. D., Gostomzyk, J., & Lieb, K. (2003). Positron emission tomography in female patients with borderline personality disorder. *Journal of Psychiatric Research*, 37(2), 109–115. https://doi.org/10.1016/s0022-3956(02)00084-5

Jung, R. E., & Haier, R. J. (2007). The Parieto-Frontal Integration Theory (P-FIT) of intelligence: converging neuroimaging evidence. *The Behavioral and Brain Sciences*, 30(2), 135–187. https://doi.org/10.1017/S0140525X07001185

Jürgens, U., & von Cramon, D. (1982). On the role of the anterior cingulate cortex in phonation: A case report. *Brain and Language*, 15(2), 234–248. https://doi.org/10.1016/0093-934x(82)90058-x

Karnath, H. O. (1997). Spatial orientation and the representation of space with parietal lobe lesions. *Philosophical Transactions of the Royal Society, Biological Sciences*, 352(1360), 1411–1419. https://doi.org/10.1098/rstb.1997.0127

Kawashima, R., Sugiura, M., Kato, T., Nakamura, A., Hatano, K., Ito, K., Taira, M., & Nakamura, K. (1999). The human amygdala plays an important role in gaze monitoring: A PET study. *Brain*, 122(4), 779–783. https://doi.org/10.1093/brain/122.4.779

Keifer, E., & Tranel, D. (2013). A neuropsychological investigation of the Delis-Kaplan executive function system. *Journal of Clinical and Experimental Neuropsychology*, 35(10), 1048–1059. https://doi.org/10.1080/13803395.2013.854319

Kennard, M. A. (1955). The cingulate gyrus in relation to consciousness. *Journal of Nervous and Mental Disease*, 121(1), 34–39. https://doi.org/10.1097/00005053-195501000-00005

Kennedy, G. (2004). Promoting cognition in multimedia interactivity research. *Journal of Interactive Learning Research*, 15(1), 43–61. https://www.learntechlib.org/primary/p/4530/

Kesselring, T. (2018). Self-awareness, self-esteem, and respect for others: The genetic perspective (in memoriam Jean Piaget, 1896–1980). *Journal of Dharma*, 43(2), 121–150.

King-Casas, B., Sharp, C., Lomax-Bream, L., Lohrenz, T., Fonagy, P., & Montague, P. R. (2008). The rupture and repair of cooperation in borderline personality disorder. *Science*, 321(5890), 806–810. https://doi.org/10.1126/science.1156902

Klingberg, T. (2006). Development of a superior frontal-intraparietal network for visuo-spatial working memory. *Neuropsychologia*, 44(11), 2171–2177. https://doi.org/10.1016/j.neuropsychologia.2005.11.019

Klingberg, T., Forssberg, H., & Westerberg, H. (2002). Increased brain activity in frontal and parietal cortex underlies the development of visuospatial working memory capacity during childhood. *Journal of Cognitive Neuroscience, 14*(1), 1–10. https://doi.org/10.1162/089892902317205276

Knight, R. T., & Grabowecky, M. (1995). Escape from linear time: Prefrontal cortex and conscious experience. In M. S. Gazzaniga (Ed.), *The cognitive neurosciences* (pp. 1357–1372). MIT Press.

Knight, R. T., Grabowecky, M. F., & Scabini, D. (1995). Role of human prefrontal cortex in attention control. *Advances in Neurology, 66*, 21–34.

Koechlin, E., Ody, C., & Kouneiher, F. (2003). The architecture of cognitive control in the human prefrontal cortex. *Science, 302*(5648), 1181–1185. https://doi.org/10.1126/science.1088545

Koziol, L., Budding, D., & Chidekel, D. (2011). From movement to thought: Executive function, embodied cognition, and the cerebellum. *Cerebellum, 11*(2), 505–525. https://doi.org/10.1007/s12311-011-0321-y

Kringelbach, M. L. (2005). The human orbitofrontal cortex: Linking reward to hedonic experience. *Nature Reviews Neuroscience, 6*(9), 691–702. https://doi .org/10.1038/nrn1747

Kroger, J. K., Sabb, F. W., Fales, C. L., Bookeimer, S. Y., Cohen, M. S., & Holyoak, K. J. (2002). Recruitment of anterior dorsolateral prefrontal cortex in human reasoning: A parametric study of relational complexity. *Cerebral Cortex, 12*(5), 477–485. https://doi.org/10.1093/cercor/12.5.477

Krueger, F., Moll, J., Zahn, R., Heinecke, A., & Grafman, J. (2006). Event frequency modulates the processing of daily life activities in human medial prefrontal cortex. *Cerebral Cortex, 17*(10), 2346–2353. https://doi.org/10.1093/cercor/bhl143

Kucyi, A., & Davis, K. D. (2014). Dynamic functional connectivity of the default mode network tracks daydreaming. *NeuroImage, 100*, 471–480. https://doi.org/10.1016/j.neuroimage.2014.06.044

Labouvie-Vief, G., DeVoe, M., & Bulka, D. (1989). Speaking about feelings: Conceptions of emotion across the life span. *Psychology and Aging, 4*(4), 425. https://doi.org/10.1037//0882-7974.4.4.425

Labouvie-Vief, G., Hakim-Larson, J., & Hobart, C. J. (1987). Age, ego level, and the life-span development of coping and defense processes. *Psychology and Aging, 2*(3), 286. https://doi.org/10.1037//0882-7974.2.3.286

Lange, C., Kracht, L., Herholz, K., Sachsse, U., & Irle, E. (2005). Reduced glucose metabolism in temporo-parietal cortices of women with borderline personality disorder. *Neuroimaging, 139*(2), 115–126. https://doi.org/10.1016/j.pscychresns.2005.05.003

Langer, N., Pedroni, A., Gianotti, L. R. R., Hänggi, J., Knoch, D., & Jäncke, L. (2012). Functional brain network efficiency predicts intelligence. *Human Brain Mapping. 33*(6), 1393–1406. https://doi.org/10.1002/hbm.21297

Langeslag, S. J., Schmidt, M., Ghassabian, A., Jaddoe, V. W., Hofman, A., Lugt, A. V., & White, T. J. (2012). Functional connectivity between parietal and frontal brain regions and intelligence in young children: The generation R study. *Human Brain Mapping, 34*(12), 3299–3307. https://doi.org/10.1002/hbm.22143

Lanius, R. A., Bluhm, R. L., Coupland, N. J., Hegadoren, K. M., Rowe, B., Theberge, J., & Brimson, M. (2010). Default mode network connectivity as a predictor of post-traumatic stress disorder symptom severity in acutely traumatized subjects. *Acta Psychiatrica Scandinavica, 121*(1), 33–40. https://doi.org/10.1111/j.1600-0447.2009.01391.x

Laufs, H., Krakow, K., Sterzer, P., Eger, E., Beyerle, A., Salek-Haddadi, A., & Kleinschmidt, A. (2003). Electroencephalographic signatures of attentional and cognitive default modes in spontaneous brain activity fluctuations at rest. *PNAS, 100*(19), 11053–11058. https://doi.org/10.1073/pnas.1831638100

Laureys, S., Boly, M., & Maquet, P. (2006). Tracking the recovery of consciousness from coma. *Journal of Clinical Investigation, 116*(7), 1823–1825. https://doi.org/10.1172/jci29172

Lawton, M. P. (1989). Environmental proactivity and affect in older people. In S. Spacapan & S. Oskamp (Eds.), *The social psychology of aging* (pp. 135–163). Sage.

Lawton, M. P., Kleban, M. H., Rajagopal, D., & Dean, J. (1992). Dimensions of affective experience in three age groups. *Psychology and Aging, 7*(2), 171. https://doi.org/10.1037//0882-7974.7.2.171

LeDoux, J. E. (1986). Sensory systems and emotion: A model of affective processing. *Integrative Psychiatry, 4*(4), 237–243.

LeDoux, J. E. (1996). *The emotional brain.* Simon and Schuster.

Lee, T. W., Josephs, O., Dolan, R. J., & Critchley, H. D. (2006). Imitating expressions: Emotion-specific neural substrates in facial mimicry. *Social Cognitive and Affective Neuroscience, 1*(2), 122–135. https://doi.org/10.1093/scan/nsl012

Leech, R., Kamourieh, S., Beckmann, C. F., & Sharp, D. J. (2011). Fractionating the default mode network: Distinct contributions of the ventral and dorsal posterior cingulate cortex to cognitive control. *Journal of Neuroscience, 31*(9), 3217–3224. https://doi.org/10.1523/jneurosci.5626-10.2011

Leigland, L. A., Schulz, L. E., & Janowsky, J. S. (2004). Age related changes in emotional memory. *Neurobiology of Aging, 25*(8), 1117–1124. https://doi.org/10.1016/j.neurobiolaging.2003.10.015

Lemer, C., Dehaene, S., Spelke, E., & Cohen, L. (2003). Approximate quantities and exact number words: Dissociable systems. *Neuropsychologica, 41*(14), 1942–1958. https://doi.org/10.1016/s0028-3932(03)00123-4

Levenson, R. W., Carstensen, L. L., Friesen, W. V., & Ekman, P. (1991). Emotion, physiology, and expression in old age. *Psychology and Aging, 6*(1), 28. https://doi.org/10.1037//0882-7974.6.1.28

Lévesque, J., Eugène, F., Joanette, Y., Paquette, V., Mensour, B., Beaudoin, G., Leroux, J. M., Bourgouin, P., & Beauregard, M. (2003). Neural circuitry underlying voluntary suppression of sadness. *Biological Psychiatry, 53*(6), 502–510. https://doi.org/10.1016/s0006-3223(02)01817-6

Levine, B. D., Arbab-Zadeh, A., Dijk, E., Prasad, A., Fu, Q., Torres, P., Zhang, R., Thomas, J. D., Palmer, D., & Levine, B. D. (2004). Effect of aging and physical activity on left ventricular compliance. *Circulation, 110*(13), 1799–1805. https://doi.org/10.1161/01.cir.0000142863.71285.74

Lewis, K. L., & Grenyer, B. F. (2009). Borderline personality or complex posttraumatic stress disorder? An update on the controversy. *Harvard Review of Psychiatry, 17*(5), 322–328. https://doi.org/10.3109/10673220903271848

Leyton, M., Okazawa, H., Diksic, M., Paris, J., Rosa, P., Mzengeza, S., Young, S. N., Blier, P., & Benkelfat, C. (2001). Brain regional α-[11C] methyl-L-tryptophan trapping in impulsive subjects with borderline personality disorder. *American Journal of Psychiatry, 158*(5), 775–782. https://doi.org/10.1176/appi.ajp.158.5.775

Lezak, M. D. (1982). The problem of assessing executive functions. *International Journal of Psychology, 17*(1–4), 281–297. https://doi.org/10.1080/00207598208247445

Lezak, M. D. (1995). *Neuropsychological assessment* (3rd ed.). Oxford University Press.

Li, B., Liu, L., Friston, K. J., Shen, H., Wang, L., Zeng, L. L., & Hu, D. (2013). A treatment-resistant default mode subnetwork in major depression. *Biological Psychiatry, 74*(1), 48–54. https://doi.org/10.1016/j.biopsych.2012.11.007

Li, W., Mai, X., & Liu, C. (2014). The default mode network and social understanding of others: What do brain connectivity studies tell us. *Frontiers in Human Neuroscience, 8*(74). https://doi.org/10.3389/fnhum.2014.00074

Liao, M., Yang, F., Zhang, Y., He, Z., Song, M., Jiang, T., Li, Z., Lu, S., Wu, W., Su, L., & Li, L. (2013). Childhood maltreatment is associated with larger left thalamic gray matter volume in adolescents with generalized anxiety disorder. *PLoS One, 8*(8), e71898. https://doi.org/10.1371/journal.pone.0071898

Lieb, K., Zanarini, M. C., Schmahl, C., Linehan, M. M., & Bohus, M. (2004). Borderline personality disorder. *Lancet, 364*(9432), 453–461. https://doi.org/10.1016/s0140-6736(04)16770-6

Liederman, J., & Meehan, P. (1986). When is between-hemisphere division of labor advantageous? *Neuropsychologia, 24*(6), 863–874. https://doi.org/10.1016/0028-3932(86)90086-2

Linehan, M. M. (2021). *Building a life worth living: A memoir.* Random House.

Loh, K. K., & Kanai, R. (2014). Higher media multi-tasking activity is associated with smaller gray-matter density in the anterior cingulate cortex. *PloS One, 9*(9), e106698. https://doi.org/10.1371/journal.pone.0106698

Lou, H. C., Luber, B., Crupain, M., Keenan, J. P., Nowak, M., Kjaer, T. W., Sackeim, H. A., & Lisanby, S. H. (2004). Parietal cortex and representation of the mental self. *PNAS, 101*(17), 6827–6832. https://doi.org/10.1073/pnas.0400049101

Lou, H., Nowak, M., & Kajaer, T. W. (2005). The mental self. *Progress in Brain Resources, 150*, 197–204. https://doi.org/10.1016/s0079-6123(05)50014-1

Luria, A. R. (1973). The frontal lobes and the regulation of behavior. In K. H. Pribram & A. R. Luria (Eds.), *Psychophysiology of the frontal lobes* (pp. 3–26). Academic Press.

Lynch, C. J., Uddin, L. Q., Supekar, K., Khouzam, A., Phillips, J., & Menon, V.

(2013). Default mode network in childhood autism: Posteromedial cortex heterogeneity and relationship with social deficits. *Biological Psychiatry*, 74(3), 212–219. https://doi.org/10.1016/j.biopsych.2012.12.013

Lyons-Ruth, K., Choi-Kain, L., Pechtel, P., Bertha, E., & Gunderson, J. (2011). Perceived parental protection and cortisol responses among young females with borderline personality disorder and controls. *Psychiatry Research*, 189(3), 426–432. https://doi.org/10.1016/j.psychres.2011.07.038

Lyoo, K., Han, M. H., & Cho, D. Y. (1998). A brain MRI study in subjects with borderline personality disorder. *Journal of Affective Disorders*, 50(2–3), 235–243. https://doi.org/10.1016/s0165-0327(98)00104-9

Machizawa-Summers, S. (2007). Childhood trauma and parental bonding among Japanese female patients with borderline personality disorder. *Journal of Psychology*, 42(4), 265–273. https://doi.org/10.1080/00207590601109276

MacLean, P. D. (1985). Brain evolution relating to family, play, and the separation call. *Archives of General Psychiatry*, 42(4), 405–417. https://doi.org/10.1001/archpsyc.1985.01790270095011

Macrae, C. N., Moran, J. M., Heatherton, T. F., Banfield, J. F., & Kelley, W. M. (2004). Medial prefrontal activity predicts memory for self. *Cerebral Cortex*, 14(6), 647–654. https://doi.org/10.1093/cercor/bhh025

Maguire, E. A., & Mummery, C. J. (1999). Differential modulation of a common memory retrieval network revealed by positron emission tomography. *Hippocampus*, 9(1), 54–61. https://doi.org/10.1002/(sici)1098-1063(1999)9:1<54::aid-hipo6>3.0.co;2-o

Mah, L., Arnold, M. C., & Grafman, J. (2004). Impairment of social perception associated with lesions of the prefrontal cortex. *American Journal of Psychiatry*, 161(7), 1247–1255. https://doi.org/10.1176/appi.ajp.161.7.1247

Main, M., & Goldwyn, R. (1998). *Adult attachment scoring and classification system* [Unpublished manuscript]. University of California at Berkeley.

Malloy, P., Bihrle, A., Duffy, J., & Cimino, C. (1993). The orbitomedial frontal syndrome. *Archives of Clinical Neuropsychology*, 8(3), 185–201. https://doi.org/10.1093/arclin/8.3.185

Malouff, J. M., Rooke, S. E., & Copeland, J. (2014). Experiences of marijuana-vaporizer users. *Substance Abuse*, 35(2), 127–128. https://doi.org/10.1080/08897077.2013.823902

Manoliu, A., Meng, C., Brandl, F., Doll, A., Tahmasian, M., Scherr, M., Schwerthöffer, D., Zimmer, C., Förstl, H., Bäuml, J., Riedl, V., Wohlschläger, A. M., & Sorg, C. (2014). Insular dysfunction within the salience network is associated with severity of symptoms and aberrant inter-network connectivity in major depressive disorder. *Frontiers in Human Neuroscience*, 7, 930. https://doi.org/10.3389/fnhum.2013.00930

Marshuetz, C., Smith, E., Jonides, J., DeGutis, J., & Chenevert, T. (2000). Order information in working memory: fMRI evidence for parietal and pre-frontal mechanisms. *Journal of Cognitive Neuroscience*, 12(2), 130–144. https://doi.org/10.1162/08989290051137459

Mason, M. F., Norton, M. I., Horn, J. D., Wegner, D. M., Grafton, S. T., & Macrae, C. N. (2007). Wandering minds: The default network and stimulus-independent thought. *Science, 315*(5810), 393–395. https://doi.org/10.1126/science.1131295

Mather, M., & Carstensen, L. L. (2003). Aging and attentional biases for emotional faces. *Psychological Science, 14*(5), 409–415. https://doi.org/10.1111/1467-9280.01455

Matsumoto, K., & Tanaka, K. (2004). The role of the medial prefrontal cortex in achieving goals. *Current Opinion in Neurobiology, 14*(2), 178–185. https://doi.org/10.1016/j.conb.2004.03.005

McGuire, P. K., Paulesu, E., Frackowiak, R. S. J., & Frith, C. D. (1996). Brain activity during stimulus independent thought. *NeuroReport, 7*(13), 2095–2099. https://doi.org/10.1016/s0920-9964(97)82485-1

McKiernan, K. A., Kaufman, J. N., Kucera-Thompson, J., & Binder, J. R. (2003). A parametric manipulation of factors affecting task-induced deactivation in functional neuroimaging. *Journal of Cognitive Neuroscience, 15*(3), 394–408. https://doi.org/10.1162/089892903321593117

Medendorp, W. P., Goltz, H. C., Crawford, D., & Vilis, T. (2005). Integration of target and effector information in human posterior parietal cortex for the planning of action. *Journal of Neurophysiology, 93*(2), 945–962. https://doi.org/10.1152/jn.00725.2004

Menon, V. (2011). Large-scale brain networks and psychopathology: A unifying triple network model. *Trends in Cognitive Sciences, 15*(10), 483–506. https://doi.org/10.1016/j.tics.2011.08.003

Menon, V., & Uddin, L. (2010). Saliency, switching, attention and control: A network model of insula function. *Brain Structure and Function, 214*(5–6), 655–667. https://doi.org/10.1007/s00429-010-0262-0

Merkl, A., Ammelburg, N., Aust, S., Roepke, S., Reinecker, H., Trahms, L., Heuser, I., & Sander, T. (2010). Processing of visual stimuli in borderline personality disorder: A combined behavioural and magnetoencephalographic study. *International Journal of Psychophysiology, 78*(3), 257–264. https://doi.org/10.1016/j.ijpsycho.2010.08.007

Mesulam, M. M., & Weintraub, S. (1987). Right cerebral dominance in spatial attention: Further evidence based on ipsilateral neglect. *Archives of Neurology, 44*(6), 621–625. https://doi.org/10.1001/archneur.1987.00520180043014

Minagawa-Kawai, Y., Matsuoka, S., Dan, I., Naoi, N., Nakamura, K., & Kojima, S. (2008). Prefrontal activation associated with social attachment: Facial emotion recognition in mothers and infants. *Cerebral Cortex, 19*(2), 284–292. https://doi.org/10.1093/cercor/bhn081

Minzenberg, M. J., Fan., J., New, A. S., Tang., C. Y., & Siever, L. J. (2008). Frontolimbic structural changes in borderline personality disorder. *Journal of Psychiatric Research, 42*(9), 727–733. https://doi.org/10.1016/j.jpsychires.2007.07.015

Minzenberg, M. J., Fan, R., New, A. S., Tang, C. Y., & Siever, L. J. (2007). Frontolimbic dysfunction in response to facial emotion in borderline personality disorder: An event-related fMRI study. *Psychiatry Research, 155*(3), 231–243. https://doi.org/10.1016/j.pscychresns.2007.03.006

Minzenberg, M. J., Poole, J. H., & Vinogradov, S. (2006). Social-emotion recognition in borderline personality disorder. *Comprehensive Psychiatry, 47*(6), 468–474. https://doi.org/10.1016/j.comppsych.2006.03.005

Misra, S., Cheng, L., Genevie, J., & Yuan, M. (2014). The iPhone effect: The quality of in-person social interactions in the presence of mobile devices. *Environment and Behavior, 48*(2), 275–298. https://doi.org/10.1177/0013916514539755

Mitchell, J. P., Banaji, M. R., & Macrae, C. N. (2005). The link between social cognition and self-referential thought in the medial prefrontal cortex. *Journal of Cognitive Neuroscience, 17*(8), 1306–1315. https://doi.org/10.1162/0898929055002418

Mitchell, J. P., Macrae, C. N., & Banaji, M. R. (2006). Dissociable medial prefrontal contributions to judgments of similar and dissimilar others. *Neuron, 50*(4), 655–663. https://doi.org/10.1016/j.neuron.2006.03.040

Molko, N., Cachia, A., Rivière, D., Mangin, J.-F., Bruandet, M., Le Bihan, D., Cohen, L., & Dehaene, S. (2003). Functional and structural alteration of the intraparietal sulcus in a developmental dyscalculia of genetic origin. *Neuron, 40*(4), 847–858. https://doi.org/10.1016/s0896-6273(03)00670-6

Moll, J., Oliveira-Souza, R. D., Garrido, G. J., Bramati, I. E., Caparelli-Daquer, E. M., Paiva, M. L., Zahn, R., & Grafman, J. (2007). The self as a moral agent: Linking the neural bases of social agency and moral sensitivity. *Social Neuroscience, 2*(3–4), 336–352. https://doi.org/10.1080/17470910701392024

Morcom, A. M., & Fletcher, P. C. (2007a). Cognitive neuroscience: The case for design rather than default. *NeuroImage, 37*(4), 1097–1099. https://doi.org/10.1016/j.neuroimage.2007.07.018

Morcom, A. M., & Fletcher, P. C. (2007b). Does the brain have a baseline? Why we should be resisting a rest. *NeuroImage, 37*(4), 1073–1082. https://doi.org/10.1016/j.neuroimage.2006.09.013

Mountcastle, V. B. (1995). The parietal system and some higher brain functions. *Cerebral Cortex, 5*(5), 377–390. https://doi.org/10.1093/cercor/5.5.377

Mowinckel, A., Alneas, D., Pedersen, M., Ziegler, S., Fredriksen, M., Kaufmann, T., Sonuga-Barke, E., Endestad, T., Westlye, L., & Biele, G. (2017). Increased default-mode variability is related to reduced task-performance in adults with ADHD. *NeuroImage: Clinical, 16*, 369–382. https://doi.org/10.1016/j.nicl.2017.03.008

Mroczek, D. K., & Kolarz, C. M. (1998). The effect of age on positive and negative affect: A developmental perspective on happiness. *Journal of Personality and Social Psychology, 75*(5), 1333. https://doi.org/10.1037//0022-3514.75.5.1333

Murphy, C., Jefferies, E., Rueschemeyer, S. A., Sormaz, M., Wang, H. T., Margulies, D. S., & Smallwood, J. (2018). Distant from input: Evidence of regions within the default mode network supporting perceptually-decoupled and conceptually-guided cognition. *NeuroImage, 171*, 393–401. https://doi.org/10.1016/j.neuroimage.2018.01.017

Nachev, P., Mah, Y. H., & Husain, M. (2009). Functional neuroanatomy: The locus of human intelligence. *Current Biology, 19*(10), R418–R420. https://doi.org/10.1016/j.cub.2009.04.002

Nagahama, Y., Okada, T., Katsumi, Y., Hayashi, T., Yamauchi, H., Oyanagi, C., Konishi, J., Fukuyama, H., & Shibasaki, H. (2001). Dissociable mechanisms of attentional control within the human prefrontal cortex. *Cerebral Cortex, 11*(1), 85–92. https://doi.org/10.1093/cercor/11.1.85

Nauta, W. J. H. (1971). The problem of the frontal lobe: A reinterpretation. *Journal of Psychiatric Research, 8*(3), 167–187. https://doi.org/10.1016/0022-3956(71)90017-3

Nedergaard, M., Ransom, B., & Goldman, S. A. (2003). New roles for astrocytes: Redefining the functional architecture of the brain. *Trends in Neurosciences, 26*(10), 523–530. https://doi.org/10.1016/j.tins.2003.08.008

Newman, S. D., Carpenter, P. A., Varma, S., & Just, M. A. (2003). Frontal and parietal participation in problem solving in the Tower of London: fMRI and computational modeling of planning and high-level perception. *Neuropsychologia, 41*(12), 1668–1682. https://doi.org/10.1016/s0028-3932(03)00091-5

Nielson, K. A., Yee, D., & Erickson, K. I. (2005). Memory enhancement by a semantically unrelated emotional arousal source induced after learning. *Neurobiology of Learning and Memory, 84*(1), 49–56. https://doi.org/10.1016/j.nlm.2005.04.001

Nietlisbach, G., & Maercker, A. (2009a). Effects of social exclusion in trauma survivors with posttraumatic stress disorder. *Psychological Trauma: Theory, Research, Practice, and Policy, 1*(4), 323–331. https://doi.org/10.1037/a0017832

Nietlisbach, G., & Maercker, A. (2009b). Social cognition and interpersonal impairments in trauma survivors with PTSD. *Journal of Aggression, Maltreatment and Trauma, 18*(4), 382–402. https://doi.org/10.1080/10926770902881489

Nitschke, J. B., Nelson, E. E., Rusch, B. D., Fox, A. S., Oakes, T. R., & Davidson, R. J. (2004). Orbitofrontal cortex tracks positive mood in mothers viewing pictures of their newborn infants. *NeuroImage, 21*(2), 583–592. https://doi.org/10.1016/j.neuroimage.2003.10.005

Nixon, N., Liddle, P., Nixon, E., Worwood, G., Liotti, M., & Palaniyappan, L. (2014). Biological vulnerability to depression: Linked structural and functional brain networks. *British Journal of Psychiatry, 204*(4), 283–289. https://doi.org/10.1192/bjp.bp.113.129965

Nobre, A. C., Coull, J. T., Frith, C. D., & Mesulam, M. M. (1999). Orbitofrontal cortex is activated during breaches of expectation in tasks of visual attention. *Nature Neuroscience, 2*(1), 11–12. https://doi.org/10.1038/4513

Northoff, G., & Bermpohl, F. (2004). Cortical midline structures and the self. *Trends in Cognitive Sciences, 8*(3), 102–107. https://doi.org/10.1016/j.tics.2004.01.004

Northoff, G., Heinzel, A., Greck, M. D., Bermpohl, F., Dobrowolny, H., & Panksepp, J. (2006). Self-referential processing in our brain—A meta-analysis of imaging studies on the self. *NeuroImage, 31*(1), 440–457. https://doi.org/10.1016/j.neuroimage.2005.12.002

Oberheim, N. A., Wang, X., Goldman, S., & Nedergaard, M. (2006). Astrocytic complexity distinguishes the human brain. *Trends in Neurosciences, 29*(10), 547–553. https://doi.org/10.1016/j.tins.2006.08.004

O'Doherty, J. (2004). Reward representation and reward-related learning in the human brain: Insights from neuroimaging. *Current Opinion in Neurobiology*, *14*(6), 769–776. https://doi.org/10.1016/j.conb.2004.10.016

O'Doherty, J. P., Deichmann, R., Critchley, H. D., & Dolan, R. J. (2002). Neural responses during anticipation of a primary taste reward. *Neuron*, *33*(5), 815–826. https://doi.org/10.1016/s0896-6273(02)00603-7

O'Doherty, J., Kringelbach, M. L., Rolls, E. T., Hornak, J., & Andrews, C. (2001). Abstract reward and punishment representations in the human orbitofrontal cortex. *Nature Neuroscience*, *4*(1), 95–102. https://doi.org/10.1038/82959

O'Keefe, J., & Nadel, L. (1978). *The hippocampus as a cognitive map*. Clarendon.

Olesen, P. J., Nagy, Z., Westerberg, H., & Klingberg, T. (2003). Combined analysis of DTI and fMRI data reveals a joint maturation of white and grey matter in a fronto-parietal network. *Cognitive Brain Research*, *18*(1), 48–57. https://doi.org/10.1016/j.cogbrainres.2003.09.003

Öngür, D., & Price, J. L. (2000). The organization of networks within the orbital and medial prefrontal cortex of rats, monkeys, and humans. *Cerebral Cortex*, *10*(3), 206–219. https://doi.org/10.1093/cercor/10.3.206

Orban, G. A., Sunaert, S., Todd, J. T., Van Hecke, P., & Marchal, G. (1999). Human cortical regions involved in extracting depth from motion. *Neuron*, *24*(4), 929–940. https://doi.org/10.1016/s0896-6273(00)81040-5

Østby, Y., Walhovd, K. B., Tamnes, C. K., Grydeland, H., Westlye, L. T., & Fjell, A. M. (2012). Mental time travel and default-mode network functional connectivity in the developing brain. *PNAS*, *109*(42), 16800–16804. https://doi.org/10.1073/pnas.1210627109

Palaniyappan, L., & Liddle, P. F. (2012). Does the salience network play a cardinal role in psychosis? An emerging hypothesis of insular dysfunction. *Journal of Psychiatry and Neuroscience*, *37*(1), 17–27. https://doi.org/10.1503/jpn.100176

Pardo, J. V., & Fox, P. T. (1993). Preoperative assessment of the cerebral hemispheric dominance for language with CBF PET. *Human Brain Mapping*, *1*(1), 57–68. https://doi.org/10.1002/hbm.460010107

Paris, J., Zelkowitz, P., Guzder, J., Joseph, S., & Feldman, R. (1999). Neuropsychological factors associated with borderline pathology in children. *Journal of the Academy of Child and Adolescent Psychiatry*, *38*(6), 770–774. https://doi.org/10.1097/00004583-199906000-00026

Park, J., Kim, Y., Chang, W. H., Park, C., Shin, Y., Kim, S. T., & Pascual-Leone, A. (2014). Significance of longitudinal changes in the default-mode network for cognitive recovery after stroke. *European Journal of Neuroscience*, *40*(4), 2715–2722. https://doi.org/10.1111/ejn.12640

Pascual-Leone, A., Rubio, B., Pallardó, F., & Catalá, M. D. (1996). Rapid-rate transcranial magnetic stimulation of left dorsolateral prefrontal cortex in drug-resistant depression. *Lancet*, *348*(9022), 233–237. https://doi.org/10.1016/s0140-6736(96)01219-6

Pasupathi, M., & Carstensen, L. L. (2003). Age and emotional experience during mutual reminiscing. *Psychology and Aging*, *18*(3), 430. https://doi.org/10.1037/0882-7974.18.3.430

Patel, R., Spreng, R. N., Shin, L. M., & Girard, T. A. (2012). Neurocircuitry models of posttraumatic stress disorder and beyond: A meta-analysis of functional neuroimaging studies. *Neuroscience and Biobehavioral Reviews, 36*(9), 2130–2142. https://doi.org/10.1016/j.neubiorev.2012.06.003

Paulhus, D. L., & Williams, K. M. (2002). The dark triad of personality: Narcissism, Machiavellianism, and psychopathy. *Journal of Research in Personality, 36*(6), 556–563. https://doi.org/10.1016/s0092-6566(02)00505-6

Paus, T., Petrides, M., Evans, A. C., & Meyer, E. (1993). Role of the human anterior cingulate cortex in the control of oculomotor, manual, and speech responses: A positron emission tomography study. *Journal of Neurophysiology, 70*(2), 453–469. https://doi.org/10.1152/jn.1993.70.2.453

Peers, P. V., Ludwig, C. J. H., Rorden, C., Cusack, R., Bonfiglioli, C., Bundesen, C., Driver, J., Antoun, N., & Duncan, J. (2005). Attentional functions of parietal and prefrontal cortex. *Cerebral Cortex, 15*(10), 1469–1484. https://doi.org/10.1093/cercor/bhi029

Peng, M., Chen, X., Zhao, Q., & Zhou, Z. (2018). Attentional scope is reduced by internet use: A behavior and ERP study. *PLoS One, 13*(6), e0198543. https://doi.org/10.1371/journal.pone.0198543

Perrin, A., & Jiang, J. (2018). About a quarter of U.S. adults say they are "almost constantly" online. Pew Research Center. https://www.weforum.org/stories/2018/03/about-a-quarter-of-u-s-adults-say-they-are-almost-constantly-online/

Petrides, M., Alivisatos, B., & Frey, S. (2002). Differential activation of the human orbital, mid-ventrolateral, and mid-dorsolateral prefrontal cortex during the processing of visual stimuli. *PNAS, 99*(8), 5649–5654. https://doi.org/10.1073/pnas.072092299

Pfefferbaum, A., Chanraud, S., Pitel, A. L., Müller-Oehring, E., Shankaranarayanan, A., Alsop, D. C., Rohlfing, T., & Sullivan, E. V. (2011). Cerebral blood flow in posterior cortical nodes of the default mode network decreases with task engagement but remains higher than in most brain regions. *Cerebral Cortex, 21*(1), 233–244. https://doi.org/10.1093/cercor/bhq090

Phan, K. L., Wager, T., Taylor, S. F., & Liberzon, I. (2002). Functional neuroanatomy of emotion: A meta-analysis of emotion activation studies in PET and fMRI. *NeuroImage, 16*(2), 331–348. https://doi.org/10.1006/nimg.2002.1087

Philippi, C. L., Pujara, M. S., Motzkin, J. C., Newman, J., Kiehl, K. A., & Koenigs, M. (2015). Altered resting-state functional connectivity in cortical networks in psychopathy. *Journal of Neuroscience, 35*(15), 6068–6078. https://doi.org/10.1523/jneurosci.5010-14.2015

Philippi, C. L., Tranel, D., Duff, M., & Rudrauf, D. (2015). Damage to the default mode network disrupts autobiographical memory retrieval. *Social Cognitive and Affective Neuroscience, 10*(3), 318–326. https://doi.org/10.1093/scan/nsu070

Phillips, L. H., & Della Sala, S. (1998). Aging, intelligence, and anatomical segregation in the frontal lobes. *Learning and Individual Differences, 10*(4), 337–350. https://doi.org/10.1016/s1041-6080(99)80131-9

Pia, L., Neppi-Modona, M., Ricci, R., & Berti, A. (2004). The anatomy of anosognosia for hemiplegia: A meta-analysis. *Cortex, 40*(2), 367–377. https://doi.org/10.1016/s0010-9452(08)70131-x

Platt, M. L., & Glimcher, P. W. (1999). Neural correlates of decision variables in parietal cortex. *Nature, 400*(6741), 233–238. https://doi.org/10.1038/22268

Pliske, R. M., & Mutter, S. A. (1996). Age differences in the accuracy of confidence judgments. *Experimental Aging Research, 22*(2), 199–216. https://doi.org/10.1080/03610739608254007

Pliszka, S. R. (1998). Comorbidity of attention-deficit/hyperactivity disorder with psychiatric disorder: An overview. *Journal of Clinical Psychiatry, 59*(7), 50–58.

Pluta, A., Wolak, T., Czajka, N., Lewandowska, M., Cieśla, K., Rusiniak, M., Grudzień, D., & Skarżyński, H. (2014). Reduced resting-state brain activity in the default mode network in children with (central) auditory processing disorders. *Behavioral and Brain Functions, 10*(1), 1–9. https://doi.org/10.1186/1744-9081-10-33

Pomarol-Clotet, E., Salvador, R., Sarró, S., Gomar, J., Vila, F., Martínez, Á., Guerrero, A., Ortiz-Gil, J., Sans-Sansa, B., Capdevila, A., Cebamanos, J. M., & McKenna, P. J. (2008). Failure to deactivate in the prefrontal cortex in schizophrenia: Dysfunction of the default mode network? *Psychological Medicine, 38*(8), 1185–1193. https://doi.org/10.1017/s0033291708003565

Porges, S. W. (2011). *The polyvagal theory: Neurophysiological foundations of emotions, attachment, communication, and self-regulation.* Norton.

Posner, J., Cha, J., Wang, Z., Talati, A., Warner, V., Gerber, A., Peterson, B. S., & Weissman, M. (2016). Increased default mode network connectivity in individuals at high familial risk for depression. *Neuropsychopharmacology, 41*(7), 1759–1767. https://doi.org/10.1038/npp.2015.342

Posner, J., Hellerstein, D. J., Gat, I., Mechling, A., Klahr, K., Wang, Z., McGrath, P. J., Stewart, J. W., & Peterson, B. S. (2013). Antidepressants normalize the default mode network in patients with dysthymia. *JAMA Psychiatry, 70*(4), 373. https://doi.org/10.1001/jamapsychiatry.2013.455

Posner, M. I., Rothbart, M. K., Vizueta, N., Levy, K. N., Evans, D. E., Thomas, K. M., & Clarkin, J. F. (2002). Attentional mechanisms of borderline personality disorder. *PNAS, 99*(25), 16366–16370. https://doi.org/10.1073/pnas.252644699

Pribram, K. H., & Luria, A. R. (1973). *Psychophysiology of the frontal lobes.* Academic Press.

Qin, P., Grimm, S., Duncan, N. W., Fan, Y., Huang, Z., Lane, T., Weng, X., Bajbouj, M., & Northoff, G. (2016). Spontaneous activity in default-mode network predicts ascription of self-relatedness to stimuli. *Social Cognitive and Affective Neuroscience, 11*(4), 693–702. https://doi.org/10.1093/scan/nsw008

Quin, P., & Northoff, G. (2011). How is our self related to midline regions and the default-mode network? *NeuroImage, 57*(3), 1221–1233. https://doi.org/10.1016/j.neuroimage.2011.05.028

Quintana, J., & Fuster, J. M. (1999). From perception to action: Temporal integrative functions of prefrontal and parietal neurons. *Cerebral Cortex, 9*(3), 213–221. https://doi.org/10.1093/cercor/9.3.213

Quirk, G. J., & Beer, J. S. (2006). Prefrontal involvement in the regulation of emotion: Convergence of rat and human studies. *Current Opinion in Neurobiology, 16*(6), 723–727. https://doi.org/10.1016/j.conb.2006.07.004

Rabinak, C. A., Angstadt, M., Welsh, R. C., Kenndy, A. E., Lyubkin, M., Martis, B., & Phan, K. L. (2011). Altered amygdala resting-state functional connectivity in post-traumatic stress disorder. *Frontiers in Psychiatry, 2*(62), 1–8. https://doi.org/10.3389/fpsyt.2011.00062

Ray, S. L., & Vanstone, M. (2009). The impact of PTSD on veterans' family relationships: An interpretative phenomenological inquiry. *International Journal of Nursing Studies, 46*(6), 838–847. https://doi.org/10.1016/j.ijnurstu.2009.01.002

Rezai, K., Andreasen, N. C., Alliger, R., Cohen, G., Swayze, V., & O'Leary, D. S. (1993). The neuropsychology of the prefrontal cortex. *Archives of Neurology, 50*(6), 636–642. https://doi.org/10.1001/archneur.1993.00540060066020

Riggs, D. S., Byrne, C. A., Weathers, F. W., & Litz, B. T. (1998). The quality of the intimate relationships of male Vietnam veterans: Problems associated with posttraumatic stress disorder. *Journal of Traumatic Stress, 11*(1), 87–101. https://doi.org/10.1023/a:1024409200155

Rilling, J. K., Gutman, D. A., Zeh, T. R., Panoni, G., Berns, G. S., & Kilts, C. D. (2002). A neural basis for social cooperation. *Neuron, 35*(2), 395–405. https://doi.org/10.1016/s0896-6273(02)00755-9

Rodrigues, E., Wenzel, A., Ribeiro, M. P., Quarantini, L. C., Miranda-Scippa, A., de Sena, E. P., & de Olíveira, I. R. (2011). Hippocampal volume in borderline personality disorder with and without comorbid posttraumatic stress disorder: A meta-analysis. *European Psychiatry, 26*(7), 452–456. https://doi.org/10.1016/j.eurpsy.2010.07.005

Rolls, E. T. (2000). The orbitofrontal cortex and reward. *Cerebral Cortex, 10*(3), 284–294. https://doi.org/10.1093/cercor/10.3.284

Rorden, C., Mattingley, J., Karnath, H., & Driver, J. (1997). Visual extinction and prior entry: Impaired perception of temporal order with intact motion perception after unilateral parietal damage. *Neuropsychologia, 35*(4), 421–433. https://doi.org/10.1016/s0028-3932(96)00093-0

Rosen, L. D., Carrier, L. M., Pedroza, J. A., Elias, S., O'Brien, K. M., Karina Kim, J. L., Cheever, N. A., Bentley, J., & Ruiz, A. (2018). The role of executive functioning and technological anxiety (FOMO) in college course performance as mediated by technology usage and multitasking habits. *Psicología Educativa, 24*(1), 14–25. https://doi.org/10.5093/psed2018a3

Rossano, M. J. (2012). The essential role of ritual in the transmission and reinforcement of social norms. *Psychological Bulletin, 138*(3), 529. https://doi.org/10.1037/a0027038

Roth, R. M., Isquith, P. K., & Gioia, G. A. (2005). *Behavior Rating Inventory of Executive Function®—Adult Version (BRIEF-A)* [Database record]. APA PsycTests. https://doi.org/10.1037/t86244-000

Ruby, P., & Decety, J. (2001). Effect of subjective perspective taking during simulation of action: A PET investigation of agency. *Nature Neuroscience, 4*(5), 546–550. https://doi.org/10.1038/87510

Ruocco, A. C., Medaglia, J. D., Tinker, J. R., Ayaz, H., Forman, E. M., Newman, C. F., Williams, J. M., Hillary, F. G., Platek, S. M., Onaral, B., & Chute, D. L. (2010). Medial prefrontal cortex hyperactivation during social exclusion in borderline personality disorder. *Psychiatry Research: Neuroimaging, 181*(3), 233–236. https://doi.org/10.1016/j.pscychresns.2009.12.001

Rüsch, N., Lieb, K., Göttler, I., Hermann, C., Schramm, E., Richter, H., Jacob, G. A., Corrigan, P. W., & Bohus, M. (2007). Shame and implicit self-concept in women with borderline personality disorder. *American Journal of Psychiatry, 164*(3), 500–508. https://doi.org/10.1176/ajp.2007.164.3.500

Rüsch, N., Schulz, D., Valerius, G., Steil, R., Bohus, M., & Schmahl, C. (2011). Disgust and implicit self-concept in women with borderline personality disorder and posttraumatic stress disorder. *European Archives of Psychiatry and Clinical Neuroscience, 261*(5), 369–376. https://doi.org/10.1007/s00406-010-0174-2

Rüsch, N., van Elst, L. T., Ludaescher, P., Wilke, M., Huppertz, H.-J., Thiel, T., Schmahl, C., Bohus, M., Lieb, K., Heßlinger, B., Hennig, J., & Ebert, D. (2003). A voxel-based morphometric MRI study in female patients with borderline personality disorder. *NeuroImage, 20*(1), 385–392. https://doi.org/10.1016/s1053-8119(03)00297-0

Rüsch, N., Weber, M., Il'yasov, K. A., Lieb, K., Ebert, D., Hennig, J., & van Elst, L. T. (2007). Inferior frontal white matter microstructure and patterns of psychopathology in women with borderline personality disorder and comorbid attention-deficit hyperactivity disorder. *Neuroimage, 35*(2), 738–747. https://doi.org/10.1016/j.neuroimage.2006.12.007

Rushworth, M. F., Krams, M., & Passingham, R. E. (2001). The attentional role of the left parietal cortex: The distinct lateralization and localization of motor attention in the human brain. *Journal of Cognitive Neuroscience, 13*(5), 698–710. https://doi.org/10.1162/089892901750363244

Rypma, B., & D'Esposito, M. (2000). Isolating the neural mechanisms of age-related changes in human working memory. *Nature Neuroscience, 3*(5), 509–515. https://doi.org/10.1038/74889

Sagar, K. A., Dahlgren, M. K., Gönenç, A., Racine, M. T., Dreman, M. W., & Gruber, S. A. (2015). The impact of initiation: Early onset marijuana smokers demonstrate altered Stroop performance and brain activation. *Developmental Cognitive Neuroscience, 16*, 84–92. https://doi.org/10.1016/j.dcn.2015.03.003

Salavert, J., Gasol, M., Vieta, E., Cervantes, A., Trampal, C., & Gispert, J. D. (2011). Fronto-limbic dysfunction in borderline personality disorder: A 18F-FDG positron emission tomography study. *Journal of Affective Disorders, 131*(1–3), 260–267. https://doi.org/10.1016/j.jad.2011.01.001

Salazar, R., Dotson, N., Bressler, S., & Gray, C. (2012). Content-specific frontoparietal synchronization during visual working memory. *Science, 338*(6110), 1097–1100. https://doi.org/10.1126/science.1224000

Salomon, R., Levy, D. R., & Malach, R. (2013). Deconstructing the default: Cortical subdivision of the default mode/intrinsic system during self-related processing. *Human Brain Mapping, 35*(4), 1491–1502. https://doi.org/10.1002/hbm.22268

Sambataro, F., Murty, V. P., Callicott, J. H., Tan, H., Das, S., Weinberger, D. R., & Mattay, V. S. (2010). Age-related alterations in default mode network: Impact on working memory performance. *Neurobiology of Aging*, 31(5), 839–852. https://doi.org/10.1016/j.neurobiolaging.2008.05.022

Sansone, R. A., Sansone, L. A., & Gaither, G. A. (2004). Multiple types of childhood trauma and borderline personality symptomatology among a sample of diabetic patients. *Traumatology*, 10(4), 257–266. https://doi.org/10.1528/trau.10.4.257.56707

Sar, V., Akyuz, G., Kugu, N., Ozturk, E., & Ertem-Vehid, H. (2006). Axis I dissociative disorder comorbidity in borderline personality disorder and reports of childhood trauma. *Journal of Clinical Psychiatry*, 67(10), 1583–1590. https://doi.org/10.4088/jcp.v67n1014

Sauseng, P., Klimesch, W., Schabus, M., & Doppelmayr, M. (2005). Frontoparietal EEG coherence in theta and upper alpha reflect central executive functions of working memory. *International Journal of Psychophysiology*, 57(2), 97–103. https://doi.org/10.1016/j.ijpsycho.2005.03.018

Scalabrini, A., Vai, B., Poletti, S., Damiani, S., Mucci, C., Colombo, C., Zanardi, R., Benedetti, F., & Northoff, G. (2020). All roads lead to the default-mode network—global source of DMN abnormalities in major depressive disorder. *Neuropsychopharmacology*, 45(12), 2058–2069. https://doi.org/10.1038/s41386-020-0785-x

Schall, J. D. (2001). Neural basis of deciding, choosing and acting. *Nature Reviews Neuroscience*, 2(1), 33–42. https://doi.org/10.1038/35049054

Schmahl, C., Berne, K., Krause, A., Kleindienst, N., Valerius, G., Vermetten, E., & Bohus, M. (2009). Hippocampus and amygdala volumes in patients with borderline personality disorder with or without posttraumatic stress disorder. *Journal of Psychiatry and Neuroscience*, 34(4), 289–295.

Schmahl, C. G., Elzinga, B. M., Vermetten, E., Sanislow, C., McGlashan, T. H., & Bremner, J. D. (2003). Neural correlates of memories of abandonment in women with and without borderline personality disorder. *Biological Psychiatry*, 54(2), 142–151. https://doi.org/10.1016/s0006-3223(02)01720-1

Schneider, F., Bermpohl, F., Heinzel, A., Rotte, M., Walter, M., Tempelmann, C., Wiebking, C., Dobrowolny, H., Heinze, H. J., & Northoff, G. (2008). The resting brain and our self: Self-relatedness modulates resting state neural activity in cortical midline structures. *Neuroscience*, 157(1), 120–131. https://doi.org/10.1016/j.neuroscience.2008.08.014

Schnell, K., Dietrich, T., Schnitker, R., Daumann, J., & Herpertz, S. C. (2007). Processing of autobiographical memory retrieval cues in borderline personality disorder. *Journal of Affective Disorders*, 97(1–3), 253–259. https://doi.org/10.1016/j.jad.2006.05.035

Schore, A. N. (2005). Back to basics: Attachment, affect regulation, and the developing right brain: Linking developmental neuroscience to pediatrics. *Pediatrics in Review*, 26(6), 204–217. https://doi.org/10.1542/pir.26-6-204

Schuermann, B., Kathmann, N., Stiglmayr, C., Renneberg, B., & Endrass, T. (2011). Impaired decision making and feedback evaluation in borderline personality disorder. *Psychological Medicine, 41*(9), 1917–1927. https://doi.org/10.1017/s003329171000262x

Schultz, R. T., Gauthier, I., Klin, A., Fulbright, R. K., Anderson, A. W., Volkmar, F., Skudlarski, P., Lacadie, C., Cohen, D. J., & Gore, J. C. (2000). Abnormal ventral temporal cortical activity during face discrimination among individuals with autism and Asperger syndrome. *Archives of General Psychiatry, 57*(4), 331. https://doi.org/10.1001/archpsyc.57.4.331

Schwartz, S., Assal, F., Valenza, N., Seghier, M. L., & Vuilleumier, P. (2005). Illusory persistence of touch after right parietal damage: Neural correlates of tactile awareness. *Brain, 128*(2), 277–290. https://doi.org/10.1093/brain/awh347

Schweinsburg, A. D., Nagel, B. J., & Tapert, S. F. (2005). fMRI reveals alteration of spatial working memory networks across adolescence. *Journal of the International Neuropsychological Society, 11*(5), 631–644. https://doi.org/10.1017/s1355617705050757

Set, Z. (2019). Potential regulatory elements between attachment styles and psychopathology: Rejection sensitivity and self-esteem [in Turkish]. *Archives of Neuropsychiatry, 56*(3), 205. https://doi.org/10.29399/npa.23451

Shallice, T., Fletcher, P., Frith, C. D., Grasby, P., Frackowiak, R. S., & Dolan, R. J. (1994). Brain regions associated with acquisition and retrieval of verbal episodic memory. *Nature, 368*(6472), 633–635. https://doi.org/10.1038/368633a0

Shapira-Lichter, I., Oren, N., Jacob, Y., Gruberger, M., & Hendler, T. (2013). Portraying the unique contribution of the default mode network to internally driven mnemonic processes. *PNAS, 110*(13), 4950–4955. https://doi.org/10.1073/pnas.1209888110

Sharp, D. J., Beckmann, C. F., Greenwood, R., Kinnunen, K. M., Bonnelle, V., De Boissezon, X., Powell, J. H., Counsell, S. J., Patel, M. C., & Leech, R. (2011). Default mode network functional and structural connectivity after traumatic brain injury. *Brain, 134*(8), 2233–2247. https://doi.org/10.1093/brain/awr175

Sheline, Y. I., Barch, D. M., Price, J. L., Rundle, M. M., Vaishnavi, S. N., Snyder, A. Z., & Raichle, M. E. (2009). The default mode network and self-referential processes in depression. *PNAS, 106*(6), 1942–1947. https://doi.org/10.1073/pnas.0812686106

Shin, J., Geerling, J. C., & Loewy, A. D. (2008). Inputs to the ventrolateral bed nucleus of the stria terminalis. *Journal of Comparative Neurology, 511*(5), 628–657. https://doi.org/10.1002/cne.21870

Shmuelof, L., & Zohary, E. (2006). A mirror representation of others' actions in the human anterior parietal cortex. *Journal of Neuroscience, 26*(38), 9736–9742. https://doi.org/10.1523/jneurosci.1836-06.2006

Shomstein, S. (2012). Cognitive functions of the posterior parietal cortex: Top-down and bottom-up attentional control. *Frontiers in Integrative Neuroscience, 6*(38), 1–7. https://doi.org/10.3389/fnint.2012.00038

Siegel, D. J. (2023). *IntraConnected: MWe (Me + We) as the integration of self, identity, and belonging.* Norton.

Siegel, D. J., & Drulis, C. (2023). An interpersonal neurobiology perspective on the mind and mental health: Personal, public, and planetary well-being. *Annals of General Psychiatry, 22*(1), 5. https://doi.org/10.1186/s12991-023-00434-5

Silbersweig, D. (2013). Default mode subnetworks, connectivity, depression and its treatment: Toward brain-based biomarker development. *Biological Psychiatry*, 74(1), 5–6. https://doi.org/10.1016/j.biopsych.2013.05.011

Simpson, J. R., Drevets, W. C., Snyder, A. Z., Gusnard, D. A., & Raichle, M. E. (2001). Emotion-induced changes in human medial prefrontal cortex: II. During anticipatory anxiety. *PNAS*, 98(2), 688–693. https://doi.org/10.1073/pnas.98.2.688

Simpson, J. R., Snyder, A. Z., Gusnard, D. A., & Raichle, M. E. (2001). Emotion-induced changes in human medial prefrontal cortex: I. During cognitive task performance. *PNAS*, 98(2), 683–687. https://doi.org/10.1073/pnas.98.2.683

Singh, K. D., & Fawcett, I. P. (2008). Transient and linearly graded deactivation of the human default-mode network by a visual detection task. *NeuroImage*, 41(1), 100–112. https://doi.org/10.1016/j.neuroimage.2008.01.051

Sirigu, A., Duhamel, J., Coehn, L., Pillon, B., Dubois, B., & Agid, Y. (1996). The mental representation of hand movements after parietal cortex damage. *Science*, 273(5281), 1564–1568. https://doi.org/10.1126/science.273.5281.1564

Smallwood, J., Brown, K., Baird, B., & Schooler, J. W. (2012). Cooperation between the default mode network and the frontal-parietal network in the production of an internal train of thought. *Brain Research*, 1428, 60–70. https://doi.org/10.1016/j.brainres.2011.03.072

Smith, E., Salat, D., Jeng, J., McCreary, C., Fischl, B., Schmahmann, J., Dickerson, B. C., Viswanathan, A., Albert, M. S., Blacker, D., & Greenberg, S. (2011). Correlations between MRI white matter lesion location and executive function and episodic memory. *Neurology*, 76(17), 1492–1499. https://doi.org/10.1212/wnl.0b013e318217e7c8

Smith, S. M., Fox, P. T., Miller, K. L., Glahn, D. C., Fox, P. M., Mackay, C. E., Filippini, N., Watkins, K. E., Toro, R., Laird, A. R., & Beckmann, C. F. (2009). Correspondence of the brain's functional architecture during activation and rest. *PNAS*, 106(31), 13040–13045. https://doi.org/10.1073/pnas.0905267106

Smith, V., Mitchell, D. J., & Duncan, J. (2018). Role of the default mode network in cognitive transitions. *Cerebral Cortex*, 28(10), 3685–3696. https://doi.org/10.1093/cercor/bhy167

Snyder, J., & Chatterjee, A. (2004). Spatial-temporal anisometries following right parietal damage. *Neuropsychologia*, 42(12), 1703–1708. https://doi.org/10.1016/j.neuropsychologia.2004.04.003

Snyder, L. H., Batista, A. P., & Andersen, R. A. (1997). Coding of intention in the posterior parietal cortex. *Nature*, 386(6621), 167–170. https://doi.org/10.1038/386167a0

Sobanski, E. (2006). Psychiatric comorbidity in adults with attention-deficit/hyperactivity disorder (ADHD). *European Archives of Psychiatry and Clinical Neuroscience*, 256(S1), i26–i31. https://doi.org/10.1007/s00406-006-1004-4

Sobanski, E., Banaschewski, T., Asherson, P., Buitelaar, J., Chen, W., Franke, B., Holtmann, M., Krumm, B., Sergeant, J., Sonuga-Barke, E., Stringaris, A., Taylor, E., Anney, R., Ebstein, R. P., Gill, M., Miranda, A., Mulas, F., Oades, R. D., Roeyers, H., . . . Faraone, S. V. (2010). Emotional lability in children and adolescents with attention deficit/hyperactivity disorder (ADHD): Clinical correlates and familial prevalence. *Journal of Child Psychology and Psychiatry, 51*(8), 915–923. https://doi.org/10.1111/j.1469-7610.2010.02217.x

Sohn, S. Y., Rees, P., Wildridge, B., Kalk, N. J., & Carter, B. (2019). Prevalence of problematic smartphone usage and associated mental health outcomes amongst children and young people: A systematic review, meta-analysis and GRADE of the evidence. *BMC Psychiatry, 19*(1), 1–10. https://doi.org/10.1186/s12888-019-2350-x

Soloff, P. H., Meltzer, C. C., Greer, P. J., Constantine, D., & Kelly, T. M. (2000). A fenfluramine-activated FDG-PET study of borderline personality disorder. *Biological Psychiatry, 47*(6), 540–547. https://doi.org/10.1016/s0006-3223(99)00202-4

Soloff, P., Nutche, J., Goradia, D., & Diwadkar, V. (2008). Structural brain abnormalities in borderline personality disorder: A voxel-based morphometry study. *Psychiatry Research, 164*(3), 223–236. https://doi.org/10.1016/j.pscychresns.2008.02.003

Sowell, E. R., Thompson, P. M., Holmes, C. J., Batth, R., Jernigan, T. L., & Toga, A. W. (1999). Localizing age-related changes in brain structure between childhood and adolescence using statistical parametric mapping. *NeuroImage, 9*(6), 587–597. https://doi.org/10.1006/nimg.1999.0436

Sowell, E. R., Thompson, P. M., Tessner, K. D., & Toga, A. W. (2001). Mapping continued brain growth and gray matter density reduction in dorsal prefrontal cortex: Inverse relationships during post-adolescent brain maturation. *Journal of Neuroscience, 21*(22), 8819–8829. https://doi.org/10.1523/jneurosci.21-22-08819.2001

Spreng, R. N., & Grady, C. L. (2010). Patterns of brain activity supporting autobiographical memory, prospection, and theory of mind, and their relationship to the default mode network. *Journal of Cognitive Neuroscience, 22*(6), 1112–1123. https://doi.org/10.1162/jocn.2009.21282

Spreng, R. N., Mar, R. A., & Kim, A. S. (2009). The common neural basis of autobiographical memory, prospection, navigation, theory of mind, and the default mode: A quantitative meta-analysis. *Journal of Cognitive Neuroscience, 21*(3), 489–510. https://doi.org/10.1162/jocn.2008.21029

Sridharan, D., Levitin, D., & Menon, V. (2008). A critical role for the right fronto-insular cortex in switching between central-executive and default-mode networks. *PNAS, 105*(34), 12569–12574. https://doi.org/10.1073/pnas.0800005105

Staudinger, U. M. (1999). Older and wiser? Integrating results on the relationship between age and wisdom-related performance. *International Journal of Behavioral Development, 23*(3), 641–664. https://doi.org/10.1080/016502599383739

Staudinger, U. M., & Baltes, P. B. (1996). Interactive minds: A facilitative setting for wisdom-related performance? *Journal of Personality and Social Psychology, 71*(4), 746–762. https://doi.org/10.1037//0022-3514.71.4.746

Staudinger, U. M., Maciel, A. G., Smith, J., & Baltes, P. B. (1998). What predicts wisdom-related performance? A first look at personality, intelligence, and facilitative experiential contexts. *European Journal of Personality, 12*(1), 1–17. https://doi.org/10.1002/(sici)1099-0984(199801/02)12:1<1::aid-per285>3.3.co;2-0

Stern, E. R., Fitzgerald, K. D., Welsh, R. C., Abelson, J. L., & Taylor, S. F. (2012). Resting-state functional connectivity between fronto-parietal and default mode networks in obsessive-compulsive disorder. *PLoS One, 7*(5), e36356. https://doi.org/10.1371/journal.pone.0036356

Sternberg, R. J. (1990). Wisdom and its relations to intelligence and creativity. In R. J. Sternberg (Ed.), *Wisdom: Its nature, origins, and development* (pp. 142–159). University of Chicago Press.

Stuss, D. T., & Benson, D. F. (1986). *The frontal lobes*. Raven Press.

Supekar, K., Uddin, L. Q., Prater, K., Amin, H., Greicius, M. D., & Menon, V. (2010). Development of functional and structural connectivity within the default mode network in young children. *NeuroImage, 52*(1), 290–301. https://doi.org/10.1016/j.neuroimage.2010.04.009

Sutherland, R. J., Whishaw, I. Q., & Kolb, B. (1988). Contributions of cingulate cortex to two forms of spatial learning and memory. *Journal of Neuroscience, 8*(6), 1863–1872. https://doi.org/10.1523/jneurosci.08-06-01863.1988

Swirsky-Sacchetti, T., Gorton, G., Samuel, S., Sobel, R., Genetta-Wadley, A., & Burleigh, B. (1993). Neuropsychological function in borderline personality disorder. *Journal of Clinical Psychology, 49*(3), 385–396. https://doi.org/10.1002/1097 -4679(199305)49:3<385::aid-jclp2270490313>3.0.co;2-4

Taber, K. H., & Hurley, R. A. (2008). Astroglia: Not just glue. *Journal of Neuropsychiatry and Clinical Neurosciences, 20*(2), 124–129. https://doi.org/10.1176/appi .neuropsych.20.2.iv

Taherdoost, H. (2022). Internet addiction: Symptoms, impacts and treatments. *Journal of Addiction and Psychology, 5*(2). https://doi.org/10.33552/oajap.2022.05.000608

Takahashi, M., & Bordia, P. (2000). The concept of wisdom: A cross-cultural comparison. *International Journal of Psychology, 35*(1), 1–9. https://doi.org/10.1080/002075900399475

Takahashi, M., & Overton, W. F. (2002). Wisdom: A culturally inclusive developmental perspective. *International Journal of Behavioral Development, 26*(3), 269–277. https://doi.org/10.1080/01650250143000139

Tang, A., Eachus, P., Szeto, S., & Royle, W. (2018). Smartphone use, executive function and psychological health among college students. In *INTED2018 Proceedings*, 2033–2040. https://doi.org/10.21125/inted.2018.0378

Tanji, J., & Hoshi, E. (2001). Behavioral planning in the prefrontal cortex. *Current Opinion in Neurobiology, 11*(2), 164–170. https://doi.org/10.1016/s0959-4388(00)00192-6

Taylor, G. J. (2000). Recent developments in alexithymia theory and research. *Canadian Journal of Psychiatry, 45*(2), 134–142. https://doi.org/10.1177/070674370004500203

Taylor, J. G. (2001). The central role of the parietal lobes in consciousness. *Consciousness and Cognition, 10*(3), 379–417. https://doi.org/10.1006/ccog.2000.0495

Teasdale, J. D., Howard, R. J., Cox, S. G., Ha, Y., Brammer, M. J., Williams, S. C. R., & Checkley, S. A. (1999). Functional MRI study of the cognitive generation of affect. *American Journal of Psychiatry, 156*(2), 209–215. https://doi.org/10.1176/ajp.156.2.209

Tentori, K., Osherson, D., Hasher, L., & May, C. (2001). Wisdom and aging: Irrational preferences in college students but not older adults. *Cognition, 81*(3), B87–B96. https://doi.org/10.1016/s0010-0277(01)00137-8

Tessitore, A., Hariri, A. R., Fera, F., Smith, W. G., Das, S., Weinberger, D. R., & Mattay, V. S. (2005). Functional changes in the activity of brain regions underlying emotion processing in the elderly. *Psychiatry Research: Neuroimaging, 139*(1), 9–18. https://doi.org/10.1016/j.pscychresns.2005.02.009

Thome, J., Frewen, P., Daniels, J. K., Densmore, M., & Lanius, R. A. (2014). Altered connectivity within the salience network during direct eye gaze in PTSD. *Borderline Personality Disorder and Emotion Dysregulation, 1*(1), 17. https://doi.org/10.1186/2051-6673-1-17

Tops, M., Koole, S. L., IJzerman, H., & Buisman-Pijlman, F. T. (2014). Why social attachment and oxytocin protect against addiction and stress: Insights from the dynamics between ventral and dorsal cortico-striatal systems. *Pharmacology Biochemistry and Behavior, 119*, 39–48. https://doi.org/10.1016/j.pbb.2013.07.015

Tremblay, L., & Schultz, W. (1999). Relative reward preference in primate orbitofrontal cortex. *Nature, 398*, 704–708. https://doi.org/10.1038/19525

Twenge, J. M., & Campbell, W. K. (2019). Media use is linked to lower psychological well-being: Evidence from three datasets. *Psychiatric Quarterly, 90*, 311–331. https://doi.org/10.1007/s11126-019-09630-7

Uddin, L. Q., Clare Kelly, A. M., Biswal, B. B., Xavier Castellanos, F., & Milham, M. P. (2009). Functional connectivity of default mode network components: Correlation, anticorrelation, and causality. *Human Brain Mapping, 30*(2), 625–637. https://doi.org/10.1002/hbm.20531

Uddin, L. Q., Kaplan, J. T., Molnar-Szakacs, I., Zaidel, E., & Iacoboni, M. (2005). Self-face recognition activates a frontoparietal "mirror" network in the right hemisphere: An event-related fMRI study. *NeuroImage, 25*(3), 926–935. https://doi.org/10.1016/j.neuroimage.2004.12.018

Ungerleider, L. G., & Haxby, J. V. (1994). "What" and "where" in the human brain. *Current Opinion in Neurobiology, 4*(2), 157–165. https://doi.org/10.1016/0959 -4388(94)90066-3

Unoka, Z., Fogd, D., Füzy, M., & Csukly, G. (2011). Misreading the facial signs: Specific impairments and error patterns in recognition of facial emotions with negative valence in borderline personality disorder. *Psychiatric Research, 189*, 419–425. https://doi.org/10.1016/j.psychres.2011.02.010

Vaillant, A. R., Zanassi, P., Walsh, G. S., Aumont, A., Alonso, A., & Miller, F. D. (2002). Signaling mechanisms underlying reversible, activity-dependent dendrite formation. *Neuron, 34*(6), 985–998. https://doi.org/10.1016/s0896-6273(02)00717-1

van Buuren, M. V., Gladwin, T. E., Zandbelt, B. B., Kahn, R. S., & Vink, M. (2010). Reduced functional coupling in the default-mode network during self-referential processing. *Human Brain Mapping, 31*(8), 1117–1127. https://doi.org/10 .1002/hbm.20920

van den Heuvel, M., Mandl, R., Kahn, R., & Pol, H. (2009). Functionally linked resting-state networks reflect the underlying structural connectivity architecture of the human brain. *Human Brain Mapping, 30*(10), 3127–3141. https://doi.org/10.1002/hbm.20737

van Elst, L. T., Hesslinger, B., Thiel, T., Geiger, E., Haegele, K., Lemieux, L., Lieb, K., Bohus, M., Hennig, J., & Ebert, D. (2003). Frontolimbic brain abnormalities in patients with borderline personality disorder: A volumetric magnetic resonance imaging study. *Biological Psychiatry, 54*, 163–171. https://doi.org/10.1016/s0006-3223(02)01743-2

Van Opstal, F., Verguts, G., & Fias, W. (2008). A hippocampal-parietal network for learning an ordered sequence. *NeuroImage, 40*(1), 333–341. https://doi.org/10.1016/j.neuroimage.2007.11.027

van Reekum, R., Conway, C. A., Gansler, D., White, R., & Bachman, D. L. (1993). Neurobehavioral study of borderline personality disorder. *Journal of Psychiatry and Neuroscience, 18*(3), 121–129.

Victor, M., & Ropper, A. H. (2001). *Adams and Victor's principles of neurology* (7th ed.). McGraw-Hill.

Vogeley, K., May, M., Ritzl, A., Falkai, P., Zilles, K., & Fink, G. R. (2004). Neural correlates of first-person perspective as one constituent of human self-consciousness. *Journal of Cognitive Neuroscience, 16*(5), 817–827. https://doi.org/10.1162/089892904970799

Wagner, A. D., Shannon, B. J., Kahn, I., & Buckner, L. (2005). Parietal lobe contributions to episodic memory retrieval. *Trends in Cognitive Sciences, 9*(9), 446–453. https://doi.org/10.1016/j.tics.2005.07.001

Wagner, D. D., Haxby, J. V., & Heatherton, T. F. (2012). The representation of self and person knowledge in the medial prefrontal cortex. *Cognitive Science, 3*(4), 451–470. https://doi.org/10.1002/wcs.1183

Walsh, V., Ashbridge, E., & Cowey, A. (1998). Cortical plasticity in perceptual learning demonstrated by transcranial magnetic stimulation. *Neuropsychologia, 36*(4), 45–49. https://doi.org/10.1016/s0028-3932(97)00111-5

Walterfang, M., & Velakoulis, D. (2005). Cortical release signs in psychiatry. *Australian and New Zealand Journal of Psychiatry, 39*(5), 317–327. https://doi.org/10.1111/j.1440-1614.2005.01578.x

Wang, L., Shen, H., Lei, Y., Zeng, L.L., Cao, F., Su, L., Yang, Z., Yao, S. and Hu, D. (2017). Altered default mode, fronto-parietal and salience networks in adolescents with internet addiction. *Addictive Behaviors, 70*, 1–6. https://doi.org/10.1016/j.addbeh.2017.01.021

Ward, A. F., Duke, K., Gneezy, A., & Bos, M. W. (2017). Brain drain: The mere presence of one's own smartphone reduces available cognitive capacity. *Journal of the Association of Consumer Research, 2*, 140–154. https://doi.org/10.1086/691462

Ward, A. M., Schultz, A. P., Huijbers, W., Dijk, K. R., Hedden, T., & Sperling, R. A. (2013). The parahippocampal gyrus links the default-mode cortical network with the medial temporal lobe memory system. *Human Brain Mapping, 35*(3), 1061–1073. https://doi.org/10.1002/hbm.22234

Watanabe, M. (1996). Reward expectancy in primate prefrontal neurons. *Nature*, *382*(6592), 629–632. https://doi.org/10.1038/382629a0

Watson, S., Chilton, R., Fairchild, H., & Whewell, P. (2006). Association between childhood trauma and dissociation among patients with borderline personality disorder. *Australian and New Zealand Journal of Psychiatry*, *40*(5), 478–481. https://doi.org/10.1080/j.1440-1614.2006.01825.x

Weniger, G., Lange, C., Sachsse, U., & Irle, E. (2009). Reduced amygdala and hippocampus size in trauma-exposed women with borderline personality disorder and without posttraumatic stress disorder. *Journal of Psychiatry and Neuroscience*, *34*(5), 383–388. https://doi.org/10.1016/j.biopsych.2004.10.004

Whalen, P. J., Kagan, J., Cook, R. G., Davis, F. C., Kim, H., Polis, S., McLaren, D. G., Somerville, L. H., McLean, A. A., Maxwell, J. S., & Johnstone, T. (2004). Human amygdala responsivity to masked fearful eye whites. *Science*, *306*(5704), 2061–2061. https://doi.org/10.1126/science.1103617

Whalley, L. J., Deary, I. J., Appleton, C. L., & Starr, J. M. (2004). Cognitive reserve and the neurobiology of cognitive aging. *Ageing Research Reviews*, *3*(4), 369–382. https://doi.org/10.1016/j.arr.2004.05.001

Whitfield-Gabrieli, S., Moran, J. M., Nieto-Castañón, A., Triantafyllou, C., Saxe, R., & Gabrieli, J. D. (2011). Associations and dissociations between default and self-reference networks in the human brain. *NeuroImage*, *55*(1), 225–232. https://doi.org/10.1016/j.neuroimage.2010.11.048

Whitney, C., Kirk, M., O' Sullivan, J., Ralph, M., & Jefferies, E. (2012). Executive semantic processing is underpinned by a large-scale neural network: Revealing the contribution of left prefrontal, posterior temporal, and parietal cortex to controlled retrieval and selection using TMS. *Journal of Cognitive Neuroscience*, *24*(1), 133–147. https://doi.org/10.1162/jocn_a_00123

Whittle, S., Chanen, A. M., Fornito, A., McGorry, P. D., Pantelis, C., & Yucel, M. (2009). Anterior cingulate volume in adolescents with first-presentation borderline personality disorder. *Psychiatry Research: Neuroimaging*, *172*, 155–160. https://doi.org/10.1016/j.pscychresns.2008.12.004

Williams, L. M., Brown, K. J., Palmer, D., Liddell, B. J., Kemp, A. H., Olivieri, G., & Gordon, E. (2006). The mellow years? Neural basis of improving emotional stability over age. *Journal of Neuroscience*, *26*(24), 6422–6430. https://doi.org/10.1523/jneurosci.0022-06.2006

Wilson, F. A. W., O'Scalaidhe, S. P., & Goldman-Rakic, P. S. (1993). Dissociation of object and spatial processing domains in primate prefrontal cortex. *Science*, *260*(5116), 1955–1958. https://doi.org/10.1126/science.8316836

Wingenfeld, K., Schaffrath, C., Rullkoetter, N., Mensebach, C., Schlosser, N., Beblo, T., Driessen, M., & Meyer, B. (2011). Associations of childhood trauma, trauma in adulthood and previous-year stress with psychopathology in patients with major depression and borderline personality disorder. *Child Abuse and Neglect*, *35*, 647–654. https://doi.org/10.1016/j.chiabu.2011.04.003

Winstanley, C. A., Theobald, D. E., Cardinal, R. N., & Robbins, T. W. (2004). Contrasting roles of basolateral amygdala and orbitofrontal cortex in impulsive choice. *Journal of Neuroscience, 24*(20), 4718–4722. https://doi.org/10.1523/jneurosci.5606-03.2004

Witelson, S. F., Beresh, H., & Kigar, D. L. (2006). Intelligence and brain size in 100 postmortem brains: Sex, lateralization and age factors. *Brain, 129*(2), 386–398. https://doi.org/10.1093/brain/awh696

Witelson, S. F., Kigar, D. L., & Harvey, T. (1999). The exceptional brain of Albert Einstein. *Lancet, 353*(9170), 2149–2153. https://doi.org/10.1016/s0140-6736(98)10327-6

Wolpert, D. M., Goodbody, S. J., & Husain, M. (1998). Maintaining internal representations: The role of the human superior parietal lobe. *Nature Neuroscience, 1*(6), 529–533. https://doi.org/10.1038/2245

Wright, C. I., Wedig, M. M., Williams, D., Rauch, S. L., & Albert, M. S. (2006). Novel fearful faces activate the amygdala in healthy young and elderly adults. *Neurobiology of Aging, 27*(2), 361–374. https://doi.org/10.1016/j.neurobiolaging.2005.01.014

Yan, C. G., Chen, X., Li, L., Castellanos, F. X., Bai, T. J., Bo, Q. J., Cao, J., & Zang, Y. F. (2019). Reduced default mode network functional connectivity in patients with recurrent major depressive disorder. *PNAS, 116*(18), 9078–9083. https://doi.org/10.1073/pnas.1900390116

Yang, J., Weng, X., Zang, Y., Xu, M., & Xu, X. (2010). Sustained activity within the default mode network during an implicit memory task. *Cortex, 46*(3), 354–366. https://doi.org/10.1016/j.cortex.2009.05.002

Yeshurun, Y., Nguyen, M., & Hasson, U. (2021). The default mode network: Where the idiosyncratic self meets the shared social world. *Nature Reviews Neuroscience, 22*(3), 181–192. https://doi.org/10.1038/s41583-020-00420-w

Yoshimasu, K., Barbaresi, W. J., Colligan, R. C., Voigt, R. G., Killian, J. M., Weaver, A. L., & Katusic, S. K. (2012). Childhood ADHD is strongly associated with a broad range of psychiatric disorders during adolescence: A population-based birth cohort study. *Journal of Child Psychology and Psychiatry, 53*(10), 1036–1043. https://doi.org/10.1111/j.1469-7610.2012.02567.x

Yoshimura, S., Ueda, K., Suzuki, S., Onoda, K., Okamoto, Y., & Yamawaki, S. (2009). Self-referential processing of negative stimuli within the ventral anterior cingulate gyrus and right amygdala. *Brain and Cognition, 69*(1), 218–225. https://doi.org/10.1016/j.bandc.2008.07.010

Zald, D. H. (2003). The human amygdala and the emotional evaluation of sensory stimuli. *Brain Research Reviews, 41*(1), 88–123. https://doi.org/10.1016/s0165-0173(02)00248-5

Zetzsche, T., Preuss, U. W., Frodl, T., Schmitt, G., Seifert, D., Münchhausen, E., Tabrizi, S., Leinsinger, G., Born, C., Reiser, M., Möller, H.-J., & Meisenzahl, E. M. (2007). Hippocampal volume reduction and history of aggressive behaviour in patients with borderline personality disorder. *Psychiatry Research: Neuroimaging, 154*, 157–170. https://doi.org/10.1016/j.pscychresns.2006.05.010

Zhang, M., & Bian, Y. (2021). An analysis of the brain structures underlying the link between pathological internet use and anxiety. *Addictive Behaviors, 112*, 106632. https://doi.org/10.1016/j.addbeh.2020.106632

Zhou, H. X., Chen, X., Shen, Y. S., Li, L., Chen, N. X., Zhu, Z. C., Castellanos, F. X., & Yan, C. G. (2020). Rumination and the default mode network: Meta-analysis of brain imaging studies and implications for depression. *NeuroImage,* *206,* 116287. https://doi.org/10.1016/j.neuroimage.2019.116287

Zhu, X., Wang, X., Xiao, J., Liao, J., Zhong, M., Wang, W., & Yao, S. (2012). Evidence of a dissociation pattern in resting-state default mode network connectivity in first-episode, treatment-naive major depression patients. *Biological Psychiatry,* *71*(7), 611–617. https://doi.org/10.1016/j.biopsych.2011.10.035

Zysset, S., Huber, O., Ferstl, E., & Cramon, D. V. (2002). The anterior frontal medial cortex and evaluative judgment: An fMRI study. *NeuroImage, 15*(4), 983–991. https://doi.org/10.1006/nimg.2001.1008

Index

About the Authors

Lou Cozolino is a psychologist who maintains a clinical and consulting practice based in Los Angeles, California. He is the author of a dozen books focused on topics including psychotherapy, neuroscience, executive functioning, education, and healthy aging, lecturing around the world on these and other subjects. To find out more about his work, his team, or to contact Lou, please visit his website, drloucozolino.com.

Chloe Drulis is an associate marriage and family therapist practicing virtually in California. She is also a writer and lecturer focusing on an integrative approach to therapy, parenting, relationships, and personal growth. To learn more about her work or to get in touch, visit chloedrulispsychotherapy.com.

Carly Trissler is a Phoenix-based writer and lecturer with expertise in interpersonal neurobiology. Her work focuses on executive functioning, parenting, and the relationship between technology and psychology.